Indian Constitution Conflicts and Controversies

Indian Constitution
Conflicts and Controversies

Subhash C Kashyap

Vitasta

Vitasta Publishing Pvt. Ltd.
New Delhi

Published by
Renu Kaul Verma for
Vitasta Publishing Pvt. Ltd.
2/15, Ansari Road, Daryaganj,
New Delhi - 110 002

ISBN 978-81-89766-41-2

First Edition 2010
Eighth Reprint 2025

MRP 895

Cover Design and Typeset by Vitasta Publishing Pvt. Ltd.
Printed by Vits Press, New Delhi

Contents

Part III

Parliament and Law Makers

Part IV

The Judiciary and the Law

Part V

Constitutional Conflicts and Controversies

Preface

To have succeeded in giving to ourselves a Constitution acceptable to all parts of our vast country and all sections of our highly pluralistic society was one of our greatest achievements since Independence. We can take even greater pride in the fact that it has stood the test of time and survived many pressures, stresses and strains inflicted on the body politic by malevolent forces, both internal and external, for nearly sixty years now. Some temporary aberrations notwithstanding, whatever problems, conflicts and crises we faced we handled them reasonably successfully within the existing constitutional framework.

In some ways, I have been privy to several developments related to the working of the Constitution and our polity ever since the first Parliament. During the last two decades, as a private citizen, I have been making some contribution to resolution of constitutional controversies. At a personal level, I have had many occasions to advise successive leaders of the government and Opposition at the Union and State levels in times of crises and on matters of national importance. While many of the contemporaneous opinions and notes on crucial matters cannot be for public domain, my public contributions have included, besides my books, more than 700 articles and numerous addresses in India and abroad. Most often these related to contemporary or ongoing problems involving understanding and interpretation of some key concepts and provisions of the Constitution. I am glad to present here a selection of articles. These were written at different points of time often in response to the controversies raised or conflict situations prevailing at the time. These have to be seen in that context and yet they retain contemporary relevance.

I am grateful to all the prominent national dailies like the *Hindustan Times, The Times of India, The Hindu, The Indian Express, The Statesman, The Tribune, The Pioneer, The Deccan Herald* and others for publishing several of these pieces as articles at a time when the events took place and difficult situations arose. Hopefully, they could impact policy and decision making at appropriate levels.

Some of the relatively longer pieces were published in journals or delivered as inaugural or keynote addresses at conferences, seminars, symposia within the country or abroad. These seek to dwell upon conceptual or systemic clarifications, institutional interrelationships and the working of the Constitution. These should be of special interest to concerned citizens.

In a work of this kind, some repetition is unavoidable to present the argument and suggest the alternative ways out under different situations. The attempt, however, has been to keep repetition to the minimum and, where possible, make cross references.

To make the text more readable and relevant to the present-day reader, liberty has been taken for some updating and editing by way of changing the narrative to past tense etc.

My publisher Renu Kaul Verma deserves to be complimented for her persistence and suave persuasion without which I would have never put these stray thoughts and writings together.

Subhash C Kashyap
New Delhi

PART I

The Concepts and the System

1

Governance and the Constitution Defined

The nation is passing through critical times. Our polity is under severe strain. Faith of the people in the quality, integrity and efficiency of governmental institutions stands seriously eroded. There has been a steep fall in the standards of conduct in public life and administration. That there is a crisis of character and values in politics and public administration, is saying the obvious. Growth of a certain cynicism towards normal democratic processes and an erosion of respect for political parties, politicians, legislators and civil servants, present a disturbing scenario. The source of many of our maladies is in the disregard of the interests of the citizen and the absence of good governance.

For some decades now, the issue of good governance has been in the forefront of political science discourse and discussions in the academia. The study of institutions that had been relegated to the footnotes is back in the reckoning and the problems of good governance have come to occupy important space and generate renewed interest. Both in the developed and developing parts of the world, there has been a welcome shift of focus from traditional concepts of mere government and politics to the paradigms of good governance, its attributes and imperatives.

Several studies were taken up by various organizations. The world development reports, 1997 onwards, underlined the effectiveness of the State as an essential prerequisite for sustainable economic growth. The Bretton Woods institutions realized even though very late in the day, that economic liberalization reform could not succeed without first ensuring quality and clean governance. In fact, the International Monetary Fund (IMF) made good governance a criterion for sanctioning loans.

Sometimes, the terms 'government' and 'governance' are used rather indiscriminately to mean the same thing. While there is no one accepted definition of governance, it means more than maintaining law and order. Besides the World Bank indicators of good governance encompassing democracy, transparency and accountability, it may be said that the whole idea of good governance is that of a participative system in which those who are called upon to govern on behalf of the people are motivated with a will to giving their best to the people.

There is nothing really new in stressing the principles and paradigms of governance in political science. The concept in ancient Indian polity of the rulers being bound by dharma was precisely that of ensuring good governance to the people. Even though monarchy prevailed, there was no place for any theory of the divine rights of the kings or of arbitrary rule. *Rajdharma* was the code of conduct or the rule of law that was superior to the will of the ruler and governed all his actions. The *Jataka* tales, *Shantiparva Anushashanparva* of *Mahabharta*, Shukracharya's *Nitisar*, Panini's *Ashtadhyayi*, *Aatreya Brahmana*, Valmiki's *Ramayana*, and not the least Kautilya's *Arthashastra* are replete with descriptions of tenets of good governance.

Ancient Indian polity recognized the rights of the people to good governance. Manu goes so far as to lay down that if the ruler ignored his responsibilities and was unjust or oppressive, the people had a right to rebellion, even regicide was accepted and the people were free to kill such a ruler 'as a mad dog".

The end of all economy and polity was social good and improvement in the quality of human life. Human beings were not to be considered as mere resource for administration or development but they were the ultimate end and all administration, development, etc., were the resources for their good. The watchword for Ashoka was Yogashkema or public welfare and, this could be achieved only through good governance. Similarly, in western thought, e.g., in Plato's Republic and Aristotle's Politics, the supreme concerns and objectives of all political activity happened to be those of providing good governance to the people and for that purpose devising the best political system and finding the best kind of rulers.

But, politics gradually degenerated into a struggle for power for its own sake. Politics became a lucrative profession and came to be regarded very much as the art and science of somehow getting to positions of power and by all possible means staying there. In this scheme of things, government was little more than the technique and the machinery of governing or ruling over the people, of keeping them under the control of the ruling classes of politicians dominating over the rest of the populace; of the masters enjoying the exercise of power over the masses. Politics became the means to power and government the manifestation of the quest for domination. Different political systems were only seen as the many alternatives for achieving the same objectives.

Things have come to such a pass that some concerned citizens and thinkers have begun to see question marks against the democratic model adopted by us and operated for more than half a century. Can we hope to achieve under it good governance, citizen-friendly administration, economic growth and nation-building? There is every need to examine where we went wrong and what needs to be done to remedy the situation.

Single party or multi-party majority government, or one-party or many-party minority government, Presidential or Parliamentary system and the like are no more the fundamental issues today. Questions relating to distribution of power (or sharing the spoils of office) between the Union and the units or between the organs of the State (Legislative, Executive and Judiciary) are also not so relevant. Even self-government or good government is not enough. What has become a categorical imperative is clean and quality governance as it affects the lives of the people. The whole idea of good governance is that of giving, of serving, of doing good to the people, of solving their problems and making their lives more livable, satisfying and enjoyable. It comes close to Gandhiji's concept of politics for service of the people and not for becoming masters of the people.

The trend almost all over the world seems to be pushing ideology to a back seat in politics. The emphasis is on providing a citizen-friendly administration and a development oriented government. People's representatives from Panchayats to Parliament must realize that the supreme sovereign power vests in the collectivity of the people. The people are entitled to demand good quality, responsive and responsible, corruption-free clean and efficient government which treats them not as subjects but as the real masters in a democracy and gives the highest priority to their needs and interests. On the other hand, the citizens at large, in whatever position, must remain awake and aware of their responsibilities and obligations.

In the so-called representative Parliamentary democracies like ours, those in Government are so pre-occupied with the struggle for survival in power that they have no time for addressing their attention to the problems of the people. Governance has become a casualty of Government. Howsoever sad, it is not surprising, therefore, that there has been such a sharp erosion in the respect of the people for politicians. In large parts of the country, Government does not exist. Mafia gangs terrorize and rule, even the thin dividing line between the politicians and criminals has disappeared. Politics has been criminalized and crime politicized. Earlier, the criminal sought the protection of the politician, now it is the politician who needs the protection of the *dada* or the two have become one and the same person. Governments have lost their credibility, legitimacy and even their representative credentials.

Good Governance and the Constitution

To a very large extent, the present-day crises and problems in governance have their source in the Constitution which we, the people of India were supposed to have given to ourselves in our Constituent Assembly on 26 November 1949. Actually, the Constitution of India is not a revolutionary document. It was not made by Indians in their Constituent Assembly. The Assembly did not have a *tabula rasa* to write on. The Constitution had had an organic growth through the various stages of the nationalist demands of self-governing institutions, struggle for freedom and reforms grudgingly and haltingly granted by the British. The primary concern of the British, naturally, was how to rule over India, keep the 'natives' weak; divided and control and govern them. Finally, the Government of India Act 1935, the Cabinet Mission Plan and the Indian Independence Act 1947, all drafted by the British to serve their interests, contributed nearly three-fourths of the Constitution of India as it came out of the Constituent Assembly.

No wonder, the entire infrastructure of the Constitution remained colonial. The focus was on organization of the State apparatus, on a political system, on institutions of government, on division of powers, on functionaries and officers—their rights and jurisdictions, etc. There was little emphasis on the principles of governance or traditional values in Indian political thought. Whatever little thought was given to governance got relegated to the non-enforceable Directive Principles part of the Constitution, perhaps, the only place where our Constitution uses the term 'governance' is in article 37 under the Directive Principles. Article 37 speaks of certain 'principles' being 'fundamental' in the 'governance of the country' but not 'enforceable by any court'. Adherence to some of these fundamental principles of governance would require the State to secure:

- a social order for the promotion of the welfare of the people with social, economic and political justice for all (article 38(1));
- minimization of inequalities in status, facilities and opportunities among individuals and groups of people (article 38(2));

- right to adequate means of livelihood for all citizens, men and women, equally (article 39(a));
- opportunities and facilities for children to develop in a healthy manner and in conditions of freedom and dignity (article 39(f));
- right to work, to education and to public assistance in cases of unemployment, old age, sickness disablement etc. (article 41);
- just and humane conditions of work and maternity relief (article 42);
- a living wage for workers with conditions of work ensuring a decent standard of life and full enjoyment of leisure (article 43);
- raising the level of nutrition and the standard of living and to improve public health (article 47);
- protection and improvement of environment and safeguarding of forests and wild life (article 48A);

These and other fundamental principles of good governance ordained by the Constitution are defiled, defaced and debunked openly almost daily and yet nobody can do anything. If these were given the status of enforceable fundamental rights, the story of the Constitution in the 21st Century, would have been very different and much less distressing than what it is today.

It is often said that there was nothing wrong with the Constitution and if it failed, those working it must be vile. But, it cannot be ignored that the vile were the products of this Constitution—its demands, constraints, compulsions and the system established under it. For example, the electoral system under the Constitution encouraged and necessitated the role of vote mathematics—of vote banks, corruption, black money, criminalization, casteism, communalism, violence and mafia power.

Nehru had told the Constituent Assembly that the first task of the Assembly was 'to free India through a new Constitution, to feed the starving people and clothe the naked masses and give every Indian the fullest opportunity to develop himself according to his capacity'. He had added that if the Constitution failed to solve the basic problems of the poor and the starving it 'will become useless and purposeless'. Even after half a century of its working, the Constitution failed to give 'clothes to the naked' and 'food to the hungry' as Nehru had wanted it to do. The number of poor and illiterates increased many-fold during the last 59 years. More than a lakh villages still do not have drinking water and in many villages, animals and human beings use the same village pond for meeting all their water needs from dawn to dusk. Still, there are fellow Indians who live on food grains retrieved from washing cow dung. However, beyond the pious wishes of the Directive Principles and hopes of men like Nehru, today, India is rated among the most corrupt nations of the world and has the largest number of illiterates and poor. A prominent Communist Party (CPI) leader and a very fine man, Shri Indrajit Gupta as the Union Home Minister in the Janata Government, despite his leftist moorings, was not ashamed of confessing that he could do nothing to remove the role of crime and criminals in politics. The Constitution contained no machinery for ensuring good governance and for solving the basic problems of under-development, backwardness, poverty, illiteracy, hunger, housing, clothing, corruption and the like.

In the midst of dismal poverty, abysmal illiteracy and alarming inequalities, a functioning participatory democracy is inconceivable. The framers of the Constitution did not seem to have foreseen a situation where the concept of collective ministerial responsibility to the Lok Sabha would tend to absolve the Ministers of all responsibility to the people at large and where the government would become so dependent on shifting party loyalties and temporary majorities. Also, they could hardly visualize how with all the electoral corruption and malpractices; with the majority of members getting elected on minority of votes, even the representative character of the rulers would come to be seriously doubted.

With a view to arrest the trend of unprincipled defections by legislators and the growing instability in governments, the Constitution of India was amended and the 10th Schedule, better known as the anti-defection law, was added. But it failed miserably and the Constitution 91st Amendment, 2003 also has not helped much. The spectacle of unethically engineered or defection-manipulated majorities or of several successive hung Legislatures or coalition governments of disparate elements coming together solely for sharing the fruits of power and including some of the goon leaders with criminal records or otherwise doubtful antecedents, are all matters of grave concern and go counter to requirements of good governance.

Things appear even more distressing when we find that in all spheres of life, in all professions, there is a general devaluation of values and de-institutionalization of institutions. Enough has been written and spoken about the problems of communalization, criminalization, casteism, growth of narrow identities and loyalties, widespread corruption, abject poverty, rampant illiteracy, over-population and lack of quality leadership.

The system under which we live has led to and nurtured an axis between the businessman, the politician, the civil servant, the police and the criminal. In large parts of India, Marx seems to have been proved right as the State appears to have withered away. There is no sign of administration. Mafia gangs rule. An ugly atmosphere of near anarchy prevails. The scepter of civil war and caste and communal war stare us in the face. We are counted among the most corrupt nations of the world. Things have come to such a pass that the other day in an open column in a national daily, a writer had no compunction in advocating take over of the nation's governance by the armed forces as the only way out to stem the rot.

The chief concern of the Constitution should be to try to evolve a polity which would attract better quality of persons—men and women of character and competence—to public service and enable them to assume political responsibility and leadership roles at various levels. They should sacrifice their normal vocations for short and fixed periods to serve the people and discharge their duties as citizens. The system should be purged of the whole-time professional politicians who have no other vocation and no known sources of making a living.

What has become a categorical imperative is clean and quality governance as it affects the lives of the people. The essential pre-requisites for quality governance are that the system should be good and suited to the needs, aspirations, background and ethos of the people concerned. Those selected for operating the system should be endowed with character and competence and motivated by the spirit of public service.

Blueprint for Good Governance

Evolve own mix

The present highly divisive system should be substituted by a suitable mix or a middle path combining the elements of stability of the Executive with accountability of the Legislature as in France, or by the German system of a constructive vote of no-confidence, whereby in effect, the Prime Minister is chosen by the whole House and continues as such unless a successor is chosen by the House. Even without any constitutional amendment, under article 86(2), the President can ask the Lok Sabha to elect the Leader of the House who can then be appointed by the President as the Prime Minister. Thus, in effect, the Prime Minister would be elected by the members of the Lok Sabha. Other ministers may, continue to be appointed on his advice but could include members or non-members. The Council of Ministers should be removable only by a constructive vote of no-confidence. If the Parliament is not able to elect a Prime Minister, it should be open to the President to appoint a government of his choice, which would continue unless Parliament can pass a constructive vote of no-confidence, while simultaneously voting to power a successor government.

We have to revive or evolve a political culture and a super-structure that is suited to our background, ethos, and even the weaknesses in our character. We should stop the fruitless and largely irrelevant debates on various western models, Presidential *vs* Parliamentary, strong Centre *vs* states' rights, accountability *vs* stability and the like. We need to look at our own historical and cultural background, our experience of working various institutions now for more than half a century and then decide upon the most suitable structures that would best meet our needs and fulfill our aspirations.

We have to consider what changes are imperative to solve the main national problems of poverty, illiteracy, corruption, over-population, criminalization of public life, devaluation of values, crisis of character, casteism, communalism, black money etc. We have to ensure our nation's socio-economic development and quality of life for all citizens. In short, we have to move towards good governance.

Unfortunately, we do not seem to have freed ourselves from the colonial hangover of thinking in terms of 'we' and they'—we the subjects and they the rulers. We talk of the conduct and responsibilities of the politicians—from Panchayats to Parliament—as things somewhat remote and different from ourselves. There is not enough consciousness of these institutions being our own and those manning and running them also being from among us. While it has become a fad to blame the politicians for all our miseries, very little is done to educate and awaken the citizens in the matter of their citizenship obligations in a representative, participatory democratic polity. Since the representatives are supposed to be responsive to public opinion and pressure, the ultimate responsibility for good and responsive governance is on us, the citizens of India. Quality of governance is dependent upon the quality of citizens. If we, the citizens, are looking for undeserved or illegitimate benefits from the system through our representatives' favours, good governance can never take shape. This is a stupendous responsibility and calls for education in the values and responsibilities of good governance in a democratic polity.

Law and Order Machinery

Security of the citizen is the primary responsibility of the state. But, the policeman in India, perceives his role as one of assisting the administration to control the people rather than of being a helper, friend and servant of the citizens. It is a matter of deepest concern that while colossal amounts of public money are spent to provide security to those, many of whom may deserve the security of jails, there is very little security for the ordinary citizen. The law and order machinery needs to be insulated from gross political influence and politicians. In this connection, the Police Commission and the Vohra Committee reports remain relevant.

The Gandhian Model

Just as economic reforms cannot succeed without political reforms, neither can separately nor together can succeed without administrative reforms, judicial reforms and educational reforms or without taking into account the likely impact of the emerging social changes, technological advances and the like. One possible option that may cover all the issues raised and merit consideration is the Gandhian model whereunder:

- politics has to be viewed as a mission for service of the peopie and maintenance of high moral standards in public life and not as a profession for wielding power and amassing wealth;
- there should be decentralization of power down to the lowest grassroots levels so that the ordinary citizen feels free and a participant in governance in keeping with the constitutional principle of the individual being the unit of Indian polity;
- instead of a pyramidical structure and concentration of power at the top with bits of it trickling down, we should have a polity of concentric circles of multi-tier governance with power spread out and shared in a bottom-up rather than top-down scenario;
- direct elections on the basis of adult franchise should be confined only to Panchayats and local bodies with all the other bodies like State Legislature, Union Parliament, President, etc., being indirectly elected. The Panchayats could elect the Zila Parishad or the like, the Zila Parishads could elect the State Legislature. The

State Legislatures, Zila Parishads and Punchayat could elect the Union Parliament and all four—Panchayats, Zila Parishads, State Legislatures and Union Parliament could elect the President.

- The President for the Republic should be elected for one fixed five or six year term. In order to be elected President, a candidate must secure more than 50 per cent of the total votes cast and a positive vote from majority of the States and the lower tiers.
- The lowest unit at the grassroots should be considered as a multi-member constituency. Besides, it could be laid down that in order to be declared a winner, a candidate must secure a minimum of 50 per cent plus votes so that it became necessary for every winning candidate to woo more than his caste, community or narrow group vote bank and seek a wider consensus. The representative credentials of those winning under this system would be above reproach;
- in keeping with the subsidiarity principle, each higher tier is entrusted with only those functions which the lower tier cannot handle.

Action Plan

A few short-term measures that may need to be examined for immediate implementation are:

- law regulating the number, setting-up, recognition/de-recognition, funding to ensure democratic and clean functioning of political parties;
- reforms to reduce the cost of elections and cleanse the system of criminalization and rid it of the role of money, muscle and mafia power;
- election of the Leader of the House (Prime/Chief Minister) by the House of the People/Legislative Assembly and adoption of the system of constructive vote of no-confidence;
- judicial and parliamentary reforms to ensure that the two apex institutions of the polity discharge their assigned functions, are

cleansed of undesirable elements and remain fully accountable to the sovereign citizens, the people of India;

- ensuring that the 73rd and 74th Constitutional Amendments are faithfully implemented and serve the objectives of strengthening democracy at the grassroots. After the 73rd and 74th Constitutional Amendments having come into operation, we can take some legitimate pride in being the only democracy with about 3.2 million elected representative rulers at various tiers of governance going down to the grassroot levels. Centralization of power and the attempt to dominate the units of the federation are at the root of much of the troubles. As a first step, therefore, radical redistribution of power between the Union and the units would be necessary. There is every case for a wholesale review of Union-State relations and decentralization of political power in a genuine four-tier system of governance down to the lowest grassroot levels. With a large number of smaller States and a four-tier system of governance, it may be possible to involve various groups in governance more closely. This may make the Union stronger and the nation more integrated emotionally and culturally.

There is no contradiction between strong units and a strong Union. A strong and stable Union Government would be necessary as much for meeting any challenges posed by separatist, secessionist or disruptionist forces, as for protecting the human rights and the rights of the smaller States and other units, and minorities throughout the country. Except that the basic constitutional values, human rights and rights of various tiers of government *vis a vis* each other may have to be guaranteed, monitored and enforced by the central authority; distribution of powers should be so designed that only the most essential or minimum necessary powers are assigned to each higher level. For example, whatever can be done by the local grassroot institutions like the village panchayats or municipalities should be left entirely in their hands. Government at a higher tier should have no power to remove or supersede a duly elected Government at a lower tier. Surrendering of powers by the Union in large areas should not mean weakening the Union. A strong and stable Union government would be necessary as much for meeting any challenges posed by divisive forces as for protecting the rights of the smaller states and ethnic minorities and human rights throughout the country.

Stop the Security Rackets

Gun-totting personal security officers and guards at residences at public expense have become a special perk and a status symbol in public life. While there is little security of life for the average citizen, literally, hundreds of millions of rupees are being spent on safeguarding the public-men—leaders and representatives of the people—from the people. Public life my have its hazards, but then, those who feel their lives threatened are free to return to private life instead of becoming a drain on the public exchequer. Security provided should be the minimum necessary and largely invisible.

Reducing Expenditure

Financial costs of parliamentary democracy have been skyrocketing. During the last five decades they have gone up by more than 100 times. Also, the figures of cost of politicians and holders of public office are fudged inasmuch as much of the expenditure gets reflected under other heads.

A matter often raised is that of the salaries, allowances, amenities, facilities etc., extended to Members. While for some entering Parliament involves financial sacrifice, for many others it provides much sought-for rewards and benefits. There are two extreme views on whether Members are heavily pampered and overpaid or they are misunderstood and grossly underpaid. According to one guess, if every member is paid Rs 200,000 per month or more in cash and all perks and direct and indirect financial benefits from the state are withdrawn, the public exchequer would be a gainer.

Educate the Citizens

While it has become a fashion to blame the politicians for all that ails the nation, little is done to educate the citizens in the matter of their own citizenship obligations in a representative, participatory democratic polity. Freedom and democracy are tender plants and demand constant vigil from the citizens. Unless nursed with great care, these are bound to wither away. In a democracy, the citizens are both the rulers and the ruled. The ultimate responsibility of good and responsive governance is, therefore, also theirs. This is a stupendous responsibility and calls for education in the values and responsibilities of good and responsive governance.

Finally, it is important to take a holistic view with regard to systemic reforms—political, administrative and constitutional; parliamentary, electoral and judicial; economic, social and educational. It is no more a question of priorities; all would have to be considered at once.

The Problem

The most difficult question is that of the mechanism for bringing about the needed reforms even if most of us arrive at some agreed suggestions. Those who can bring about the changes are the very people who have the greatest vested interest in the status quo. If more radical remedies are not to be advocated, we would have to be content with keeping up the efforts for creating greater awareness and building public opinion in the fond hope that one day, before it is too late, the elite and the people would wake up, arise and act to bring about the dawn of good and responsive governance and save our nation, freedom and democracy.

The country may be divided into 40 to 50 states of almost equal size and with near-equal representation in Parliament. This would lead to greater stability, more accountability, stronger union and better administered and more developed or faster developing states. It may help in getting over the malady of caste and communal divide and the increasing role of sub-national and narrower ethnic identities.

Reform options suggested may call for no major constitutional amendment, no change in the basic or any other features of the Constitution nor are any fundamental alterations in the political system suggested. It seems that what is really imperative is a total change in the attitude and approach of the rulers, the politicians and bureaucrats, who have usurped the powers of the sovereign people and instead of remaining the servants of the people, have become their masters. The political reform proposals mooted here may be a matter only of reinterpretation or proper implementation of constitutional provisions and intent of the founding fathers. Some of the suggestions may require only legislative or executive action or modification in rules of procedure. Even in the few cases, where Constitutional Amendments may be called for, it should be possible to effect them within the terms of article 368 of the Constitution itself. Also, if a national consensus on any reform agenda can be evolved, no Court can come in the way of the duly expressed sovereign will of the people.

It is only when we fulfill the basic duty of politics of restoring the power of the Constitution and its institutions back to their legitimate owners, the people, that things will begin to change. Really, no reforms shall succeed and nothing can change unless the sovereign power is exercised by the people and they use it to discharge their citizenship responsibilities.

Mere setting the agenda for action would not be enough. We cannot leave it to the government either. Blaming the politicians and the bureaucrats also would not do. We need to develop an awakened and aware activist citizenry. What we should be talking about is a citizen's movement against corruption, criminalization and concentration of power, or, in short, a crusade for good governance. Unless the people themselves are prepared to fight it out, the vested interests shall never allow a citizen-friendly administration. After all, why would the beneficiaries of bad governance give up their benefits?

Good governance is limited governance. Paring down the state to its bones is necessary so that it concentrates on its essential functions and divests itself of all non-essential functions. For example, doing business is not the business of government.

Citizens must not be made to feel dependent on the state; they should be able to feel like free citizens of a free country. Politicians and bureaucrats should realize that they are also citizens of India first before anything else and as public servants are fully accountable to their fellow citizens. Their self-interest agenda must not overshadow people's interest.

Serious efforts should be initiated to provide orientation and training to politicians and bureaucrats to prepare them for leadership roles. Building quality leadership is a crying need. India needs nothing more than leaders of high integrity, calibre and competence. Political management skills, techniques and tools have to be developed. Governance capacity is not a static quantity. It has to be raised by means of systemic reforms, training and reorienting the political and administrative leadership.

At the root of many problems in governance is the desire of any central authority, dominant party, social segment, caste, region or group to concentrate and monopolise power and to try to dominate other fellow citizens. This applies as much to institutions, organs and functionaries of State as to others.

People need education in democracy and for democracy. Without an educated populace, democracy is a sham. All of us need intensive education in citizenship values, in the duties and obligations of citizens. The first and foremost duty of every citizen is to be an active participant in the business of democratic government. Governance is too serious a matter to be left entirely in the hands of politicians and bureaucrats.

It has to be remembered that in a country like ours, good governance recipes have to take care of the poorest of the poor. International Monetary Fund and World Bank models of market-oriented global village and good governance based on maximization of production and consumption—competitive consumerism leading to sustainable development may not do. We may have to consider the old Indian concepts of a global family based on caring for the disadvantaged members, limitation of wants, sustainable consumption, the Gandhian principle of trusteeship and a private sector motivated by public purpose. Lastly, man treated not as a resource but as the end purpose.

Some of the problems are systemic. Case for reforms is unassailable. We need economic and political reforms, reform in education, judicial, social and cultural reforms and perhaps a bit of Constitutional reform. An integrated approach is necessary as all these are interrelated and interdependent and necessary parts of ensuring good governance. If we want good governance then beyond a minimum representational requirement, we do need a few capable and honest persons of character who come to public life with a spirit of service. There is a contradiction between good governance and viewing democracy as merely a matter of distribution of spoils or of purchasing loyalties by bribery in terms of money, ministerships or other allurements. If sharing corruption as widely as possible is democracy then only the corrupt and criminal elements would be more likely to get to power as representatives of the people.

Whether it is the Executive or the Legislature or the Judiciary, all must be fully accountable to 'We, the people of India'. All those who serve these institutions must consider themselves as citizens first and responsible to fellow citizens for whose service they are there.

There is much to despair. But all is not lost. Not all politicians are crooks, nor all bureaucrats or businessmen are corrupt. Some will listen and respond. India's future is bright. Misgovernance can abort all hope and good governance can actualize our great national potential. It should not be left to a power-hungry dictator or coup leader to come to remind us of this truism. Time to wake up and act is now, tomorrow may be too late.

Nations are made only when people rise above their narrow self-interests and are prepared to make sacrifices for their fellow citizens. Unless we, the citizens of India at large, are vigilant and conscious of our obligations as citizens, there is no reason why freedom and democracy should continue for ever. These plants are very fragile and unless nursed with care they are bound to wither away. If we fail to protect and promote the principles of good governance as the bedrock of our polity not only we will lose our freedom and democracy, but as a nation we may be forever thrown in the dust bin of oblivion.

2

Law and Justice in Kautilya's *Arthashastra*

Law, Justice and Dharma

Need for 'law' for regulating relationships between individuals and with the authority of the state has been felt from the earliest beginnings of civilization and structured human society. The quest for 'justice' has been equally old and perennial. In our jurisprudential academia and law school curricula, however, the concept of 'law and justice' in Indian legal thought has not so far received the attention it deserves.

Law and justice as a single integrated concept or as two separate but interrelated concepts came to be understood differently at different points of history and in the hands of different scholars in India. In order to appreciate those thoughts, it is imperative to remember the time and age when they were conceived and the then existent societal realities. Also, it is most advisable to so interpret the perspectives of old that they relate to the modern notions of jurisprudence and legal framework and become relevant to our present day needs and thinking.

Law is 'the expression of a principle of order to which men must conform in their conduct and relations as members of society'. Its objective is to so harmonize interests, rights and obligations of individuals and groups as to achieve justice. Even Dean Pound was intrigued by the ambiguity of the term 'law' used 'for the legal precepts which were actually recognized and applied in the tribunals of a given time and place, and for the more general body of doctrine and tradition from which those percepts are chiefly drawn, and by which we criticize them'. 'Justice' also meant different things to different people. Aristotle made a distinction between corrective, distributive and general justice. But, in a more fundamental sense, 'justice' is that to which law must conform (Cardozo, 31, 86-87,140). Under ancient Indian polity, law as the 'general body of doctrine and tradition' and 'justice' to which 'law must conform' were given the name Dharma.

The Sanskrit word Dharma is difficult to define. It includes concepts of duty, justice, law, righteousness, good, morality and much else. It is the code of laws both for the rulers and the ruled. In the practice of Dharma lies the well being of the individual and the State. Law did not emanate from the will or the authority of the ruler. It did not depend on the decree of a sovereign or other political authority. Both law and justice had their source in the foundational concept of Dharma.

Dharma as Rule of Law

The king was the protector and guardian of Dharma. He was himself bound by Dharma. He had to enforce it strictly on himself and the people and had no powers to overrule or contradict it. If he violated the laws ordained by Dharma or exceeded his jurisdiction, he was also subject to punishment. The basic principle was that the government should be conducted not by the wish of an individual but with the aid of councillors and in accordance with Dharma. The *Arthashastra* says that sovereign powers cannot be exercised without the cooperation of others. The sovereign must, therefore, appoint councillors and act on their advice. It could be said that Dharma was the true sovereign laying down the rules of conduct to be followed by all the people irrespective of their religion. It was not religion. Perhaps, the modern concept nearest to Dharma is the 'rule of law'.

Believed to belong to a period some 300 years before Christ, Kautilya's *Arthashastra* is replete with references to Dharma as the foundation of the concepts of law and justice. Dharma was both the source and the sanction of law. *Rajdharma* was more specifically the code of conduct or law governing the powers and duties of the ruler. It was superior to his own will and all his actions had to be tested on the anvil of *Rajdharma*. All laws and orders emanating from the ruler (king) had to be in keeping with the spirit and tenets of Dharma. In modem terminology the same principle could be expressed thus: the legitimacy of all statute law depends on its being in conformity with the norms of the rule of law. Duguit (as cited by Cardozo) says:

> "I am convinced that law is not a creation of the state, that it exists without the state, that the notion of law is altogether independent of the state, and that the rule of law imposes itself on the state as it does upon individuals."

Civil and Criminal Law before Kautilya

Even before Kautilya, civil and criminal justice were to be administrated by the king in accordance with the laws laid down in the *Dharmasutra* and *Arthashastra* systems. Manu enjoins the people to protect Dharma because it protects those who protect it. Those who act against Dharma or destroy it will themselves be destroyed. Society remains orderly and rights of all individuals are protected so long as everyone acts according to Dharma. Rules of Dharma are meant to so regulate the conduct of every individual as to protect the rights of all other individuals in society. Inasmuch as Dharma regulated the mutual obligations of the individual and society, protection of Dharma was in the interest of both the individual and society. Also, it embodied the entire content of the concept of the Rule of Law (Rama Jois 31-32).

धर्म एवं हतो हन्ति धर्मो रक्षति रक्षितः ।
तस्माद्धर्मो न हन्तव्यो मानो धर्माहतोऽवधीत् ।।

(Manu VIII-15)

The *Mahabharta* (*Shantiparva*) describes the evolution of *Rajdharma* in the context of the origin and objective of the state, the rule of law, kingship and rules of conduct for the king. If everyone acted according to Dharma, there would be no need for the kingdom or the king, there would neither be any guilty person nor any punishment.

नैवं राज्यं न राजोऽऽसीन्न दण्डो न च दाण्डिकः ।
धर्मेणैव प्रजाः सवां रक्षन्तिस्म परस्परम् ।।

The two chief sources of law at this time were the *Smritis* and *Shrutis*. The *Dharmasutras* came to be known as *Smriti* (that which is remembered) distinct from the earlier Vedic literature called *Shruti* (that which is heard). The *Dharmasutras* by Gautama, Bandhayana, Vashishtha and Apastama were the earlier *Smritis*. Later expanded and revised versions which were called *Dharmashastras* (instructions in law) were written by Manu, Yajnavalkya, Vishnu and Narada. These were basically commentaries and were second in line of prominence to the *Shruti*.

Dandaniti in *Arthashastra*

Kautilya's *Arthashastra* is among other things, a comprehensive treatise on law—both civil and criminal. Also, it is a classic work on political economy and statecraft in ancient India. But, Kautilya's *Arthashastra* differs from the *Smriti* way of writing and is considered to be written in a more secular form (Basham 114). According to Arthashastra, the concept of the protection and security of the state extends to the realm of the people.

Kautilya recognizes the concept of *danda* (punishment) as the most important means of control. The basic philosophy behind *dandaniti* (theory of punishment) was the already existent and accepted concept of the early political thinkers about the nature of man in the state of nature. This state explained by the analogy of fishes was called *matsyanyaya* whereunder we have the big fish eating the small. In this state of anarchy there is no protection or safety for the weak. Hence to come out of this state of nature a ruler is required to enforce the law or Dharma through *danda*. As Kautilya says:

> 'But when the law of punishment is kept in abeyance it gives rise to disorders as is implied in the proverb of fishes for in the absence of a magistrate the strong will swallow the weak but under his protection the weak resists the strong.'

Realizing that mere creation of the State and the ruler (the king) was not enough, the *Brihadaranyakopanishada* lays down that law (Dharma) is a power above the king and is meant to protect the people—the weak. Law is defined as the king of kings, that enables the weak to prevail over the strong. Kings become subordinate to Dharma or the rule of law. The duty of king under *Rajdharma* is to rule according to law so that law reigned supreme and was accepted as the ultimate authority. Under Kautilya's *dandaniti*, no body is above the law.

तदेतत् क्षत्रस्य क्षत्रं यद्धर्मः।
तस्माद्धर्मात्परं नास्ति।
अथो अबलीयान् बलीयांसमाशंसते धर्मेण।
यथा राजा एवम्।।

Rajdharma and Welfare State

The first and foremost duty of the ruler is to ensure the protection of the people. *Rajdharma* requires, as Manu put it, that equal protection should be given to all the people without any discrimination. As the earth holds all living beings equally, the ruler should support all without any discrimination.

यथा सर्वाणि भूतानि धरा धारणयते समम् ।
तथा सर्वाणि भूतानि बिभ्रतः पार्थिवं व्रतेम् ।।

(*Manusmriti,* IX, 31)

Raksana (रक्षण) or *palana* (पालन) meant primarily the protection of the person and property of the people and ensuring their welfare and material well-being. The ruler must maintain order. Discipline lay at the root of all success. Disorder and offences against the law must be repressed without undue severity or leniency. Justice is the bedrock of society. Kautilya's whole conception of the duties of the rulers is positive and explicitly suggests improvement of every aspect of social life. The principle is the observance of the qualities of exertion, dutifulness and impartiality culminating in a doctrine of the ruler's complete identification of his interests with those of the people.

Under *Rajdharma*, the ruler is for the service of the people. धर्मा राजा भवति न कामकाणाय तु । [*Mahabharata*, *Shantiparva*, Chapter 90, 3(1)]. The job of the king is to serve Dharma (law) and not to indulge in pleasures. He may have to desert even his wife for the sake of his people.

Rules of administration are aimed at the over all development of the people and at building an institutional structure of government that provides rule of law and justice and protects the State. Dharma or rule of law was enforced by the king. Also, his powers were limited by the will of the people and customs, usages and injunctions of the *Dharmashastras*. The king was required to take an oath of loyalty to the law and constitution of the realm and to hold in trust the State for achieving the welfare of his people, both material and moral.

Kautilya attaches prime importance to the preservation of the State. His whole *Arthashastra* devolves round this objective. For this very purpose, he gives to the ruler utmost powers in matters of statecraft. The notion of justice has to be derived from the objective of *Arthashastra*. As Kautilya says, *danda* is the law of punishment or science of government (*dandaniti*). As the essential duty of the government is to maintain order Kautilya includes both maintenance of social order as well as order in the sense of preventing and punishing criminal activity. (Rangarajan 378).

The earlier *Arthashastras* had developed four sources of state law. These were the sacred canons (Dharma or *Dharmashastra*), the current law (*vyavahara* or *vyavaharika shastra*) usage (*samastha*) and reasoning (*nyaya*). Kautilya placed *Rajshasana* or *Rajdharma* above all other kinds of law. Along with the earlier *Arthashastra* sources of law, Kautilya developed a new concept of the king's quasi-legislative authority. But this did not mean that the king was regarded as the law maker. The king could not make fresh laws in suppression of those already existing.

II

Legal Justice System

Kautilya's ideal was to have a crime free society governed by law with assurance of justice to all without discrimination. Books III and IV of *Arthashastra* deal specially with the judicial administration and justice system and also set forth the laws to be administrated by the courts. The books cover civil law (including family law, law of contract and labour law) and criminal law (including the Penal Code). A broad distinction can be discerned wherein Book III covers most of the Civil Law and Book IV is concerned with Criminal Law. Though a strict differentiation between Civil and Criminal Law is not envisaged by Kautilya, a broad distinction as to the nature of the crime is certainly intended. Moreover, many offences which are deemed to be criminal today are dealt with under Civil Law of the *Arthashastra*. Book III is called '*Concerning Upholder of Dharma*' and Book IV '*The Removal of Thorns*', that is, elimination of anti-social activities (Rangarajan 378). The *Arthashastra* lists the types of crimes and corresponding punishments. Different kinds of penalties are discussed in great detail.

Structure of Courts

The proper identification of crime with differentiation of the courts to deal with them and the reach of the justice system are characteristic of Kautilya's *Arthashastra*. Two types of courts are provided in Kautilya's *Arthashastra*. To use modern terminology, these are the Civil Courts and the Criminal Courts. The Civil Courts are envisaged for major cities and at places where districts meet. A *janapadasamdhi* is the frontier post where the districts meet. *Sansaham* is the headquarter of 10 villages, *dronamukhi*, the headquarter of 400 villages, and *sthaniya*, the chief city among 800 villages, which in effect is the capital of the State. Gradation among the courts at different places is not clear. Since there is no such reference, it appears that all courts at the various places mentioned are at the same footing (Kangle 215). Civil courts consisting of three judges and three jurors shall judge civil cases arising from disputes between two parties. Special royal courts of criminal jurisdiction known as *kantakasodhana* courts shall entertain cases of serious crime against the state and society. These courts will consist of three commissioners (*pradeshtarah*) or three ministers (Shamashastri 229, Rangarajan 381, Altekar 250).

Judges

There are some problems of translation in the matter of the number and the background of judges. Shamashastri makes a reference to three members acquainted with sacred law and three ministers (*amatyas*) of the king who will carry the administration of justice in the civil courts. Kangle equates the three members to the ministers (*amatyas*) whereas Altekar refers to three jurors and three judges. Again it is not clear whether the bench consisted of three judges or they sat independently.

The method of appointment of judges is not mentioned in the *Arthashastra* but it can be inferred. Kautilya is very keen on who and who should not be appointed to ministerial positions. If the appointment of judges has to be made from among the ministers, obviously, it is for the king to select and appoint the judges. In Chapter 8 of Book I, Kautilya deals with the selection of ministers by the king. It follows that the judge must also be qualified as a minister. He should be born in a respectable family and must possess wisdom, purity of purpose, bravery and loyal feelings, and must be proficient in the science of polity. Apart from all this, he must also be well-versed in the knowledge of sacred laws (Shamashastri 13, 169).

Kautilya lays down certain don'ts which the judges have to follow, the violation of which will attract punishment for them which shall be in the nature of fines or corporal punishment or removal from office.

The judges shall not:

- threaten, intimidate, send out or unjustly silence disputants;
- defame or abuse any disputant;
- ask what ought not be asked;
- leave his own questions;
- teach to answer, or remind facts or statements;
- inquire into unnecessary circumstances and instead probe necessary ones;
- delay suits on any pretext resulting in the tiring of parties;
- re-hear cases that are settled;
- impose unjust fines in gold;
- impose unjust corporal punishment;
- falsify truth and declare true what is false.

Jurisdiction of Courts

The *Arthashastra* has determined the scope and jurisdiction within which the courts will function and the broad procedure that they would follow. In the matter of territorial jurisdiction, the courts established in the *sthaniya* city will have jurisdiction over 800 villages.

In *dronamukha* cities, the court will exercise jurisdiction over 400 villages. In the *sangrahana* cities, the courts will exercise jurisdiction over 10 villages. This jurisdiction is in relation to civil cases. (*Arth.* Book III, Chap I). The territorial jurisdiction of the *Kantakaksodhana* courts dealing with criminal cases in not specified.

Ratione Personae

The *Arthashastra* lays down that the purpose of courts in general is to ensure the welfare and security of the people. Persons responsible for violating the law of Dharma or the writs of the king, and whosoever threatens the security of the State or causes breach of peace will be brought to trial. Courts could take even *suo motu* notice in matters of public welfare.

Ratione Materiae

The *Ratione Materiae* (jurisdiction on crimes) of the courts or the justice system in *Arthashastra* consists of the jurisdiction in civil and criminal matters and the issuing of writs. The civil jurisdiction consists of:

- Determination of forms of Agreement and Legal Disputes: These include valid and invalid transactions.
- Law concerning marriages: These include the duty of marriage, the property of a woman and compensation for remarriage, duty of a wife, maintenance of a woman, cruelty to women, enmity between husband and wife, wife's transgression, forbidden transactions, vagrancy, elopement and sojournments.
- Law on division of inheritance: Includes time of dividing inheritance and shares in inheritance.
- Law on buildings (*Vastu*): Includes sale, boundary dispute and determination and miscellaneous hindrances.
- Law on destruction of pasture land, fields and roads, and non-performance of agreements.

- Law on recovery of debt and deposits.
- Law on rules regarding slaves and labourers and co-operative undertakings.
- Law relating to recession of purchase and sale.
- Law relating to resumption of gifts sale without ownership and with ownership.
- Law relating to robbery: Defamation, assault which includes striking, hurting and robbery.
- Law relating to gambling and betting and miscellaneous offences.

Criminal jurisdiction is contained in Book IV. It consists of:

- Law on protection against artisans: The artisans include weavers, washer men, scavengers, medical practitioners, musicians.
- Law on protection against merchants.
- Law on suppression of the wicked living by foul means.
- Law on detection of youths of criminal tendency by ascetic spies.
- Law on seizure of criminals: The grounds may include suspicion, seizure of stolen articles and circumstantial evidence.
- Law on examination of sudden death.
- Law on trial and torture to elicit confession.
- Law on protection of all kinds of government departments.
- Law on fines in lieu of mutilation of limbs.
- Death with or without torture.
- Sexual intercourse with minor girls.
- Punishment for violating justice.

The royal writs (*shasana*) or the command of the king can be issued regarding 13 purposes. These are:

- Calumination (*ninda*) or speaking ill of one's family, body and acts
- Commendation (*prasansha*) or praising one's family, body and acts

- Inquiry—to inquire about something
- Narration (*akhyima*)—to point out the way
- Request—to entreat to 'give'
- Refusal—to say, 'I do not give'
- Censure (*upalambhah*)—to say, 'it is not worthy of thee'
- Prohibition (*pratishodha*)—to say, 'do not do so'
- Command (*chodana*)—to say, 'this should be done'
- Conciliation (*santvam*)—to say, 'what I am, thou art that'; 'whichever article is mine is thine also'
- Promise of help (*abhyavapaltin*)—to hold out help in trouble
- Threat (*abhibhartsanam*)—pointing out the evil consequences that may occur in future
- Persuasion—this is of three kinds: that made for the purpose of money; that made in made of one's failure to fulfill a promise; that made on occasion of any trouble.

Trial Procedure

Trial proceedings will be held in public. The exceptions to this rule consist of matters relating to division of inheritance, sealed or unsealed deposits, marriage, women afflicted with disease or who do not stir out, persons of unsound mind, and those transactions done during the first part of the night (Shamashastri, 169). Agreements between persons living in forests, between members of an association, by dependants and unauthorized persons are invalid. Agreements under provocation, anxiety, or intoxication, by lunatics or convicted persons are also void.

For any trial of civil matters, the first requirement is that the plaintiff and defendant must be fit to sue and defend. The case will be then registered by the court clerk, which should contain the following particulars: the year, the season, the month, the fortnight (*paksha*), the date, the nature and place of the deed, the amount of debt as well as the country, the residence, the caste, the *gotra* and the name and occupation of both the plaintiff and the defendant. The statement of the parties will then be taken down in such order as may be required by the case. These statements then shall be thoroughly scrutinized. The burden of proof lies on the plaintiff. Normally, the defendant will get three to seven fortnights to prepare his defence, failing which fine will be imposed. An extended time till three fortnights can be given to the defendant, on the faltering of which he will be fined for *parokta* and the plaintiff will recover the amount of the case from his property. Both the parties must be consistent with their statements, must not ask for third person's opinion, must answer in full the questions at issue, must not introduce new questions, must agree with their own witnesses. On faltering, the party will be fined for the offence of *parokta* (the fine of five times the amount). If the plaintiff runs away or does not substantiate his case he will be guilty of *parokta*. No countersuits except those of duel, robbery or dispute among merchants or trade-guilds will be entertained against the plaintiff or the defendant (Shamashastri 170-171). Testing the self-assertion (*svayamvada*) of the opposite parties, examination (*amiyoga*), honesty (*arjava*), evidence (*hetu*) and asseveration by oath are employed during the trial of the case.

Evidence and Witnesses

Evidence refers to all kinds of evidence, documents, witnesses and so on. As the transactions were not carried out in written documents, the witness to it were the 'listeners'. When they come to the court, they are 'eyewitnesses'. Witnesses are not thought to be those who depose signatures to documents. A testimony of witnesses is given more importance than documentary evidence (Kangle 218-220).

It was the responsibility of the parties to bring three witnesses (*sakshi*) of their own. Two witnesses may be allowed if the parties agree but never one in cases of doubt. These witnesses should be accessible and should not be living too far. They must be reliable, honest and respected. Certain persons do not qualify to be admitted as witnesses.

These are wife's brothers, co-partners, prisoners, creditors, enemies; maimed persons or persons once punished by the government.

Other persons such as persons legally unfit to carry on transactions, the king, persons learned in the *Vedas*, dependants, lepers, persons suffering from bodily eruptions, outcaste persons, *chandals*, persons of mean avocation, the blind, the deaf, the dumb, egotistic females or government servants, are barred as witnesses except in cases of transactions in one's own community.

Witnesses are required to take oath before deposing in a court. The procedure for taking oath varied for different categories of people. They are bound to depose evidence within seven days, the failure of which will make them liable to a fine of 12 *panas* and after three fortnights a fine of the decreetal amount (Kangle 219).

For perjury, the witness is liable for a fine of 24 *panas* if he gives false evidence and 12 *panas* for refusing to give evidence at all (Shamashastri 203).

The law of evidence takes into account both witnesses and documents, but as documents were not the norm in ancient times, personal witnesses got more weightage. Hence, to prevent miscarriage of justice, checks and balances in terms of fines and compulsory attendance of witnesses are provided in the *Arthashastra*.

In case of differences among witnesses, statement of a majority is accepted. The evidence of a witness shall be final in a case where the plaintiff is careless, the witness cannot hear properly during transaction, when there is bad writing or when the debtor is dead (Shamashastri 203).

The payment of fees to the witnesses is to be made by the defeated party. It will be one-eighth of a *pana* (*astanga*) or proportional to the amount sued or both (Shamashastri 171).

Decision

Judges are expected to settle disputes free from all kinds of influences and with a stable and reasonable mind. The decision should be pleasing to all. Kautilya enumerates five elements which would help the judges in arriving at decisions: a party being manifestly in the wrong, a free admission of the charge, straight-forwardness in the question and answers between the two parties, reasoning and oath.

In case a matter finally goes to the king, he should decide the matter in accordance with Dharma, evidence (*vyavahara*), history (*samastha*) and earlier royal edicts (*nyaya*). Whenever there is disagreement between history and Dharma or between evidence and Dharma, then the matter shall be settled in accordance with Dharma. Dharma is the supreme law but whenever, Dharma is in conflict with rational law (*dharmanyaya*), according to Kautilya, the latter should prevail (Shamashastri, 173). But here we are on delicate grounds. Also, it is not clear whether the standard set for the king to come to a decision is also applicable to the judges.

It seems that while the judges have to decide cases on the basis of facts and circumstantial evidence, the king being the superior and the final court decides on the basis of law and principles of legal jurisprudence. It is also possible that the customary law applicable to every case is in conflict with the *rajashasana*. In such a situation judges will have to decide the case according to the edicts of the king. This shows that the judges must also follow the broader principles set in the *Arthashastra*.

Punishment

Kautilya mentions 13 kinds of criminals who should either be banished or made to pay adequate compensation according to the seriousness of the offence. Punishment is to be inflicted with impartiality and in proportion to the guilt. In keeping with the social realities of the times, punishment for the same offence varied on the basis of the position of the offender. Taking into consideration the social position of persons, the nature of offence, the cause, whether grave or slight, (that led to the perpetration of the offence), the antecedents and present circumstances of the accused, the time and the place where offence was committed and noticing equitable distinction among offenders, whether belonging to royal family or to the common people, shall the commissioner determine the propriety of imposing the first, middle-most or highest punishment. Fines and punishment in cases of robbery, defamation and assault shall be given in accordance to the gravity of the crime. Thus, the intention and condition under which crime was committed is taken into consideration in determining the crime and the punishment for the crime committed. Death punishment shall be awarded in cases of murder and grievous hurt leading to murder. However, Kautilya provides for relaxing the punishment in cases of those offenders who have not been cruel (Shamashastri 173, 219-225, 258-261).

III

System of Law

While enumerating the various instances relating to the commission of offences of civil and criminal nature, Kautilya lays down broad generalizations to be applied to categorization of offences. The criteria take into consideration personal factors, human psyche and needs of the stability of the state.

The age of adulthood or majority laid down by Kautilya is for women 12 years and for men 16 years. Persons of this age or above are liable to be fined for the disobedience of lawful authority distinguishing them from the minors.

Inheritance

Kautilya may be considered the first secular law giver in Indian legal history. He tried to separate religion and its practices from mundane worldly pursuits. He discusses in depth the Dayabhaga system of inheritance. Kautilya lays down the laws of inheritance and the lineage. Personal customs are given more weightage. There is a strong underlining principle that recognizes the local customs in cases of inheritance, for it will be in accordance with the customs prevalent in the country, caste, guild or the village of the inheritors that succession will be determined. In the absence of a son, property may be inherited by brothers and in their absence, by daughters. In case of division, minor's share shall be free from all, encumbrances. Sons, even the eldest, may lose their share in part or full under certain circumstances or failings in conduct.

Urban Planning

Kautilya was well aware of the problems of crowding, congestion, fire hazards, environmental violation, etc., in cities. He emphasizes the need for planning urban buildings and lays down municipal laws ensuring that hygiene is maintained and the essential services or infrastructure, are not disturbed or damaged. He suggests incentives in the form of remission of taxes to build dams and disincentives in the form of levies of fine if hygiene is not maintained, mischief is done to other's property and roads or flow of water from dams are obstructed (Shamashastri 190-197). Kautilya disapproved of unjustified or reckless felling of trees.

Contracts and Agreements

Kautilya restricts the contracts of sale and mortgage to be made within certain classes, e.g., among those who pay taxes. Agreements or contracts made are to be fulfilled, nonperformance will invite fines. Agreements which are ill-considered and improper *prima facie*, shall not succeed. It is provided that such agreement or promises will be subject to verification and proper settlement by the experts (Shamashastri 197-198, 211).

In case of losses due to neglect or putting off work or breach of contract, appropriate fines and damages will be recovered depending upon the merit of the case. In cases of partnership or company, the principle followed in relation to the sharing of the income is that of equal distribution, of earning or the amount agreed upon. Discoverers of mines, precious stones, treasure troves, etc., are entitled to a percentage share in the find.

Debts and Deposits

Similar rules are laid down for guiding matters concerning debts and deposits. Kautilya says that the nature of transactions between creditors and debtors, on which the welfare of the kingdom depends shall always be scrutinized. He distinguishes between and prescribes different rates of interest for non-commercial and commercial debts and deposits. Also, different rules are prescribed for trade in forestry goods and for sea-traders in their dealings. Charging of excess rate of interest will be liable to be punished by way of fine. The prevalent interest rates varied between 5 to 20 per cent per month. An interest of 15 per cent per year was generally just and proper and in accordance with Dharma according to Kautilya. Limitation as to neglect of recovery of debt has been laid down as for ten years. Thereafter, one would not be able to claim back the debt.

The exceptions to this rule are certain class of persons such as the minors, the aged, the deceased, those involved in calamities, those sojourning abroad or, those who fled the country during disturbances. The responsibility of paying the debts lies on the sons and grandsons of the deceased except where it is barred by the limitation of time and space. Some debts such as between husband and wife, father and son are not recoverable. It makes provisions for suing for the recovery of debt but no debtor can be sued for multiple debts. The suit should follow the order in which the debts were taken. In cases of deposits, only those can be claimed which are misappropriated for self. Deposits lost during plunder, invasion or natural calamities cannot be claimed. So is the case with pledges. Rules regarding debts are also to be followed in cases of resumption of gifts (Shamashastri 201-216).

Slaves, Labourers, Prisoners and Servants

Kautilya bans and outlaws all selling or mortgaging of human lives except under certain conditions. The *Arthashastra* protects the rights of the slaves to their privileges and to freedom against employment in polluting or degrading jobs or against violation of chastity in case of the female slaves. The slave also has the right to his earned labour and inheritance from his father. Also, a slave can be released from the bondage against the payment of his value. Moreover, no slave of eight years old, shall be sold against his wish, nor any pregnant woman can be sold without making provisions for her confinement. Welfare and rights of landless labourers, wage-earners and prisoners are protected. The servants are guaranteed the right to agreed wages. The wages are settled using the parameters as to work done in relation to time and the prevalent market rates (Shamashastri 208-210).

Consumer Protection

Kautilya had a poor opinion about the honesty of traders and thought that they sought to cheat the consumers. In *Arthashastra*, provision is made for a Superintendent of Commerce charged with the responsibility of inter alia supervising weights and measures to prevent deception by the unethical merchants. The Superintendent of Commerce has to fix a profit of five per cent on local products and 10 per cent on foreign products: Merchants making higher profits are to be punished. The sale of articles of quality inferior to what is claimed is punishable by eight times the value of the article sold. Stringent punishment is provided for adulterators of goods and for middlemen who cheat a merchant or consumer (Book IV, Chapter II). Kautilya prescribes punishment for the non-performance or the mal-performance of duties by the artisans, washer men, goldsmiths, musicians, merchants and others. He cites nine ways in which the artisans, for example, may cheat their clients. It is most interesting that Kautilya's consumer protection law covers the medical practitioners also. Punishment is provided to a doctor for negligence in treating a patient. Kautilya is sensitive towards the exploitative nature of economy and thus emphasizes state control over economic activities: Where necessary, he does not hesitate to suggest even to centrally regulate economic activities. He lays down rules for the performance of duties for various categories of people. The rules are directed towards the protection of the consumer from exploitation. He calls for quality check-up of all goods from grains to gold, toll amount, interest-fixing of prices for which state shall appoint a special office/officer.

Vigilance

Kautilya's most important source of gathering information relating to corruption (including among government officers) and other criminal activities is the system of spies or in modern terminology we can say 'intelligence agencies'. The ruler is supposed to exercise vigilance and make his omnipresence felt through the spies. The spies hold an important position in the overall scheme of justice and to further this, they are given wide powers and exemptions. Detecting criminal tendencies, investigating crimes and identifying and bringing to book persons living on foul means and constituting a danger to the State and to society are some of the jobs to be performed by the intelligence agencies. Kautilya has words of admiration for the spirit of sacrifice and patriotism among those entrusted with espionage responsibilities.

Post mortem Investigation and Behaviour towards the Dead

In cases of sudden death of a person, investigation/examination is to be carried out to ascertain the identity of the person as well as to get to know 'why' and 'how' the death occurred (Shamashastri 247-249). Kautilya discourages 'suicide' attempts as being illegal. He lays down prohibition of cremation rights of the person who has committed suicide. Kautilya also lays down stringent rules against mistreatment of the dead body by dragging it on the public road.

Though some torture is allowed by Kautilya as a means of investigation during the trial to elicit confession from the accused, he does not approve of third degree methods leading to death in custody. For custodial deaths, the guilty will be punished. Certain categories of persons shall be fully exempted from torture. These are—the youngsters, the aged, the afflicted, those under intoxication, lunatics, hungry persons, those thirsty or fatigued from journey or those who have confessed on their own accord (Shamashastri 250-252). Such concerns exemplify Kautilya's notion of legal justice and the humanitarian approach to law.

Women's Rights and Matrimonial Matters

Kautilya is very progressive in his conception of marriage, divorce, remarriage, inheritance and family laws. He provides for rights of women. Given the social and political conditions of the times, it was natural that the *ganikas* were used by the State for espionage work. But, rights of *ganikas* also were protected. Married women were allowed to remain in touch with their parents even after marriage. Heavy fines are provided for molesting the dignity or outraging the modesty of a woman. Kautilya recognizes eight kinds of marriages and establishes the right of woman to her *stridhana*. The *Arthashastra* recognizes the freedom of a young girl to choose her husband. In this, Kautilya showed himself to be far ahead of his times. He also lays down conditions in which both women and men will have the right to sever matrimonial ties or to divorce or remarry. A wife may abandon her husband if he is of bad character, abroad for long, a danger to her life, impotent or fugitive in law. Divorce can also be obtained by mutual consent. It gives the woman the right to maintenance. Brides cannot be rejected or the contract of marriage broken down after certain rituals have been performed. Special protection is provided for women in captivity particularly those in ill health.

Separate provisions are made for working women with regard to their emoluments (Shamashastri, 174-179, 215).

Punishment for Rape

Kautilya prescribes capital sentence for the offence of rape against woman in custody committed by an officer of the State. Also, there is provision of heavy punishment for rape on minor girl and if the victim dies, Kautilya prescribes death punishment. There are certain categories of sexual intercourse which are strictly prohibited both for men and women, e.g., 'no man shall have intercourse with any woman against her will' (Shamashastri 262-264). Kautilya's position in this matter appears to be very modern and in fact, is an improvement on what our criminal law provides. The primary issue is willingness or consent irrespective of rights and relationship. A woman could refuse to allow her husband to cohabit if she did not feel the 'desire'. Even where consent might have been given, there are certain instances where Kautilya considers the act illegal and provides punishment. Despite the amendment of Section 376 IPC by the Criminal Law Amendment Act, 1980, present law in the matter of rape does not provide as rigorous punishment as Kautilya does.

IV

Overview and Conclusion

The part of Kautilya's *Arthashastra* dealing with issues of law and justice encompasses a very wide area. It covers almost all matters where laws need to deal with the governance of the state machinery and maintaining order in society. Kautilya cites specific instances, drawing legal principles, and prescribing punishments keeping in view the needs of the security and stability of the state. His concern is to provide justice for the people through proper governance by means of law and its enforcement through the sanction of force behind it. Other texts of *Dharmashastras* contain only scrappy rules on only some of the topics and can hardly be regarded as genuine codes of law. Kautilya's *Arthashastra* however gives us a fairly complete code.

> 'It is perhaps a pity that the full code of law which we find in Kautilya and which could have been the basis even of modern legislation on a number of topics came to be ignored and that its breadth of outlook despite its adherence to Varna system, its warm humanitarianism and its understanding of the realities of actual life, were set aside in favour of the rather one-sided and narrow-minded teachings of Apastamba, Manu and others.' (Kangle)

Kautilya's *Arthashastra* is a secular text suggesting remedies for the actual administration of law and justice in the state. It is not only ahead of its own times but also at some levels it may seem to have an edge even over our modern legal system. Public interest litigation is often lauded as an example of creative jurisprudence and judicial activism. But Kautilya, 300 years before Christ, envisaged courts taking *suo motu* notice in matters of public interest and welfare without any aggrieved person or other approaching them for redress. Kautilya is very modern when he deals with certain issues such as women's rights, espionage, consumer protection, duties of citizens, rights of landless labourers, wage earners, servants, prisoners, and concerns like forestry, environmental protection and water resource management.

Kautilya gives to Dharma as the code of laws a more scientific, procedural and factual basis. Though he gives the king wide powers and makes him the 'wholesole' in the affairs of the state, yet the king is not to be an autocratic ruler. He is bound by the laws of Dharma to rule the people by law, so as not to create disaffection among people and to preserve harmony and welfare among them. The coercive authority of the king or what is called *dandaniti* is not an arbitrary authority. It has to be used in such an appropriate and equitable manner that coercion commands obedience and raises the authority of the king over his subjects.

The various levels of intelligence agencies for espionage and vigilance over the subjects as well as officials and bringing them to justice in cases of violation of the prescribed law serves the basic purpose of good governance and proper administration of the state.

The process followed to cleanse the system of corruption is another unique feature of Kautilya's statecraft. His analysis of corruption and suggestions for its eradication sound very modern. Even the judges are not immune from the watchful eyes of his spies and are expected to perform their functions in an honest manner. Any violation of trust would make the officer liable to punishment or removal from office. Kautilya wanted to ensure that the officers remain accountable to the people. Even poverty is attributed to bad governance. Kautilya attaches considerable importance to issues like public sanitation, management of natural disasters like floods, famines, fire and epidemic.

As the dictum goes, 'justice delayed is justice denied'. Kautilya seems to follow this rigorously as he has prescribed immediate filing of cases and speedy judgements. In some cases the judgements are to be delivered on the same day. Another dictum that fits very appropriately in case of Kautilya is 'justice should not only be done, but it should be seen to be done', he calls for justice and speedy justice so that the people at large see and feel that justice has been done. Also, the judgements delivered must be such that the parties involved too should not feel bad about the decision given by the judges.

Though the ancient concepts were largely duty-based with each person enjoying to perform certain duties for the fulfillment of a better life. Kautilya derived rights from these duties and provided them to the destitute, the weak, women, labourers, slaves and so on. The matrimonial rights of the women and the rights against sexual abuse appear very contemporary and at some points better than what we have. When providing remedies for the violation of rights, or non-performance of duties, Kautilya takes care to exempt certain categories of people.

To conclude, Kautilya's *Arthashastra* provides an in-depth formulation of laws based on experience, facts, reason and a concept of justice and of right and wrong. Legal justice system is the backbone of the whole administrative machinery of the Kautilyan state. It is unfortunate that Kautilya's *Arthashastra* has not received the attention it deserves. More so, theoretical analyses of this work as a legal treatise are practically non-existent. There is need to go deeper to look into epistemology and perspectives of law and justice in Kautilya. We may end up finding a 'treasure-trove filled with precious gems of wisdom'.

It can be nobody's case that what was written by Kautilya three centuries before Christ can be applied without any change to present-day problems in the field of the study or dispensation of law and justice. Nevertheless, there is every case for a sustained in-depth study of Kautilya's *Arthashastra* as a classic book in law and jurisprudence and as an important landmark and reference point in Indian legal history. There is much in Kautilya that relates to some of the most modern and emerging concerns. His insights and prescriptions are almost as relevant to today's predicaments as they were during the times of Chandragupta Maurya.

3

Federalism

Union-State Relations

Federal Polity

Federal polity usually refers to the political system in a country with a written Constitution defining and delimiting the powers and functions both of the central or federal legislature and government on the one hand and local or state legislatures and governments on the other. In a classical federation like that of the United States, sovereignty is divided between the federal and state institutions, both partaking of sovereign powers in their respective spheres.

Federation, literally and historically is the result of an agreement. It is when two or more sovereign States resolve to surrender a part of their sovereignty and join hands to constitute a new union, a federal polity is born. It is a union without the constituting units losing their own identities. However, there are also instances where an existing unitary system may decide to share powers with the units under an agreed system of devolution or distribution of powers. Canada and India are examples of such polities. But, in every case of federalism—classical or otherwise—(i) the Constitution occupies the supreme position. It is written and relatively rigid, that is, not easily amendable; (ii) there are at least two levels at which government functions. In other words, two separate governments—federal and state—coexist, and (iii) as the arbiter of any disputes between the federation and the units as also between the units themselves, the highest judiciary—federal court or Supreme Court—enjoys great authority and prestige.

Many countries in the developing world which do not strictly fit in the definition of a federal polity and yet have many of its features are variously described by scholars as some kind of a federation or a polity covered by some variant of federalism. Today, one hears of all kinds of 'innovative' federalisms—cooperative, executive, emergent, responsible, parliamentary, populist, legislative, competitive, fiscal, restructured, reluctant or quasi-federalism are some of these. Mention is also made of federations without federalism.

The western mind particularly is anxious to reduce everything to a model or to fit every phenomenon into one of the models of its own conception. The tyranny of models, however, may be dangerous. That apart, federalism is basically an integrative device intended to keep different communities or divergent religious, linguistic, racial, tribal or other group identities together united under one nation state. Problems of social pluralism or of diversities in a pluralism or of diversities in a plural society are sought to be resolved by an arrangement or agreement to share political power. Irrespective of any variant of federal polity that we may be thinking of, the most important fact to be remembered is that federalism is relevant only in a situation where the pluralism is territorially based, that is, where particular groups are concentrated in separate territorial units or where the societal diversities are territorially identifiable, definable and separable. In other words, federalism as a political system can be a meaningful performer only for a society faced with territorial diversities. It is an arrangement between separate territorial entities to come together or to avoid break-up and stay united by sharing power through free democratic will.

Indian Federation

There is perhaps no other comparable example of a classic plural society and a massive federal polity that is representative, republican and parliamentary, uniting and protecting under its umbrella numerous religious, linguistic, regional and other diverse identities. As has been well said, India is a continental federal polity constituted into a single territorial sovereignty as a result of historical forces.

The underlying principle of the Indian politico-social system from the ancient times down to the beginning of the British rule was, as Sri Aurobindo says, that of a synthesis of autonomies of the village, the town, the local or regional, territorial or other administrative units. The kingdom or a confederated republic was often a means of holding together and synthesizing a free and living organic system of autonomies.

The only function of the unionizing agency was to establish paramountcy with a view to strengthening security against external enemies and ensuring greater oneness, peace, trade and prosperity among the participating autonomies. Thus, during the ancient and medieval times, all major political units were sort of unions of autonomies and in modern terminology, they could be called federal or confederal states.

When the British power was established in India, it was highly centralized and unitary. To hold India under its imperial authority, the British had to control it from the centre and ensure that power remained in their hands. A strong central authority was for the British both an imperial and an administrative necessity. The Joint Committee on Constitutional Reforms in 1934 observed:

> "Notwithstanding the measure of devolution on the provincial authorities which was the outcome of the Act of 1919, the Government of India is and remains in essence a unitary and centralized Government, with the Governor-General-in-Council as the keystone of the whole constitutional edifice."

In the British House of Commons, the problems of princely states and of British commercial interests were raised as grounds for the continuation of a strong central authority under the direct control of the British masters.

It was only when the nationalist movement for independence on the basis of pan-Indian nationalism and a united India became powerful that the British rulers started talking of the federal principles. By definition, an integrative device, federalism in British hands was used to weaken and disintegrate what then was India.

The Government of India Act of 1935 proposed to set up a federal polity in India, with a Central government and Provinces deriving their jurisdiction and powers by direct devolution from the Crown. The 1935 Act sowed the seeds of Pakistan and the many maladies and difficulties we are faced with today.

The Federation envisaged by the 1935 Act never came into being. Only the Provincial autonomy part of the 1935 Act was put into operation. Even this experiment was short-lived. The country as a whole continued to be ruled under the 1919 Act by a central authority only until 1947.

When the Constituent Assembly first met in 1946 and early 1947, the idea was to have a federation with a Centre having limited powers. For the Congress, it was a compromise to prevent the partition of the country on communal lines. Before the Union Constitution Committee could transact any worthwhile business, the Mountbatten Plan of 3 June 1947 was announced whereby all hopes of preserving the unity of India vanished and the partition of the country on communal lines became a settled fact.

Once partition had become a reality, there was no need to appease the Muslim League and restrict the powers of the Union Government. Also, after the partition, there were no ethnic groups which could be readily territorially identified although there was plenty of non-territory linked diversity. The Union Constitution Committee meeting of 6 June 1947 tentatively decided that the Constitution should be a federal structure with a strong Centre and that there should be three exhaustive lists with residuary powers vesting in the Centre.

The Drafting Committee decided in favour of describing India as a Union, although the federal façade or the outer trappings of a federal structure remained as a historical hang-over. The emphasis on India being a 'Union' was to convey the fact that it was not the result of a compact or agreement between the constituent units but a declaration by the Constituent Assembly deriving its authority from the one people of India.

Moving the Draft Constitution for the consideration of the Constituent Assembly on 4 November 1948, Ambedkar explained the significance of the use of the expression 'Union' instead of the expression 'Federation'. He said:

> "...what is important is that the use of the word 'Union' is deliberate... The Drafting Committee wanted to make it clear that though India was to be a federation, the federation was not the result of an agreement and that the federation not being the result of an agreement, no State has the right to secede from it. The federation is a Union because it is indestructible. Though the country and the people may be divided into different States for convenience of administration, the country is one integral whole, its people a single people living under a single imperium derived from a single source. The Americans had to wage a civil war to establish that the States had no right of secession and that their federation was indestructible. The Drafting Committee thought that it was better to make it clear at the outset rather than to leave it to speculation or to dispute."

Dr Ambedkar added that rigidity and legalism were the two serious weaknesses of federalism. Indian system was unique inasmuch as it created a dual polity with a single Indian citizenship and it can be both unitary as well as federal according to requirements of time and circumstances. Federal in structure and functions during normal times, it can be transformed into a unitary State during Emergency. Also, even in normal times, it gives primacy of powers to the Union Parliament in many ways, the amending procedure is not rigid, there is considerable uniformity of laws and judicial procedures, one unified judiciary and common all-India Services.

The Drafting Committee clearly attached great importance to the use of the term 'Union' as symbolic of the determination of the Assembly to maintain the unity of the country. The supreme value in the minds of the founding fathers was to build a united India and an integrated nation. The Union of India was designed to achieve this aim.

Finally, when the Constitution was adopted on 26 November 1949, it provided for India being a Union of States and its states and territories being as specified in the First Schedule. The Schedule specified four types of units—Parts 'A', 'B' and 'C' states and Part 'D' territories. The conceptualization was clearly intended to convey the federal nature of the structure of polity but with a subordinate position to the states and structural-functional balance in favour of the supremacy of the Union. The point was upheld by the Supreme Court in *West Bengal vs Union of India* (AIR 1963 SC 1241).

The hard fact of history is that the Union of India was put into shape in a hurry and all through the period following the commencement of the Constitution; it is being refined and reshaped. Categorization of States has disappeared, names of many territorial units called States have vanished from the map of India, many new States have been formed on linguistic and other criteria, boundaries, areas, names, etc., of several States have been changed and many relationships have been transformed.

The major achievement of the Union has been that despite all the pressures, pulls and strains, despite the many crises caused by internal disturbance and foreign aggressions and despite its still being in the making, the Indian Union has survived with its freedom and democracy reasonably intact. A number of separate States have been constituted in the North-East and elsewhere. Three States—Uttarakhand, Jharkhand and Chattisgarh—were the latest additions to the list of States. As at present, the Union consists of 28 States and seven Union Territories. Some unique solutions of regional councils, development boards, etc., have been attempted with varying degrees of success. Movements continue for Vidarbha, Bodoland, Bundelkhand, Telengana and others.

During the six decades and more, a great deal has been written and talked about federalism and Centre-State relations in India. But, the Constitution practically nowhere uses the term 'federalism' or the term 'Centre'.

The predominant concern of the founding fathers as also of the various Commissions and Committees appointed since Independence to consider reorganization of State or Union-State Relations—the JVP Committee, the Dar Commission, the States Reorganization Commission, the Rajamannar Committee, the Sarkaria Commission, etc.—has been that of the unity and integrity of India. We are still engaged in the stupendous task of national integration which is also an admission of the hard reality of our having not become a nation and of our Union being still in the making. The SRC report concluded:

> "It is the Union of India which is the basis of our nationality… States are but limbs of the Union, and while we recognize that the limbs must be healthy and strong… it is the strength and stability of the Union and its capacity to develop and evolve that should be the governing consideration of all changes in the country."

According to the SRC, not only in the political but in economic sphere also, the supremacy of the Union must be accepted.

It is common in federal systems that the administrative relations between the Union and the States are fraught with difficulties. The Constitution of India seeks to achieve a smooth working relationship between the two levels by tilting heavily in favour of the Union. It provides that the executive powers of the State Government are to be exercised in such a way as to ensure compliance with the laws made by Parliament. The Union Executive is also empowered to give such directions to a state as may appear to the Government of India to be necessary for the purpose. Any extra expenditure incurred by the State for the purpose of fulfilling directives is to be reimbursed by the Union to the State. The provision in article 261, directing that full faith and credit shall be given to public acts, records and judicial proceedings of the Union and the States in all parts of the Indian territory, adds a lot to the smooth working of Union-State relations. Parliamentary control over inter-State rivers and provisions for adjudication of any inter-State water disputes were intended to take away a whole host of possibilities of friction between Union and States and between States themselves. In fact the Constitution-makers did not want anything to be left to chance; hence the arrangements for Inter-State Councils and Zonal Councils.

With regard to the financial relations between the Union and the States too, one can find the general tendency of Indian federalism for centralization. The Union may be said to be financially more powerful but given the nature of the country's needs for growth through planned economy this was considered not only very desirable but entirely necessary. Although, the States are having their own resources, the Union is providing substantial amounts to them by way of grants-in-aid, share proceeds of certain taxes, etc. The provision for the appointment of a Financial Commission every five years to examine the distribution of tax proceeds between the Union and the States and to determine the principles which should govern the grants-in-aid has contributed to the generally smooth financial relationship between the Union and the States. It is pertinent to recall that one of the critical issues which led to the break up of the Soviet Union was the unsatisfactory arrangement with regard to the distribution of resources and considerable dependence of the Union on constituent republics in budgetary matters.

The Indian Union obviously does not fit into any of the accepted federal models. Some scholars have suggested that India be viewed as a civilizational State and not as a nation-state. Another suggestion has been that it be called a federal nation-state. We are, no doubt, a highly pluralistic society but our pluralism is not territory based. It is of a special kind. We have many diversities of various sorts pulling us at once in the same or in opposite directions. Indian society is fragmented and segmented at every level on different grounds. Our basic problem was never that of territorially based diversities or pluralisms. Our diversities are within and cut across territorial units.

In a sense, our diversities themselves are plural and our pluralism is diverse, both horizontally and vertically. What seems to divide, also unites. In fact, our diversities are our greatest strength and a great cementing force for national unity. Diversity is not division and unity does not mean uniformity or conformity. Also, unity of India and integrity of the nation as concepts are very different from national or political integration.

During the colonial period, the Congress talked of linguistic units as a device to contain and counter the communal divide. After independence, linguistic States were accepted under pressure and against the Congress perception and because the process became irreversible and because of a need in the struggle for political power.

In the first phase after our Independence there were several strong unifying factors:

- the members of the recent struggle for freedom and the sacrifices made for national unity;
- the trauma of the partition, the riots, the unprecedented migrations and the gigantic problems of rehabilitation, integration of States, tackling the food crises;
- strong charismatic leadership both at the Union and the State levels with excellent rapport among them;
- one-party dominance practically all over the country;
- needs of social engineering, central planning, Planning Commission, grants-in-aid to the States etc.

In the second phase, however, cracks in the system began to appear and many divisive, fissiparous, regional or sub-national loyalties and tendencies came to the fore to weaken the Indian Union concept but at the same time as a reaction reinforcing centrist urges,

- the linguistic States changed the entire political paradigm;
- departure of charismatic leaders form the scene; the leadership both at the Union and the State levels became mediocre and weak;

- the end of one-party dominance; several new regional parties were born in different parts and even came to power; national parties became weaker;
- widespread craving for a more federal structure implying need for greater sharing of power and patronage;
- rise of a larger and more powerful middle class with political ambitions and conflicts regarding employment opportunities;
- craving for regional or sub-national identities as the means to political power;
- rise of a rich farmer class with trading interest conflicts with the other states, lobbying for pricing policies for farm products, royalties for natural resources etc.

In the present scenario also, both integrational and distintergrational, centripetal and centrifugal forces are at work at the same time at various levels—political, economic, administrative and emotional. Thus, some of the factors standing for national unity are:

- history of a common ancient civilization and culture and record of political organization as single State attempted repeatedly and often achieved, for example, by Ashoka and Akbar and later by the British colonial masters;
- development of communications, modern technology and economic development factors with an indivisible and interdependent economy;
- the new economic policy of liberalization, market economy and globalization;
- needs of multi-nationals, business and industry as also interests of industrial labour;
- administrative and legal unity through all-India Services, common laws and unified judiciary continuing faith in the higher judiciary as a fair arbiter;
- despite experiments of multi-party minority coalition Governments (of NDA and UPA) with the predominance of regional parties, fortunately, major parties like the Congress,

BJP, CPI, CPM, BSP, SP and Janata Dal all stand for a vision of national unity, notwithstanding their tantrums and aberrations intended to capture votes to get or stay on in power;

- dynamics of centre-aided projects implemented locally through the State machinery;
- fragmented nature of diversities constituting a strength for unifying forces.
- dependence of politicians in all parties on the instrumentalities and authorities under the control of the Union Government to protect them in the course of criminal cases of corruption and other serious crimes.

On the other hand, the divisive factors are language, religion, politics and political parties. It is said that throughout history, strong centralized governments have never lasted long in India. Even the British tried to recognize the territorial principle by ruling through Governors.

Today the case for a strong Union Government rests on the need to protect the interests of weaker or smaller units against the big ones, to protect human rights all over the country, to protect the interests and rights of minorities, to ensure that democratic rule and will of the people prevail against arbitrary power assumption by an unscrupulous oligarchy or the like and to ensure needed transfer of resources and removal of economic growth imbalances and regional disparities.

The National Commission to Review the Working of the Constitution (NCRWC) which made its report in 2002 said:

> "There is no dichotomy between a strong Union and strong States. Both are needed. The relationship between the Union and the States is a relationship between the whole body and its parts. For the body being healthy it is necessary that its parts are strong. It is felt that the real source of many of our problems is the tendency of centralization of powers and misuse of authority."

That fundamental principles of good governance ordained by Part IV of the Constitution are daily defiled, debased and debunked openly, has nothing to do with India being a federal polity or otherwise. It is, however, certain that problems of governance in a country of India's size cannot be satisfactorily handled without greater decentralization of economic and political powers to lower and lower levels, with several tiers of functioning and the people at the grassroots having the real powers with the system growing up from there rather than coming down from above. The only way to strengthen the Union is to make it lose its extra weight, to shed monopoly of power in all areas and concentrate on essentials. With economic liberalization must come decentralization of political power and management.

We have to go in for a different variant of the parliamentary system which is compatible with the new federalism, which should build a united nation of a large number of autonomies considered not as subordinates or subsidiaries but as federal partners at various levels, rooted in our culture, ethos and genius, and taking into account our weaknesses and needs of making the federal Union an ever-developing and lasting reality. In short, the only way to preserve 'India, that is Bharat' as a 'Union of States' is to work for building it as a 'federal Union' with multiple tiers of government and sharing of powers from the lowest grassroot levels of Panchayats to the Parliament and the Government of the Union.

Federalism of Growth

Governance means dignity, development and growth of the individual to its highest potential. This calls for decentralization of power ultimately to the individual. Struggles for separate identities or greater federalism in pluralist societies are really not a fight for social justice, for the promotion of the interests of the disadvantaged sections of society or for protecting the rights of the units against the Union. The real issue is not even that of separate cultural or ethnic group interests. The entire conflictual situation revolves round the issue of sharing the fruits of political power. Ethnicity, language, religion and the like are politicalized to be used merely as the means to legitimize one's claims in the struggle for political power.

The Constitution of India, as it stands today, has both unitary and federal features. It is a compromise between the two. Sometimes, it is described as amphibian, as federal in structure but unitary in spirit or as federal in normal times but convertible to unitary in Emergency.

The federal features are (a) separate Union and State Governments with distribution of legislative, executive and financial powers, (b) provision of the Supreme Court to adjudicate disputes between the Union and the States or between the States, and (c) non-amendability of constitutional provisions affecting State powers without ratification by the States.

On the other hand, it cannot be considered federal in the classical sense and may seem to be more unitary if we consider that (a)residuary powers vest in the Union, (b) the names, boundaries, areas etc. of the States can be changed by Union Parliament by ordinary law, (c) Union Legislature can invade the State List under certain circumstances, (d) Union Government can issue directions to States, and (e) Governments of the States can be taken over by the Union.

Articles 245 to 255 contain a charter of the distribution of legislative powers between the Union and the States. Parliament may make laws for the whole or any part of India. The legislature of a State may make laws for the whole or any part of the state. The 7th Schedule to the Constitution embodies three lists, viz., the Union List, the State List and the Concurrent List consisting of 97, 66 and 47 items respectively. Both the Union and state legislatures could legislate in the area of items included in the Concurrent List. In case of any inconsistency between laws made by Parliament and those made by the legislature of a state in respect of items in the Concurrent List, the Union law shall prevail and the State law shall be void to the extent of inconsistency except where a State law is reserved for the consideration of the President and receives his assent (article 254). In the three-fold distribution of legislative powers, residuary powers of legislation have been left with the Union (article 248). Also, Parliament had been given the power to make any law for the whole or any part of the country to give effect to any international treaty, agreement, convention or decision (article 253).

Under article 249, if the Rajya Sabha declares by a Resolution supported by two-thirds of the members present and voting that it is necessary or expedient in the national interest that Parliament should make laws with respect to any matter enumerated in the State List, Parliament is competent to make laws on that matter for the whole or any part of India. Such a resolution remains valid for a year; it can be extended by another year by a subsequent resolution. Any law passed under this provision would cease to have effect on the expiry of six months after the resolution ceases to be in force.

Again, under article 250 Parliament is empowered to make laws on any item included in the State List for the whole or any part of India while a Proclamation of Emergency is in operation. The maximum duration of validity of such laws will be six months after the expiry of the Emergency.

In case of inconsistency between laws made by Parliament under articles 249 and 250 and laws made by State Legislatures, the law made by Parliament shall prevail and the State law shall be inoperative to the extent of repugnancy while the law made by Parliament remains in effect (article 251).

According to article 252, two or more State legislatures by passing a resolution may ask Parliament to make laws on any matter in the State List. Such laws can be extended to other states provided the concerned State legislatures pass resolutions to that effect.

Articles 256 to 265 seek to regulate administrative relations between the Union and the States. The Constitution provides that the executive powers of the Union are coextensive with its legislative powers. Also, executive powers of the State Government are to be exercised in such a way as to ensure compliance with the laws made by Parliament. The Union Executive is empowered to give such directions to a State as may appear to the Government of India to be necessary for the purpose.

Article 257 similarly provides that the executive power of every State shall be so exercised as not to impede the exercise of the executive power of the Union and the Union may issue necessary directions in that regard.

Under article 258, the President may, with the consent of a State Government, entrust to that government or its officers functions in relation to any matter to which the executive power of the Union extends. Similarly, under article 258A, the Governor of a State may, with the consent of the Union Government, entrust to that Government or to its officers functions in relation to any matter to which the executive power of the State extends.

While, there is no dichotomy between a strong Union and strong states, the way Union Governments have operated during the 60 years that have gone by and misused their powers blatantly for political and partisan end, particularly under articles 352 and 356—Proclamations of Emergency and imposition of President's rule in the States—have weakened the case of the Union beyond repair.

It is the constitutional duty of the Union to protect its States against external aggression and internal disturbance and to ensure that the government of every State is carried on in accordance with the Constitution (article 355). If, on receipt of a Report from the Governor or otherwise, the President is satisfied that government of the State cannot be carried on in accordance with the Constitution or that the constitutional machinery has failed, he may issue a proclamation taking over any of the functions and powers of the State Government including those of the Governor and other State authorities (article 356). The satisfaction of the President, of course, means the satisfaction of the Union Government and President's rule is actually rule by the Union Government.

Article 356 has been one of the most criticized and controversial provisions of the Constitution. Under this provision, State governments were taken over on nearly 120 occasions, that is, on an average more than two states each year. Opposition members and critics have said that the article has been misused, more often than not for political and partisan purposes by the party in power at the Union level, usually to dismiss state governments of parties in opposition. In the Constituent Assembly, while replying to the critics of this provision, Dr Ambedkar had expressed the hope that it might remain a dead letter and might never be used except as a last resort, after everything else had failed.

It is important that article 356 is read with articles 355, 256, 257, 253 and 365. This is usually not done. Insofar as article 355 speaks of the duty of the Union to ensure that government of every state is carried on in accordance with the provisions of the Constitution, it is obvious that article 356 is not the only one to take care of a situation of failure of constitutional machinery. The Union can also act under article 355, that is, without imposing President's rule. Article 355 can stand on its own. Also, Union Government can issue certain directions under articles 256, 257 and 353.

Article 365 says that where a State fails to comply with Union directions (under articles 256, 257 and others) "it shall be lawful for the President to hold that a situation has arisen in which the government of the State cannot be carried on in accordance with the provisions of this Constitution". It is unfortunate that before rushing to issue a proclamation under article 356, no effort appeared to have been made to ensure that (i) the Union had done all that it could in discharge of its duty under article 355 and (ii) that the state had 'failed to comply with, or give effect to' those directions. It seems in many cases recourse to article 356 has been taken without keeping other provisions in view.

In *State of Rajasthan vs Union of India* (AIR 1977 SC 1361), the Supreme Court held that a Proclamation under article 356 depended on the subjective satisfaction of the President and the court could not substitute its own satisfaction for that of the President nor could it, in view of article 74(2), enquire into the advice given to the President by the Council of Ministers. The court, however, significantly added that if the satisfaction of the President was *mala fide*, based on extraneous or irrelevant considerations or no satisfaction at all, it could interfere. Thus, exercise of President's power under article 356 was brought under judicial review to that extent.

In the *Bommai* case, the Court went much further. It was held (i) that the question of the State Government losing the confidence of the House should be decided on the floor of the House and until that is done, the Ministry should not be unseated, (ii) that dissolution of the Assembly by Presidential Proclamation is subject to judicial review, and (iii) that if the court finds that relevant material justifying the proclamation did not exist or that *mala fide* was involved, it may strike it down and restore the Ministry (*Bommai vs Union of India*, JT (1994) 2 SC 215).

The Constitution Commission (2002) recommended (a) greater consultation between the Union and the States through the Inter-State Council under article 263; (b) establishment of an Inter-State Trade and Commerce Commission; (c) treating inter-State river waters as national assets and enacting legislation for dispute resolution; (d) appointing only persons of eminence and with detached outlook as Governors in consultation with concerned Chief Ministers and respecting their five-year term; (e) using article 356 only as a last resort after action under 256, 257, 355 etc., fails; (f) deciding questions of majority support only on the floor of the House; and (g) in case of a hung house, election of the Chief Minister by the House.

The federal structure has come to stay and needs to be strengthened. The central problem today is not of Union-State relations but of greater decentralization of economic and political powers. A bottom-up rather than a top-down approach. It is heartening and nothing short of revolutionary that after the 73rd and 74th Amendments coming into operation, India has 3.20 million elected rulers—over a million of them women. But, the States by and large seem unwilling to transfer power lower down and the MPs and MLAs feel uncomfortable and threatened by the new grassroot leadership. The Union and the States should concentrate on essentials following the subsidiarity principle. With economic liberalization must come decentralization of political power and of management. To preserve 'India' as a 'Union of States', it is necessary to work for building it as a 'federal Union of Autonomies' with multiple tiers of government and sharing of powers from the lowest grassroot level of Panchayats to the Parliament and Government of the Union. Incidentally, this would be the most rational and practical way of operationalizing the Gandhian vision of a Constitution for India which recognizes the sovereign power vesting in the people at the grassroots and builds from below.

In conclusion, it may be iterated that during the historical evolution of Indian polity, both centripetal and centrifugal forces have been at work simultaneously. While the concept of Indian unity is age old, the Indian Union is still in the making. We have had periods of ups and downs even during the recent post-independence history. At one time, there were strong secessionist movements. All these were contained and successfully managed. Sustainable national unity with the units enjoying reasonable devolution of powers was ensured. Diversity was suitably subsumed or appropriately organized within unity. While subordinate or subsidiary relationships had to be defined, what was considered to be of paramount importance was the indestructible nature of the Indian Union, its unity, integrity and indivisible sovereignty.

4

Parliamentary System

India can be legitimately proud of having been a functioning democracy for six decades. The nation had to face a plethora of difficulties and a succession of external aggressions and internal crises. That we were nevertheless able to work a vibrant and democratic system, in a country of India's size and diversity, without any major breakdown, for so long, has been in itself a tremendous achievement particularly when we compare it to the experience of other nations that became independent during the same period. That parliamentary institutions have endured in India for sixty years is a great tribute also to their strength and resilience.

On the attainment of independence from British colonial rule on the midnight of 14-15 August 1947, India became one of the youngest members of the comity of nations. With the commencement of the Constitution on 26 January 1950, she became a 'Sovereign, Democratic, Republic' with a representative parliamentary system of government. The concepts of nation and representative parliamentary institutions as modern constructs are said to owe their origin and growth in India to our British connection for some two long centuries.

It would, however be wrong to premise, as some scholars do, that India adopted the Westminster system of parliamentary democracy in its entirety as it operated in Britain.

Some sort of parliamentary institutions were already functioning in India both at the central and provincial levels. When the founding fathers sat down to frame a constitution for free India, they said goodbye to British rule, but embraced the colonial model of the British system as was developed in India. Nearly 75 per cent of the text of the Constitution was derived from the Government of India Acts 1919 and 1935, the Cabinet Mission Plan and the Indian Independence Act 1947. The Constitution of India was thus made more by the British than by we, the people of India.

To some extent, it was also natural that we looked up to the system and the institutions of our rulers as the best. Even during the early days of the freedom struggle, one of the nationalists' chief demands used to be that the British should concede to their Indian subjects the same institutions and freedoms that they themselves enjoyed back home. The seeds of the colonial model of the parliamentary system in India can be traced back to this demand. In fact, the beginnings of the system of parliamentary democracy and its institutions in India could be seen in the successive stages of the freedom movement—the nationalist demands for representative, responsive and responsible institutions—and the halting doses of constitutional reforms grudgingly granted by the British rulers from time to time.

The psychology of the slave makes him consider everything that belongs to the master to be necessarily good and desirable. He aspires to achieve all that and to be like the master. His struggle is also not so much for freedom as for ruling over other men like his master. Also, the background of the sad experiences of the arbitrary colonial rule made them prize responsibility of the administration more than anything else. They, therefore, adopted the system of ministerial responsibility to the popularly elected House. As Dr Ambedkar said, they were conscious of the fact that they were sacrificing stability for the sake of more responsibility and accountability. They did not, however, seem to have foreseen a situation where the concept of collective ministerial responsibility to Lok Sabha would tend to absolve the ministers of all responsibility to the people and where the government would become so very desperately dependent on shifting party loyalties and temporary majorities in the august House that the ministers would have to remain preoccupied with efforts to continue in power and would have little time or patience left for the business of governance or development. Also, they could hardly visualize how, with all the electoral corruption and malpractices and with the majority of members getting elected on minority of votes, even their representative character would come to be seriously doubted.

Probably, the founding fathers thought that for a country of India's size, diversity, background and needs, a system of representative parliamentary democracy with universal adult franchise would be the most suited. They repeatedly emphasized that their vision of democracy was not merely political and that the polity envisaged by them was relevant only as an instrument for social engineering and for ushering in an era of economic democracy and a more equitable society.

The British parliamentary system was never designed or structured. It evolved through a long struggle between a hereditary monarchy and feudal lords in a small island with a large overseas empire during the post-industrial revolution period of great economic prosperity and affluence. It is not easy to transplant foreign institution on native soil. Also, it is not necessary that a system that succeeds in one country would succeed in another as well. For the success of parliamentary democracy of the British type, there are certain essential pre-requisites like (a) the people should have already been a sovereign nation, (b) there must be general commonality of interests and agreement on fundamental national issues, (c) some economic stability and a certain level of prosperity must have been achieved already, (d) there must be relative absence of social tension and an atmosphere of reasonable peace, (e) there must exist some democratic traditions, a more or less homogenous population and political consciousness among the people at large, (f) there should be a well-organized ideologically oriented, fairly stable system of two major national parties, and lastly (g) there should be an institution of a hereditary constitutional monarch, a king, who can do no wrong. Unfortunately, none of these pre-requisites existed in India at the time of the commencement of the Constitution. They do not exist today either.

In the classical parliamentary system of the British type, Parliament, at least in theory, is supposed to be supreme and repository of the sovereign power of the people. Unlike the UK, India has a written Constitution where the powers and position of the three organs are clearly defined and delimited and none of them is supreme or sovereign. India was not a sovereign nation when the colonial system of parliamentary democracy was imposed. The parliamentary system, if anything, proved to be divisive. Unity of the nation and national integration and an Indian identity were merely clichés or slogans for speeches from public platforms. It was difficult to pinpoint any issues on which there was national unanimity or consensus. A healthy two-party system had not developed thus far. We had widespread deprivation and destitution. The leadership seemed to have had a vested interest in keeping the people poor, illiterate and backward. When voters cannot understand the value of their votes and cannot appreciate national problems, to talk of representative parliamentary democracy is a farce.

Questions about the suitability of the parliamentary system of the British type for India are being raised right from the times of the Constituent Assembly and the commencement of the Constitution. Some members of the Constituent Assembly had expressed fears that the Constitution they had framed might give rise to a new class of professional politicians which could be its undoing inasmuch as these people and begin to live on their ministerships, memberships of legislatures, etc., with nothing else to fall back upon. Adult suffrage may prove to be a monstrous experiment if it unleashes forces which work in favour of sectional interests instead of working for national good.

In the years 1956 and 1957, two national seminars were held on the theme of the future of Parliamentary Democracy in India. Nehru himself participated and referring to the growing complexities of administration said:

> "The business of government and the business of Parliament become more and more complicated and it becomes a little .doubtful how far parliamentary democracy can solve such problems... Unsolved problems are dangerous."

Even today, we are facing the same stupendous problems of governance and nation-building with which the founding fathers had to grapple. If anything, the problems have become more acute. The tall leadership of that generation is no more around and we are shattered from within.

The post-independence history of our polity can be divided into two periods—the first of erecting structures and institution building and perhaps of over-institutionalization and the second of gradual de-institutionalization of politics and demolition of legitimate structures. However, very little, if any, attention seems to have been paid to analysing with objectivity and honesty what ails our parliamentary polity and why it seems to have brought us to a blind alley or to the edge of the precipice. There has been in recent years quite some thinking and debate about decline of Parliament, devaluation of parliamentary authority, falling standards of debate, deterioration in the conduct and quality of members, poor levels of participation and the like. A certain cynicism towards parliamentary institutions and an erosion in the respect for normal parliamentary processes, the parliamentarians and the system of parliamentary democracy, present a disturbing scenario.

The system under which we live has led to and nurtured an axis between the businessman, the politician, the civil servant, the police and the criminal. For the new breed of professional parliamentary politicians, national interest is the last priority. Power for its own sake or for personal ends has become the supreme value. Those in government under the parliamentary system remain so occupied in the struggle for sheer survival that they have no time for serving the people. Populism has acquired respectability.

People talk of happenings in Parliament and of the conduct of politicians as things quite remote and different from themselves. There is little consciousness of Parliamentary institutions being their own and members being from among themselves. A senior parliamentarian speaking of politics generally, bemoans:

> 'It will not be far wrong to say, sorrowfully, that there never was a time in living memory when politics and politicians were, almost rightfully, as denigrated, even degraded, and sometimes detested, in the eyes of our people as they are at the moment.'

This should cause the greatest concern and anguish to all lovers of freedom and democracy. When the representatives of the people themselves lose the respect of the people, democracy cannot last long. It is essential for parliamentary institutions and public men to regain their traditional esteem and honour in the affection of the people. Reforming parliamentary polity in essential respects is already a categorical imperative.

It is often said that there is nothing wrong with the system, the fault lies with the people who operate it. The argument ignores the facts that (1) the people operating the system today are largely the products of this system, (2) the system is for the people and not the other way round, the system has to be adjusted to the needs of the people, (3) we cannot keep waiting for angels to descend from heaven, our people cannot be changed or others imported to work the 'excellent' system, and (4) both the system and its operators are responsible for the failure. If parliamentary democracy and individual freedom are to endure and representative institutions made impregnable, both the system and the character of those operating it would have to be transformed.

The latest developments affecting the economy of the nation underline the need for greater responsibility and accountability of the political executive and the administrators through the representative institutions. On the other hand, the spectacle of several successive hung parliaments and state legislatures and minority governments and frequent general elections naturally cause grave concern for stability.

While quite understandably, the chief concern of the politicians in power is always somehow to retain power and to work for ways to ensure greater stability, in a democracy stability alone is not enough nor is it the highest value. The need for emphasis on ministerial responsibility has become more imperative in the dismal political scenario of today when credibility of ministers and politicians in power has been badly eroded with scams after scams being exposed and with allegations of corruption and crimes of all kinds—forgery, cheating bribery, conspiracy and the like—being levelled against senior leaders who only till yesterday occupied the highest positions as cabinet ministers, chief ministers, prime minister, etc.

At the root of all variants of democratic polity is the concept of sovereignty vesting in the people, of citizen being both the ruler and the ruled at the same time, of people ruling over themselves through their freely elected representatives. Every Member of Parliament represents the people and has the same credentials irrespective of the ruling or opposition party to which he may belong. He may be elected from a territorial constituency, but once elected, in principle, he is a member of the nation's parliament and custodian of the interests of the entire nation. In a representative parliamentary democracy like ours, Parliament collectively is the supreme representative institution through which the sovereign will of the people finds expression. The house directly elected by we, the people, throws up a government with the leader commanding the support of the majority in the house constituting the cabinet. The cabinet which becomes the Government of the country is responsible to the House of the people and through it to the citizenry at large.

A modern Parliament is a multifunctional institution and of its many roles, the representational role has of late become the most important. To what extent it can perform this role effectively depends on the representative credentials of individuals elected to Parliament and of Parliament in its collectivity.

Although political parties were not mentioned in the Constitution until the 1985 52nd Constitutional Amendment, the fact remains that our representative democratic polity under the Constitution presumed a well-organized system of political parties. The source of many of our troubles during the decades gone by has been our failure to evolve a healthy two-or-three party system based on some political ideologies or economic programmes. At election time, there are hardly any issues of policy or even programme before the electorate. All the campaigning and contests are personality and power oriented. Parties vaguely talk about development, national pride, security, secularism, etc. But on these laudatory principles, there seem to be hardly any difference among the parties.

If the political parties become merely power machines with the sole purpose of getting to power and once there somehow sticking to it, people soon realize that such democratic polity is only for the politicians sharing the spoils at the cost of the populace. They begin to lose faith in the system and in their representatives who are seen as not devoted to public service but engaged in seeking narrow personal ends of wielding power and amassing wealth with service to the people not being any part of their priorities. There can be nothing sadder in a democracy than the representatives of the people losing their representative credentials and the respect of the people.

The phenomena of hung parliaments, post-election group defections, instability and toppling of governments leading to frequent elections, etc., adversely affected the representative credentials of Parliament itself. Parliament belongs to the people and not to MPs. The latter themselves are responsible to Parliament and to the people outside. It is the ordinary people who have to be enabled to feel that through Parliament their voice can reach the Government and that it counts.

If corruption is suspected inside the portals of legislatures, the press and the public must be free to question it and expose it without being threatened under the law of parliamentary privileges. In their own long-term interest, parliamentary institutions cannot afford to place themselves beyond all scrutiny. There is every need for a parliamentary ombudsman. Stories current about payments demanded, offered or made for a variety of favours, need to be thoroughly investigated and, if untrue, publicly contradicted.

Responsibility to Parliament has ceased to have much meaning in a situation where no party commands a clear majority. Therefore, we need new mechanisms and devices for ensuring and enforcing responsibility of ministers and members of Parliament to the people at large. The hard operative reality of our polity today is that it is no more representative or parliamentary or even a democracy. But, the greatest merit of the parliamentary system is that it is not static. It keeps constantly evolving and adjusting to changing needs. While we would not like to dilute the element of responsibility, all are agreed that the country can ill-afford frequent general elections which apart from other implications, cost colossal amounts of money. The choice before us, therefore, is to find ways and means of ensuring greater stability within the parliamentary system with the ultimate objective of meeting the needs and aspirations of the people and solving the main national problems of poverty, illiteracy, corruption, population, backwardness and disunity.

The structure of Indian polity is unique. Though we adopted the parliamentary system, we have given to ourselves a written Constitution which means that the position, powers and jurisdictions of the Executive, Legislature and Judiciary are only as defined and delimited by the Constitution. The Executive or the Government is part of Parliament, comes out of it and remains responsible to it. On the other hand, independence of the Judiciary is guaranteed in several ways.

The structure at the State level is also broadly parliamentary, similar to the Union. Relationship between the Union and the States is determined by distribution of legislative powers. India is described as a Union of States but the Union is indestructible and indissoluble. We are a representative parliamentary democracy and a republic with a President at the head. All executive powers vest in the President but are to be exercised only with the advice of the Council of Ministers responsible to the Lok Sabha.

Indian polity is based on the premise of sovereign power vesting in the hands of the people. It has been polluted by the ugly role of casteism, communalism, criminalization and vote bank politics. The question is to what extent these are relatable to the political system and what political reforms are dictated? The reforms ultimately must lead to making the state and its organs—Legislature, Executive and Judiciary—to so conduct themselves as to put the citizen at the centre of our polity, restore credibility and respect to institutions of governance and ensure that the entire administration becomes citizen-friendly and leads to building a more united and integrated nation.

We have to evolve a political superstructure that is suited to our background, ethos and weaknesses, one that can bring forth men of character and competence to represent the people in positions of leadership. We have to ensure the nation's socio-economic development, improve the quality of life for all citizens and provide good, democratic, citizen-friendly governance with accountability to the people. The present system has failed to protect and promote the basic values and objectives enshrined in our Constitution. It has resulted in unstable governments, corruption, horse-trading, populism, casteism and communalism and criminalization of politics.

The present highly divisive system should be substituted by a suitable mix of a middle path combining the elements of stability of the executive with accountability to the legislature as in France or by the German system of a constructive vote of no-confidence whereby in effect the Prime Minister is chosen by the whole House and continues as such unless a successor is chosen by the House. The Prime Minister should appoint his ministers and should be removable only by a constructive vote of no-confidence passed by a two-third-majority vote. Also, there is every case for real transfer of power to the people at the grassroots. They have yet to feel the glow of freedom or power in their hands. The three or four tier governance model has to be strengthened and given more meaning in the Gandhian sense of building from below or following what the Germans now call the subsidiarity principle. What can be done at the lower level should be left to be done only there. Ultimately, parliamentary system can succeed only if the masses of people become active participants. Also, there is every case for a review of Union-State relations in the context of parliamentary federalism. There is no dichotomy between a strong Union and strong States. If necessary, India can have 40-50 small States.

Since the anti-defection law has proved unworkable, it should be removed from the Constitution. Freedom to vote may be restored. At best, whips may apply only in matters like no-confidence motion affecting the life of the Government.

During the last few years, it has come to be clearly recognized that the present model of our parliamentary democracy has failed to meet the hopes, aspirations and requirements of the people and that a fresh look at our political system is necessary. The case for some fundamental systemic changes is unassailable. Piecemeal reforms or patchwork solutions will not do. We may have to go in for a reformed parliamentary polity more in tune with our needs and character. It must be clearly understood that advocacy of a review of the system does not necessarily mean a switch over to the Presidential system or altering any of the basic features of the Constitution.

Limiting direct elections, having multi-member constituencies, making 50 per cent plus votes necessary for success at the polls, enlarged electoral college for the Presidential election, restricting the number of political parties, regulating their structure and functioning by law to ensure inner party democracy, audit of party accounts, etc., may be some other suggestions.

Parliamentary democracy in India will hopefully get over the present crises and emerge stronger. What we need is an awakened and activist citizenry fully participating in the decision-making, legislative and governance processes of their country.

5

Formation of Government

Under the scheme of the Constitution of India, the President is the constitutional head of the State in whom all executive power of the Union vests. The political or real executive of the nation is the Council of Ministers with the Prime Minister at its head.

Under article 75, the Prime Minister is appointed by the President and other ministers are appointed by him on the advice of the Prime Minister. The ministers hold office during the pleasure of the President. The Council of Ministers is collectively responsible to the Lok Sabha.

Appointment of the Prime Minister

While the President is to be fully guided in the discharge of all his functions by the advice of the Council of Ministers with the Prime Minister at its head, it is not clear as to on whose advice he performs the most crucial function of appointing the Prime Minister. So far as the letter of the Constitution goes, the President can appoint almost anyone as the Prime Minister but he has to remember that under the

Constitution the Council of Ministers headed by the Prime Minister has to be responsible to the House and would have to go if it loses the confidence of the Lok Sabha. The President therefore would appoint only a person who, in his best judgement would be acceptable to the House. If a party or a pre-election alliance commands absolute majority support in the Lok Sabha, there is no difficulty. For, the President in such cases, following well established parliamentary practices and conventions, has to invite the leader of the majority party, front or alliance to take over as the Prime Minister and form a government. But, where no single party or coalition is in a position to form a government on its own, the role of the President in choosing the Prime Minister becomes most delicate and difficult. He may have to use all his abilities to decide on the leader most likely to command the confidence of Lok Sabha. But, even in such a difficult situation, it would be best for the President to follow some norms and established precedents. The Sarkaria Commission has suggested that the President/Governor should invite the leaders in the following order of priority:

- Leader of the largest pre-poll alliance of parties
- Leader of the single largest party
- Leader of a post-poll alliance

He may call the leader of the single largest party or of the pre-poll alliance—whichever is larger—first followed by the other. If both of them are unwilling or unable to form a government, the leader of a post-poll alliance may be called only at the end, as the last alternative because such alliances are only marriage of convenience for sharing power.

Where the government is defeated on the floor of the House on a no-confidence motion, first opportunity to try to form an alternative government should be given to the Leader of the Opposition. As precedents go, there has been no uniformity in the approach of different Presidents and Governors in this regard. Sometimes the leader of the largest single party has been called first to explore the possibility of forming a government while in some cases the leader of an alliance has been given the first such opportunity in preference to the leader of the largest single party. At the Union level, the first critical situation in this regard arose in 1979 when the then Prime Minister Morarji Desai resigned following defections and a split in the ruling Janata party and a no-confidence motion moved by the Leader of the Opposition, YB Chavan of the Congress. President Sanjiva Reddy called Chavan to form the alternative government but after exploring the possibility for a few days, he expressed his inability to do so. The leader of the breakaway Janata(S) group, Charan Singh formed a new alliance and staked his claim to be called to form the government. Morarji Desai was still the leader of the largest single party. In this situation, President Sanjiva Reddy took the unusual step of asking both Charan Singh and Morarji Desai to submit to him the lists of their supporters. Since the list of Charan Singh had more names, even though not absolute majority, he was called to form the government and to prove his majority on the floor of the House within three weeks. As it turned out, Charan Singh could not face the House, resigned but was continued as head of a caretaker government while fresh elections were held. President Sanjiva Reddy was rightly criticized for making the leader of a group of defectors with very doubtful support in the House the Prime Minister of the country and later, before dissolving the House, of not giving an opportunity to the then Leader of the Opposition and of the largest single party, Jagjivan Ram to form an alternative government.

The Constitution does not make any specific provision in regard to a sudden vacancy in the office of Prime Minister due to death or otherwise. The eventuality is to be governed by the general provision of article 75(1) under which the Prime Minister is to be appointed by the President, and by conventions that may be developed.

When the first Prime Minister, Jawaharlal Nehru died in 1964 and also when Prime Minister Lal Bahadur Shastri suddenly passed away at Tashkent in 1966, the senior-most Cabinet Minister, Gulzari Lal Nanda was appointed to take care until the formal election of the Leader of the ruling party. However, when Prime Minister Smt Indira Gandhi was assassinated by her own guards in 1984, a departure from convention was made and following the provision of article 75(1), Rajiv Gandhi was appointed Prime Minister by President Zail Singh on the advice of constitutional experts, senior Congress leaders and ministers. Obviously, the President was satisfied that Rajiv Gandhi would be able to win the confidence of the Lok Sabha. In any case, ideally, the President should not involve himself in any head counting exercise, checking of lists or verification of signatures of the supporters or of letters of support from party leaders to determine the majority support credentials of respective claimants. Also, once the Prime Minister/Chief Minister is appointed by the President/Governor, it is between the PM/CM and the Lok Sabha/State Assembly.

Since in any case, ultimately it is necessary for the Prime Minister to have the confidence of the Lok Sabha and it is President's responsibility to find out who can command such confidence. The most logical and above-board solution would be that, instead of getting involved in political controversies, appointing someone and then asking him to seek a confidence vote in the House, the President can ask the House to elect its leader who can then be appointed by the President as the Prime Minister. This was what was later recommended also by the National Commission to Review the Working of the Constitution (2002).

Appointment of Other Ministers

While the Ministers, other than the Prime Minister are also appointed by the President and said to hold office during the pleasure of the President, in actual effect, it means they are selected by the Prime Minister—the President cannot appoint anyone not recommended by the Prime Minister—and hold office at his pleasure. If the Prime Minister is unhappy or dissatisfied with any minister, he can advise him to resign, advise the President to dismiss him or tender the resignation of his Council of Ministers and then reconstitute it after deleting the name of the minister in question. Vesting of such power in the Prime

Minister for choosing and retaining his colleagues in the Council of Ministers is necessary also in the context of the principle of collective responsibility of the Council of Ministers to Lok Sabha.

Holding Office during Pleasure

Article 75(2) says that the 'Ministers' shall hold office during the pleasure of the President. It is to be noted that

- Clause (2) is preceded by clause (1) which provides separately for the appointment of 'Prime Minister' and of' 'other ministers';
- Clause (2) speaks of only the ministers and does not say anything about the Prime Minister;
- Inasmuch as Ministers are appointed on the advice of the Prime Minister, they can continue only during the pleasure of the Prime Minister; It is clear that the word 'ministers' in clause (2) does not cover the Prime Minister;
- Clause (2) does not cover the Council of Ministers either, that is, because under clause (3) it is responsible to the Lok Sabha and not to the President. The Council of Ministers cannot therefore, under normal circumstances be dismissed by the President, only individual ministers have to go on the withdrawal of pleasure by the Prime Minister;
- Continuance in office of the Prime Minister and the Council of Ministers depend on their enjoying the confidence of the House and not on the sweet will of the President. The only situation where the President may legitimately dismiss a Council of Ministers can be where it has lost the confidence of the House, has been defeated on a vote of no-confidence/confidence motion on the floor of the House but refuses to resign.

Responsibility

It is important to remember that once the Council of Ministers is constituted, it is responsible to the House of the People and not to the

President. Its continuance or otherwise is a matter between it and the House. The President should normally not come in. As recommended by the Sarkaria Commission and the National Commission to Review the Working of the Constitution as also held by the Supreme Court in the *Bommai* case, the question of the Council of Ministers commanding or losing majority support in the House of the People (or State Assembly) should be decided only on the floor of the House.

Coalition Government

For the major part of the last half-a-century and more, single party governments were in power at the Union level. That the Congress Party itself was an umbrella organization and always a conglomeration or coalition of different ideologies and interests is another matter. In fact, when Janata Party with Morarji Desai as Prime Minister came to power, it was also a sort of coalition of all anti-Congress forces and included such disparate elements as the Communists on the one end and the Jan Sangh on the other. Several of the States had coalition governments from as far back as 1967. The Constitution has no provision in regard to single party or coalition governments. It only speaks of the Prime Minister/Chief Minister being appointed by the President/Governor and the Council of Ministers being responsible to Lok Sabha/State Assembly.

Coalition is the *ad hoc* coming together or entering into an alliance of two or more separate parties, persons or interests, for a temporary period and with a specific objective of taking combined action like formation of government and carrying on the activities of the State. Coalition arrangements presume that the parties coming together retain their distinct identities but they usually agree on a common minimum programme or a national agenda to be followed by their government.

At the Union level, the first coalition government in a formal sense was the one formed in 1989 by a United Front of several parties and headed by VP Singh. It was supported from outside by the BJP and the Left parties. With none of the parties having secured an adequate number of seats to be able to form a stable government on its own, and as the single largest party still, Congress not laying any claim to be allowed to explore the possibility of forming a government, the President invited the Leader of the United Front, VP Singh to form a coalition government and to prove his majority support on the floor of the Lok Sabha within a month. This was done but the government fell within less than a year following withdrawal of support by the BJP and the United Front losing the support of the majority of members. Under the directions of the President, VP Singh sought the decision of the House on a fresh confidence motion. The motion was defeated and VP Singh resigned. Duly sounded by the President, none of the parties in the House, was in any position to form a government. Chandra Shekhar, the Leader of the breakaway Janata Dal claimed majority support in the House and ability to provide a stable government. With the outside unconditional support promised by Congress (I), Chandra Shekhar was appointed Prime Minister. He proved his majority on the floor of the House. But, in fact, Chandra Shekhar Government was also a minority government dependent on outside support. On withdrawal of Congress support, Chandra Shekhar resigned. Fresh elections brought another minority government headed by Narasimha Rao into office. Rao was invited by the President to form the Government as the leader of the single largest party. Pursued by no-confidence motions, Narasimha Rao gained in strength by securing defections every time such a motion came. In fact, with some group defections in its favour, the United Front Government acquired majority and lasted practically its full term.

The phenomenon of hung Lok Sabha continued when at the general election of 1996, there was no party or leader able to command majority support in the House. The BJP emerged as the single largest party in the Lok Sabha but failed to secure a clear majority. A post-poll United Front of 13 parties elected Deve Gowda as its leader. The Congress extended full support to the United Front. The President, however, rightly called the leader of the single largest party, the BJP, to form the government and seek confidence of the House within 15 days. Sensing that he did not have majority with him on the confidence motion, Vajpayee resigned after being in office for only 13 days. What followed was a succession of minority governments with the support of the Congress, the Leftist parties, regional parties and other disparate elements. The President invited the Leader of the United Front, Deve Gowda to form the Government. But Deve Gowda government fell after 11 months when the Congress withdrew its support. IK Gujral was elected leader of the United Front as a compromise candidate acceptable to the Congress, the Left and other partners in the Front. Gujral formed the second United Front Government. But, he could last only some seven months and fell after the Congress withdrew its support. This was followed by a dissolution of the House and fresh elections.

At the 1998 elections, the BJP and its pre-poll allies together secured a clear majority in the Lok Sabha. However, instead of straight-away calling the BJP alliance leader, Atal Bihari Vajpayee to form the government, President Narayanan consulted leaders of the various political parties and asked Vajpayee to submit documents in regard to the support enjoyed by him. After being fully satisfied, he appointed Vajpayee as Prime Minister for the second time. However, this time also, the coalition could not survive for long. After an alliance partner, AIADMK withdrew its support, Vajpayee Government fell after 13 months. When President Narayanan asked Vajpayee to seek a fresh vote of confidence, Vajpayee Government was defeated on the floor of the House by a solitary vote.

Another fresh general election was forced on the nation. The BJP led National Democratic Alliance (NDA) emerged as the largest pre-poll alliance. The TDP extended support from outside. The third Vajpayee Government formed on 13 March 1999 proved quite stable and nearly lasted its full term. Probably on a political miscalculation, it preponed the general elections at which the NDA failed to secure a majority of seats. It was also not the single largest party, with the Congress having secured five more seats. BJP led NDA, however was still the largest pre-poll alliance. The Congress put together a post-poll alliance under the name 'United Progressive Aliiance' (UPA). The

UPA supported by the Leftist allies from outside, had a clear majority support. Mrs Sonia Gandhi who was the leader of the single largest party as also of the largest alliance (even though a post-poll one) could claim to be called to form the new government. President Kalam, however, appointed Dr Manmohan Singh as the Prime Minister apparently on the advice of Mrs Gandhi. What actually transpired between the President and Mrs Gandhi and why the latter could not be appointed Prime Minister is still not in the public domain. But, in a clear departure from all past practice, it was not the leader of the party or the alliance but the nominee of the leader who was appointed Prime Minister, obviously thereby eroding the constitutional status of the office. It would have been another matter if Mrs Gandhi had decided to really make a sacrifice and resigned from the leadership of the Congress Legislature Party and the UPA, and Dr Manmohan Singh was elected as the new leader to be in that capacity invited by the President. Much worse, from the constitutional angle was to follow when a super extra-constitutional body called the National Advisory Council was formed with Mrs Gandhi at the head and charged with the responsibility of monitoring the implementation of the Common Minimum Programme of the UPA. To the extent that the Council of Ministers is the supreme body to aid and advise the President, the constitution of another body above it was again an affront to the constitutional position of the Council of Ministers.

The National Democratic Alliance government which was in power for over six years (1998-2004) at the Union level as also the United Progressive Alliance government (2004) are examples of coalitions of several parties functioning on the basis of an agreed national agenda of governance.

Caretaker Government

At the level of states, if the government cannot be carried on in accordance with the Constitution, there is provision for President's rule. But, at the Union level, the Constitution envisages that there shall always be a Council of Ministers to aid and advise the President who shall act in accordance with the advice tendered. There is no provision in the Constitution for anything like a caretaker government. The term has come to be used in common parlance to describe the status of a Council of Ministers that has resigned on having lost the confidence of the Lok Sabha or otherwise but is asked by the President to continue till alternative arrangements are made. If an alternative government cannot be formed immediately and general elections have to be held, the outgoing Council of Ministers may have to hold charge till the conclusion of elections and formation of new government. In any case, the presumption is that such an arrangement is for as short a period as absolutely necessary, that elections, if necessary, are held at the earliest possible and that during the interregnum, no new schemes are launched or major policy decisions taken by the government unless dictated by demands of national security and the like. It must, however be added that the so-called caretaker government is also the fully competent government under the Constitution and can take even the most crucial decisions as was evident from the exemplary role of such a government headed by Atal Bihari Vajpayee during the Kargil war.

6

Coalitions and Minority Governments

It is believed that one party, the Indian National Congress, has been in power at the Union level for nearly half a century since independence. Until 1967, the same party dominated the scene and formed governments in most of the States also. Only after the 1967 general elections, in many States, non-Congress coalition governments were formed by parties and groups coming together on anti-Congress platforms of Samyukta Vidhayak Dals (SVD).

At the Union level, one-party monopoly of power of the Congress was first broken in 1977 when in the wake of Emergency excesses, Congress was badly mauled. Under the JP movement, the Janata Party achieved spectacular victories. Morarji Desai became the Prime Minister at the head of a Janata Government. Confronted by a no-confidence motion, Morarji resigned on 15 July 1979. Another non-Congress Council of Ministers, this time headed by Charan Singh, was installed. Lok Sabha was summoned to meet on 20 August 1979 to enable Charan Singh Ministry to seek a vote of confidence. But, Charan Singh never faced the House and resigned. The Janata experiment had failed badly. Non-Congressism did not prove strong enough as a cementing force between disparate groups.

The 1980-1989 decade was again of Congress monopoly of power at the Union level. The second breakthrough for anti-Congress parties came towards the end of 1989 when the common platform of Janata Dal was forged. Congress (I) performance at the general election was dismal. For the first time in India's parliamentary history, no party had secured a clear majority to be called upon to form the government. A minority government of the Janata Dal was formed in December 1989 by VP Singh with the support of the BJP and the left parties from outside. It was the first time that a minority government was formed at the Union level in India. It secured a vote of confidence on 21 December 1989. It was for the first time that such a motion was moved and passed to test the legitimacy of the government on the floor of the House. But, VP Singh Government could not complete even a year in office. Following the withdrawal of support by BJP and its allies, VP Singh lost majority support in the House. His government was defeated on a confidence motion on the floor of the House. In November 1990, leader of a breakaway group from Janata Dal, Chandra Shekhar formed another minority government with the outside support of the Congress (I) Party.

Later, when in March 1991, Congress (I) members staged a walk-out and announced boycott of proceedings of the House, Chandra Shekhar resigned. The second Janata experiment of a non-Congress front had failed. Also, the experiment of minority governments run by outside support had flopped. At the tenth general election, a clear majority to form a stable government again eluded every party. Congress (I) was returned as the single largest party but short of an absolute majority. It formed a minority government with Narasimha Rao at the head. This was the third minority government and continued as such for nearly two-and-a-half years but Rao succeeded in gaining majority by generating splits in other parties and securing group defections to his side by offering money, ministerships, etc. The Rao government lasted nearly its full five-year term.

During 1996-1998, there were two general elections, both returning fractured mandates. In both these elections, Congress (I) for the first time, was relegated to the second position having secured only 140 seats each time. The BJP rose and continued to be in the first position as the single largest party even though without a clear majority. Atal Bihari Vajpayee who was appointed the Prime Minister in 1996, failed to prove majority support on the floor of the House and resigned after being in office merely for 13 days. This was followed by two successive Janata Dal-led United Front minority coalition governments headed by Deve Gowda and IK Gujral and supported by the Congress from outside. Thus, these could be said to be the first two coalition governments at the Union level and the coalition era could be said to have begun in 1996 and continued. Vajpayee government of the BJP-led alliance that assumed power after the 1998 elections was the third coalition government in three years.

Following withdrawal of support by one of the alliance partners, AIDMK, Vajpayee government lost on the floor of the House by a single vote after a life of 13 months in office. The adverse vote turned out to be a blessing in disguise for the Vajpayee Government inasmuch as the thirteenth general election held in September-October 1999 returned the BJP led National Democratic Alliance (NDA) with a convincing majority. The Congress Party which became the main opposition under the leadership of Sonia Gandhi was further decimated to the lowest ever position in Lok Sabha. The NDA formed its government and experiment in a new kind of coalition government provided by a pre-election alliance of some 24 parties. Inasmuch as the NDA partners had sought the mandate of the people on a common agenda, the new Vajpayee Government assumed special legitimacy and also remained stable and with proper political management lasted close to a full term. This was the third Vajpayee government and the fourth coalition government in four years followed by the UPA coalition government led by the Congress from 2004 onwards. This could be said to be the fifth coalition government since 1996.

But, coalition is the *ad hoc* coming together or entering into an alliance of two or more separate parties, persons or interests, for a temporary period and with a specific objective of taking combined action like formation of government and carrying on the activities of the State. Coalition arrangement presumes that the parties coming together retain their distinct identities but some sacrifice of individual principles and strongly-held opinions is naturally involved. For the purists in politics, there is something basically wrong in coalitions because sacrificing principles for the sake of political power may not be the best of things to do.

Some scholars are prone not to differentiate between minority and coalition governments. It is important to stress that the two are genetically different and cannot be equated; minority governments are not a variant of coalition government or vice versa.

Those who believe that the era of coalition politics in India began in 1996, perhaps forget that in a sense, Indian politics has always been coalitional. In a country of India's size, diversities and pluralities, any attempt at nation-building or at political management is bound to be an exercise in trying to bring together different groups or persons, principles and interests. The one party dominance that we often talk of, was, if fact, the result of the Congress itself having evolved as a coalition.

The Indian National Congress before independence, was essentially a freedom movement under which people of diverse beliefs and backgrounds came together. The Swaraj Party, the Socialist Party and for a long time even the Communist Party were within the Congress. It was a sort of an 'umbrella organization' with the all embracing single aim of achieving the country's emancipation from foreign rule. The Congress was not a political party; it was something much less or much more. When independence came, Gandhi would have liked the Congress to dissolve or be transformed into a social service organization so that a healthy, ideologically oriented party system could grow in India. But, the Congress leaders then—including the tallest among them—disagreed with Gandhi. Perhaps they thought the Congress was necessary for running the government or that there was no other alternative or that it was after all a going concern and that was the season of harvest. The going was good for the dominant Congress Party till 1963 or 1967 while it continued to be coalitional in nature.

It may be recalled that following the split in the Congress in 1969, Mrs Gandhi's government was in a minority for some time. Throughout the period of its dominance, the real strength of the Congress Party was not its ideological or programmatic orientation or its performance in providing good governance—it could claim few credits on either count—but its coalitional and consensual character which made it an alliance of different castes, communities and minorities of various sorts with their varying religious, regional, linguistic, ethnic, cultural and economic interests. All the parties that replaced the Congress at the parties that replaced the Congress at the states' level were also coalitions of political convenience. The non-Congress governments at the Union level during 1977-79 and 1989-91 attempted to be close proximate of the Congress coalitional model. Thus, not only was Prime Minister Morarji Desai a product of the Congress culture and a life-long Congressman, the Janata Party was a coalition of several parties—Congress (O), Jan Sangh, Socialist Party, Bharatiya Lok Dal and the Congress for Democracy (another Congress splinter group, headed by Jagjivan Ram). Before the government could settle down to positive business, serious fissures appeared between the leaders and diverse groups constituting the Janata Party.

Again, in 1989, the minority Janata Dal government headed by VP Singh, another former Congressman and a protégé of Indira Gandhi and Rajiv Gandhi, was a coalition of the Janata Party, Lok Dal (A), Lok Dal (B) and others.

Finally, the so-called first coalitions headed by Gowda and Gujral were really minority governments and an ugly parody of coalitionism and a fraud on representative democracy inasmuch as the two largest parties in Parliament with the best and the second best mandate from the people remained outside the government. By no stretch of imagination, could Gowda and Gujral be said to have received the people's mandate for government formation.

Coalition governments in India have been generally unstable and short-lived. Of the 138 State governments between 1977-1996, 40 were coalitions and their average life was a mere 26 months. Also, in a coalitional arrangement, adjustment and accommodation are regarded as the greatest virtues and many compromises with beliefs and principles – sometimes even in matters of national interest – may have to be made. Described deridedly as a "soft State", India may tend to grow softer under coalition governments. But, there is nothing intrinsically wrong with coalitions nor is it necessary that they should not last long. Important thing is the nature of coalition arrangement and the character of coalition partners. Coalitions may be ideological or opportunistic. If the coalition is pre-election and the constituent parties have some basic ideological compatibility and agreement on a common programme calculated to serve the best interests of the nation, there is no reason why it should not be successful. Most lasting coalitions in continental Europe are entered into by political parties before the elections and are based on ideological similarities or nearness. The fairly long experience with coalition governments at the level of states in India shows that pre-election alliances among similarly oriented parties as in West Bengal, Tripura and Kerala are success stories.

For success:

- Coalitions must be based on a pre-election alliance between parties.
- There must be a large party to form the nucleus round which some smaller parties may revolve.
- Coalition partners should have a general ideological affinity. It is best to have agreement on a common programme and preferably a common election manifesto.
- A Coordinating Committee, Steering Committee or Consultative Committee consisting of the representatives of all the constituent parties should meet at regular intervals to sort out differences of perception, if any, and to hammer out common approaches ideally, the smaller the number the better.
- Temperamental compatibility between the leaders of the constituent parties is important.

- A coalition is bound to lose some of its relevance if even after some parties getting together, a majority eludes it.

The country is passing through a period of unending political instability, expensive general elections becoming almost an annual ordeal. The resultant hung Houses and post-election coalition governments are devoid of principles and political legitimacy. The phenomenon is directly related to the political system that the founding fathers gave us and the ways in which we have operated it during the last nearly 50 years.

We are supposed to be working a system of representative parliamentary democracy broadly patterned on the British colonial model. Also, we have adopted the British majority or first-past-the post system of elections. Under this system, the person getting the largest number of votes cast—not necessarily the majority of votes cast—is accepted to have received the popular mandate. To transplant foreign institutions on the native soil is always a dicey business. The essential pre-requisites for the success of British parliamentary system are non-existent in India.

Among other things, we do not have a system of two major parties with clear ideological and programmatic orientation. Instead of a two-party system, we have the unsavoury spectacle of nearly 900 registered parties and nearly 50 recognized parties. The hard bargaining and play the game of brinkmanship, bluff and blackmail to get the best price for their support in government formation or in 'operation topple'. In one of the most corrupt and illiterate societies in the world, our legislators can be freely bought and sold.

In a two-party situation, the first-past-the-post electoral system makes sense because most often the winning candidate is likely to have received the majority of votes cast. Applied to the Indian scene, it has proved to be very divisive and one that is seriously distorting the people's verdict by returning to the legislatures persons who may have got only 20 per cent or less of the votes cast, with more votes cast against them than in their favour.

In UK during a period of 100 years, there had been only five occasions when none of the parties could obtain a clear majority of seats in the House of Commons. On all these occasions, minority governments were formed and coalition not considered a better option.

In India, if we wish to work the Westminster system, we would have to take drastic measures to restrict the number of political parties and suitably regulate their working. In the alternative, we may have to adopt some kind of proportional representation system with single transferable vote and its concomitant of coalition governments of the type known in the continental countries of Europe. But, as it is, that is hardly a viable alternative in our situation.

We have to begin by accepting the hard reality that the people have lost faith in the present political system, political parties and politicians. Coalitions of all hues appear to them to be mere convenient alliances for sharing power and public office most often for getting-rich-quick and for serving their other personal, narrow, selfish interests.

In a situation where political parties are every now and then born and nurtured around personalities or caste and get split, merged or dissolved frequently, their commitment in a coalition alliance can hardly mean much. Sometimes, the only interest of a party joining a coalition or supporting it from outside may be to protect the interests of its supreme leader, like ensuring withdrawal or soft-pedalling of pending criminal cases. Ideological compatibility, principles or ability to serve the people are the lowest, if any, priorities for them.

Some of the parties have themselves become mafia gangs. Very often, coalition is another name for a sharing arrangement between criminals, the police, the bureaucracy, businessmen and politicians, Under the circumstances, there are many systemic constraints and no coalition arrangement can help unless there is a fundamental attitudinal change and a wide ranging review and reform of the political system including the administrative set-up and electoral processes.

It should be possible to simplify electoral laws and processes, the number of parties can be limited by law making it obligatory for recognition as a national party to secure at least five per cent votes cast all over India and in not less than half the states. For recognition as state parties, the same percentage of votes should be necessary in the state concerned. Only federal alliances or national parties or pre-election coalitions may be allowed to contest elections for Lok Sabha while state parties may contest for state legislatures and the Rajya Sabha.

It is also worth considering whether the Gandhian model of multi-tier governance with a bottom-up approach and the German subsidiarity principle may not be a more viable policy option for us. In that case, the number and frequency of direct elections could be drastically reduced and limited to the lowest grassroots level of self-governing institutions with lower levels electing representatives for each higher level going up to the office of the President and the institution of the Union Parliament.

In the interregnum, since the Westminster system has little room for post-election coalitions and somehow we do now have—if not two major parties—two major pre-election political alliances, if should not be difficult to cope with the post-election scenario, subject to political will and some basic liberal values of integrity of character among the political class. If one of the two alliances wins a clear majority of seats in the Lok Sabha, there is no problem. The leader of the winning alliance can form the new government. But, if the House is again hung and none of the alliances or parties gets a clear majority, then the alliance or party getting the largest number of seats must be invited and allowed to form the new government on the ground of its having received the best, even if not absolute, mandate of the people. The other alliance getting the second largest number of seats must accept the position of a responsible opposition. This is the only way a parliamentary polity can really operate.

In keeping with the democratic ethos, it is absolutely necessary that the two major parties/alliances recognize each other's relevance and legitimacy. It is also in the mutual interest of the two major national parties alliances that they remain the only viable alternatives to each other. It is outright undemocratic and puerile to regard as 'untouchable', any party that secures the largest or second largest number of seats and votes all over the country. Whether we like it or not, the people's verdict must be respected. If that is done, government formation should pose no problems nor should it be necessary to encourage unprincipled post-election coalitions where parties fighting each other at the polls, join hands after the polls to share power thereby clearly cheating the public.

As another option, it should be possible without making any constitutional amendments or fundamental political reforms to resolve the problem of instability of governments, frequent elections and hung houses by (i) the President asking the Lok Sabha to elect its leader so that he could be appointed the Prime Minister (this can be done by the President sending a message to the House under article 86(2)), and (ii) the House simply amending Rule 198 of its Rules of Procedure to provide for a constructive vote of no-confidence, that is, the motion expressing no-confidence in a Prime Minister simultaneously naming an acceptable successor.

7

Secularism, Hinduism and Minorities

Sardar Patel's Perspective

It would be specially relevant in today's context to try to understand Patel's vision of independent India and his perspectives on the issues of secularism, Hinduism and Hindu-Muslim unity.

Sardar Vallabhbhai Patel's ancestors who became leading *patidars* in Karamsad (Gujarat) were believed to have descended from Punjab with a robust agricultural background. The great son of the soil, Vallabhbhai learned to plough fields as a boy, at 25 he started legal practice at Godhra—a town that has most recently made prominent media headlines and stirred the entire nation. The societal structure, the nature of the population and the inter-community relations in Godhra must have had some impact on his thinking. But, he left Godhra fairly early and established a lucrative legal practice at Ahmedabad.

In October 1916, Vallabhbhai was to enter public life almost accidentally. He was in his early forties. Gandhiji had returned from South Africa. A conference devoted to Hindu-Muslim unity was being held in Ahmedabad, close to Patel's house. Gandhiji was there. Jinnah presided. Patel attended, may be only out of curiosity. The conference was followed by the Congress and the Muslim League meetings in Lucknow and the 1916 Congress League Pact. Patel was there and was a witness to the pact that conceded separate electorate to the Muslims—something that was one day to culminate in the tragic partition of the country. It is not known if the Lucknow experience influenced Patel's later thinking on Hindu-Muslim issues.

Beginning his political career with the membership of Ahmedabad city board, Patel was to share the dais with the Ali brothers and preside at the Gujarat Political Conference at Ahmedabad in the summer of 1921. As early as that, Vallabhbhai gave expression to his vision of independent India when he said that "no one would die of starvation in independent India", its leaders would not "use a foreign language", "military expenditure would not be heavy", "army would not subjugate its own people or other lands", "its best-paid officials would not earn a great deal more than its lowest paid servants" and "finding justice in it would be neither costly nor difficult". One wonders if during the last 62 years (1947-2009) of India's independence, we have succeeded in realizing Sardar's vision in any measure or we have largely betrayed it with impunity in every respect.

Unfortunately, the Ahmedabad conference was followed by the Moplah rebellion, forced conversions to Islam and declaration of an independent Muslim Moplah state. Thousands lost their lives in the strong military action by the British Government. An inevitable fall-out was Hindu reaction and worsening of Hindu-Muslim relations despite the closeness attempted during the Khilafat movement under Gandhiji's leadership.

Like Mahatma Gandhi, Patel stood steadfast for Hindu-Muslim harmony and unity and integrity of the nation. At one stage he had gone as far as to say that let the British transfer power to anyone in India, even the Muslim League, and he would be happy to see the Congress dissolved.

Patel has often been misunderstood because he was not a romantic idealist visionary like some others but a down-to-earth realist. He did not like Gandhiji's policy of going out of the way to try to appease the

Muslim League. For example, during 1944 after his release from jail, Gandhiji went to Jinnah 14 times during a single month while Jinnah remained unrelenting. Patel did not talk too much but when he spoke, he called a spade a spade. Rajmohan Gandhi says, Patel was allergic "to anything that looked like appeasement of the Muslim League".

> "Unlike Jawaharlal, who sometimes imagined Hindu-Muslim unity when it did not exist, Vallabhbhai was frank about the reality. Also, he felt it unnecessary to give a 'secular' wrapping to his utterances....
>
> "Vallabhbhai never tried or claimed to represent Muslims. And he found it natural to speak as a Hindu."

When after the formation of the Interim Government, Viceroy Wavell spoke of the possibility of the Muslim League also joining, Patel bluntly told him that "Jinnah was an impossible personality to negotiate with." Soon thereafter, on 16 August, the League unleashed a reign of terror and mayhem in Bengal in the name of direct action. There was widespread orgy of violence, 'murder, arson, rape and looting' in Calcutta. According to British Government estimate, 5,000 persons were killed and 15,000 wounded. When massive Hindu reaction followed, Patel minced no words and noted that it was a good lesson for the League, because he had heard that the proportion of Muslims who had died in the aftermath of the 'direct action' was much larger.

Patel was opposed to League's entry into the Interim Government without its agreeing to join the Constituent Assembly. Somehow Nehru was persuaded by the Viceroy and the League became a partner in the Government. As Patel had foreseen, it was a disaster. Patel found sharing power with the Muslim League in the Interim Government disgusting. The League was determined not to cooperate. With some exceptions, Muslim officials from the top down to the *chaprasis* were working for the League. Liaquat Ali, as Finance Minister, controlled the purse-strings and made it impossible for Congress ministers to function. In fact, as Shankar puts it, all the departments controlled by the League had become 'entrenched Muslim camps'.

Patel never forgave Viceroy Wavell for manipulating Nehru to agree to the induction of the League in the Interim Government. He wrote to Cripps in December 1946 that every action of the Viceroy "since the great Calcutta killing has been in the direction of encouraging the Muslim League and putting pressure on us towards appeasement".

In the communal carnage in Noakhali, Hindus were forcibly converted to Islam or killed, temples were destroyed and women raped. Hindu reaction again was massive. Many Muslims suffered in Bihar and UP. Speaking at the Congress Session at Meerut towards the end of November 1946, Patel had advised the advocates of Pakistan to follow methods of love and peace. He had added that "sword will be met by the sword".

Gandhiji was so upset by the reports of Patel's speech that he wrote a strong letter to Patel saying how he disliked his inflammatory speeches which made no difference between violence and non-violence and asked people to meet the sword by the sword.

In his reply in January 1947, Patel told Gandhiji that his habit was to tell unpalatable truths but his statement suggesting violence was taken out of context. When Gandhiji later pressed him in favour of the appointment of a Commission to inquire into the Bihar riots of November 1946, Patel held his own and told Gandhiji that nothing would be gained by appointing it and there would be some harm instead.

When partition became imminent, Patel was not really very upset. The experience of running a coalition government with the League had taught him that it would be better to have a divided India than an India at civil war. With the constitution of Pakistan, the rest of India could hope to live in peace. When a British officer suggested 'great generosity' towards the League, Patel in his characteristic style retorted:

> "If you think that generosity will placate the Muslim Oliver Twist, then you do not understand either the Muslim mind or the situation."

Speaking towards the end of a very heated and communally charged debate on a draft clause which sought to bar any conversion from one religion to another 'by coercion or undue influence' or of 'a minor under the age of 18', Sardar Patel said that it was a hard fact that in India there were mass conversions; conversions by force, conversions by coercion and undue influence and that children and orphans were also being converted.

As Chairman of the Advisory Committee on Fundamental Rights, Minorities in the Constituent Assembly, Sardar Patel played a crucial role in finalizing and piloting all the relevant clauses regarding minority rights. In particular, through his statesmanship and dexterity he was able to seek agreement on discarding separate communal electorates, reservations and quotas. Seats in legislatures were to be reserved only for the Scheduled Castes and Scheduled Tribes. Muslim members were the last to agree to give up separate electorate and reservation of seats for them. It was distressing, though not surprising for Patel to see the Muslims left in India after partition still clinging to the sinister two-nation theory and pressing for separate electorates which had led to the partition. Speaking with certain emotion, Sardar Patel said while replying to the debate on the interim Report of the Advisory Committee on 27 August 1947:

> "But today, after agreeing to the separation of the country as a result of this communal electorate, I never thought that proposition was going to be moved seriously, and even if it was moved seriously, that it would be taken seriously. Well, when Pakistan was conceded, at least it was assumed that there would be one nation in the rest of India—the 80 per cent India—and there would be no attempt to talk of two nations here also. It is no use saying that we ask for separate electorates, because it is good for us. We have heard it long enough. We have heard it for years, and as a result of this agitation we are now a separate nation. The agitation was that 'we are a separate nation, we cannot have either separate electorates or weightage or any other concessions

> or consideration sufficient for our protection. Therefore, give us a separate State.' We said, 'All right, take your separate State.' But in the rest of India, in the 80 per cent of India, do you agree that there shall be one nation? Or do you still want the two-nations talk to be brought here also? I am against separate electorates. Can you show me one free country where there are separate electorates? If so, I shall be prepared to accept it."

Patel was transparent and forthright. He believed that all those who adhered to the two nation theory had no place in India and should move to Pakistan. Replying to the debate on his report on Minority Rights on 28 August 1947 Sardar Patel had this to say:

> "If the process that was adopted, which resulted in the separation of the country, is to be repeated, then I say: those who want that kind of thing have a place in Pakistan, not here (applause). Here, we are building a nation and we are laying the foundations of one nation, and those who choose to divide again and sow the seeds of disruption will have no place, no quarter, here, and I must say that plainly enough... (Hear, Hear)... Therefore, my friends, you must change your attitude, adapt yourself to the changed conditions… Let us face the realities. Ask yourself whether you really want to stand here and cooperate with us or you want again to play disruptive tactics.. Forget what has happened. You have got what you wanted. You have got a separate state and remember, you are the people who were responsible for it, and not those who remain in Pakistan. You led the agitation. You got it. What is it that you want now? I do not understand. In the majority Hindu provinces, you, the minorities, you led the agitation. You got the partition and now again you tell me and ask me to say for the purpose of securing the affection of the younger brother that I must agree to the same thing again, to divide the country again in the divided part. For God's sake, understand that we have also got some sense… There will be no injustice done to you. There will be generosity towards you, but there must be reciprocity. If it

is absent, then you take it from me that no soft words can conceal what is behind your words. Therefore, I plainly once more appeal to you strongly that let us forget and let us be one nation."

Patel sometimes joked that Nehru was 'Congress's only nationalist Muslim'. He was convinced that the great majority of Muslims believed in the two nation theory. But, a clear enunciation of his attitude to the Muslims and to Hindus was reserved for a meeting at Lucknow on 6 January 1948 when he said:

"I believe in plain speaking. I do not know how to mince matters. I want to tell them frankly that mere declarations of loyalty to the Indian Union will not help them at this critical juncture. They must give practical proof of their declarations. I ask them why they do not unequivocally denounce Pakistan for attacking Indian territory with the connivance of the Frontier tribesman. Is it not their duty to condemn all acts of aggression against India? I want to say a word as a friend of Muslims and it is the duty of a good friend to speak frankly. It is your duty now to sail in the same boat and sink or swim together. I want to tell you very frankly that you cannot ride two horses. Select one horse. Those who want to go to Pakistan can go there and live in peace. I appeal to Hindu Mahasabhaites to join the Congress... If you think you are the only custodians of Hinduism, you are mistaken. Hinduism preaches a broader outlook."

Speaking in Bombay on 16 January 1948 Patel dwelt on the theme further when he said:

"We have just heard people shouting that Muslims should be removed from India. Those who do so have gone mad with anger. I am a frank man. I say bitter things to Hindus and Muslims alike. At the same time I maintain that I am a friend of the Muslims".

Sardar Patel was a Hindu. He was proud to be a Hindu. But, it would be entirely wrong to think that he was anti-Muslim, communal or anti-secular. In fact, many instances can be cited of Muslims being appointed to coveted posts by Sardar Patel and of his being on the most cordial terms with many prominent Muslims. He was secular but, in the words of HM Patel, "He was not prepared to equate secularism with injustice to the majority community". He was truly secular and respected all religions because he was a good Hindu. Hinduism is nothing if not tolerant of different paths to the Godhead. Problems arise when the other participants in the democratic process believe neither in democracy nor in secularism but are only anxious to be beneficiaries thereof while strongly believing that their path alone is true and all those not following it must be brought around, if necessary by force.

Sardar Patel stood for equal political rights for all citizens irrespective of religion, race, caste, gender, place of birth or the like, while conceding various linguistic, religious or other minority rights, he was opposed to any political rights—like seats in legislatures—being sought on grounds of ones religion or on grounds of belonging to a minority or majority. Political rights can be claimed only as citizens of India. Every citizen—Hindu, Muslim or other—is entitled to same rights.

Sardar Patel did not subscribe to the idea of a theocratic state. After the country's partition on communal lines became settled and Pakistan was soon to become an Islamic State, BM Birla suggested (on 5 June 1947) that India should become a Hindu State with Hinduism as the State religion. Patel brushed the proposal aside as not possible because, he said, the State must exist for all, irrespective of caste or creed and protection of minorities was also its responsibility. We find Sardar Patel writing to the Chief Minister of Mysore on 30 November 1947, "We should see that the minorities feel a sense of security and confidence in the majority".

In Sardar's thinking, ideology took a back seat. He was practical and pragmatic, a patriot par excellence wedded to building a strong and united nation. He said, he did not believe in any caste or community, the whole of India was his village and men of all communities were his friends and relations. He believed that stability was the surest foundation of progress. Stability could come only when there was unity. The lot of the common man could not be improved unless there was 'peace and communal harmony'. In July 1948, he once said:

> "It is the duty of the majority community to protect the minority whose interests, as it were, come as part of a trust to the former. Muslims, after all, number only four crores, Hindus about thirty crores."

On 12 January 1949 delivering a speech at Gandhiji's samadhi at Rajghat, Sardar Patel appealed to all Indians to live as brothers. He said:

> "Whatever our community, all of us—Hindus, Muslims, Sikhs, Parsis, Christians—should remember that we belong to one country.... Let us get together and create in India an atmosphere of amity... Let us all recognise like Gandhiji that we are creatures of one God, subjects of one divine King."

Speaking in the Constituent Assembly on 25 May 1949 on the final report of the Advisory Committee on Minorities etc. Sardar Patel said that in the interest of laying down 'real and genuine foundations of a secular state in the country', nothing is better for the minorities than to trust the good sense and sense of fairness of the majority and to place confidence in them. Likewise the majority must think of what minorities feel. Patel expressed the fervent hope that in the long run, "it would be in the interest of all to forget that there is anything like majority or minority in this country, and remember that in India there is only one community." Again speaking in the Constituent Assembly the next day, Patel was even more clear and categorical. He said:

> "Those who claim that in this country there are two nations and that there is nothing common between the two, and "that we must have our homeland where we can breathe freely", let them do so. I do not blame them. But those who still have that idea that they have worked for it, that they have got it and therefore they should follow the same path here, to them I respectfully appeal to go and

> enjoy the fruits of that freedom and to leave us in peace. There is no place here for those who claim separate representation…
>
> "…For a community to think that its interests are different from that of the country in which it lives, is a great mistake. Assuming that we agreed today to the reservation of seats, I would consider myself to be the greatest enemy of the Muslim community, because of the consequences of that step in a secular and democratic state."

The *Ram janmabhumi*-Babri Masjid dispute involving the sentiments of Hindus and Muslims has continued to bedevil solution for the last 54 years. As early as 9 January 1950 writing to the then UP Premier Govind Ballabh Pant, Sardar Patel had said:

> "I feel that the issue is one which should be resolved amicably in a spirit of mutual toleration and goodwill between the two communities. I realize there is a great deal of sentiment behind the move which has taken place. At the same time, such matters can only be resolved peacefully if we take the willing consent of the Muslim community with us. There can be no question of resolving such disputes by force."

When in March 1950, Jawaharlal Nehru wrote a long letter to Sardar Patel expressing his great anguish at the differences of approach between them, Sardar Patel, despite his failing health took pains to send a comprehensive reply. Among other things, on the point of secularism, he made a very lucid statement which merits somewhat *in extenso* recall. He said:

> "As regards the differences of our approach, as far as I know there has been none as regards the secular ideals to which we all subscribe and for which we all stand; in fact I have throughout emphasized the need for full protection of minorities in India and condemned violence. At the same time I have not ignored the basic cause of such violence, namely, what is happening in

Pakistan and the bitterness which it engenders in the country. When we consider stern action to deal with trouble on our side we have to take into account this fact, for to ignore it would mean our depending on coercion and suppression to deal with the psychology of deep-seated grievances and prejudice as regards our neighbors which unfortunately has repercussion on the followers of Islam in this country. You yourself have recognized this in your correspondence with the Pakistan Prime Minister. I have also laid stress on the fact that our secular ideals impose a responsibility on our Muslim citizens in India—a responsibility to remove the doubts and misgivings entertained by a large section of the people about their loyalty, founded largely on their past association with the demand for Pakistan and the unfortunate activities of some of them. It is in this light that to my mind some tangible steps to deal with the present situation become urgent and that is why I have been insisting on a well-considered, firm and determined line of approach."

In one of his last public speeches delivered in Hyderbad on 7 October 1950, Sardar Patel summed up his stand by saying that "every Indian citizen, whether he is a Hindu or a Muslim, will have to behave as an Indian and act as an Indian, and sooner they realize this the better."

Patel felt proud and hoped the House would be proud to lay the foundations of a true secular democratic state where everybody had equal chance. Today, after 58 years (1950-2008) of the life of our Republic, the whole nation remembers with deep gratitude to Sardar Patel, how he rid us of the scourge of separate communal electorates and religion-based reservations and quotas.

We miss the Sardar today. We need a Sardar who has the love, interest and service of the nation uppermost in his mind and heart and who can speak the truth and take firm action where needed, without any fear of being labelled communal and without seeking to build a vote bank and derive other political advantage.

8

Institutionalization of Grassroots Governance

Power to the People

The most fundamental tenet of democratic polity is that sovereign powers vest in the people. It is in the exercise of that power that they are supposed to frame a constitution for themselves. That is why the Preamble to our Constitution speaks of 'We, the people of India... hereby adopt, enact and give to ourselves this Constitution'.

The transfer of power from the hands of the British masters took place on 15 August 1947. The Constitution was adopted on 26 November 1949. With its commencement on 26 January 1950, the Sovereign Democratic Republic of India was born. On that day, if not earlier, power was supposed to have come to the people. From being subjects of a foreign power, they were supposed to have become citizens of a free country. But the very fact that even after sixty years scholars keep talking of transfer of power to the people is proof enough that all these years power has been in the illegitimate hands of some usurpers. It has still to reach the people where it really belongs. The ordinary Indian in his hut and hamlet still has to feel the glow of freedom or the transfer of power to his hands. Masters have changed but the colonial model of the rulers and the 'subjects' continues. In a genuine democracy, the ordinary people should be respected as the real masters and all the administrators, legislators, ministers and judges should regard themselves as their servants.

The philosophy, motivation and historical evolution of the Panchayati Raj institutions as also the structural-functional parameters and nuts and bolts of the entire machinery in operation need to be studied in depth and widely debated, not only in the academia or among professional seminarians but by the people at large. The ethos of democracy can find real nourishment only when power reaches the grassroots level. For the ordinary citizen, it is local democracy which can have real meaning and significance. In a vast country where large masses are still unlettered, village panchayats and participative democracy can do wonders. If the aim is to establish a democratic society, where change is brought about by voluntary consent and willing cooperation and not by the force of arms, there may be no alternative to Panchayati Raj or Local Self Government institutions. In that sense, the most revolutionary measures in recent decades have been the 73rd and 74th Constitutional Amendments. With 3.5 million elected rulers today—over a million of them women—Indian democracy could become a unique model for the rest of the world.

Panchayat as an institution of local self-government at the village level had its origin in ancient India. A sort of village council or an association of the residents of the village often consisting of the village elders, Panchayat or *Gram Sangha* performed administrative and judicial functions. Sometimes, the *Gram Sanghas* or Panchayats were elected from among the villagers who regulated their own lives through these bodies. We find references to *Gram Sanghas* in the *Manusmriti* (code of Manu), Kautilya's *Arthashastra* (400 BC) and the *Mahabharata*. The *Shanti Parva* of *Mahabharata* refers to a *sabha* named *sansad*. This consisted of the common people and was, therefore, called the *jan sansad*. Valmiki's *Ramayana* speaks of the *Ganapada* which was a sort of federation of village republics. Only those persons could become its members who had the general welfare of the people at their hearts; the membership was denied to *durjana* or impious persons. Later, village commonwealths are mentioned in *Sukra Niti* (Sukracharya's *Nitisara*). In fact, the institution of village panchayats in one form or the other, has had an unbroken continuity almost all over India and throughout her long history. Facts and fiction gathered round the institution and legend and literature grew. Some British writers contributed to presenting an idealized and somewhat sentimentalized image of village communities in India. Thus, Sir Charles Metcalf said:

> "The village communities are littlè republics, having nearly everything they can want within themselves and almost independent of any foreign relations. They seem to last when nothing else lasts. Dynasty after dynasty tumbles down, revolution succeeds revolution but the village communities, each one forming a separate little state in itself has contributed more than any other cause to the preservation of the people of India."

With the beginning of British rule in India came centralization of administration and gradual erosion of surviving local self-governing institutions. This was resented by the people at large. From the earliest stages of India's national struggle for representative institutions and freedom from foreign rule, the nostalgia in the Indian psyche for Panchayati Raj was the result of this resentment against administrative centralization. The mere mention of panchayats brought back fond memories of the distant past immortalized in folklore going back to 5,000 years and to the era when there flourished a network of village republics and panchayats in the country. Jawaharlal Nehru also referred to the existence of democratic institutions at the village level in ancient India and said that India's strength really lay in 'her widespread system of village republics or self-governing panchayats'. These panchayats, he noted, were 'elected by the village folk and thus there was a basis of democracy in this system'. Nehru was rather surprised to find out that these panchayats enjoyed both executive and judicial powers 'and their members were treated with the greatest respect by the king's officers'.[1]

On a philosophical plane, the value of a decentralised system of government and village self-sufficiency was upheld and propagated by thinkers like Annie Besant and Rabindra Nath Tagore. The *Gandhian Constitution for free India* drafted by SN Agarwal envisaged self-sufficient, self-governing village communities. Gandhiji was an ardent exponent and devotee of village *swaraj* (self-rule). Under the Gandhian concepts of a constitutional scheme for India, the village panchayat was visualized as the primary political unit enjoying maximum autonomy in internal village administration including full control over the village watchman, *patwari*, police and schools, assessing and collecting land revenue, supervising cooperative farming, irrigation, interest rates, khadi and other village industries. Members of village panchayat were to be elected by all adults in the village. The village was to be the primary unit and the foundation of development planning. A hierarchical pattern linking the *taluka*, district, provincial and central governments was envisaged which provided for indirect election of various office bearers at all levels except that of the village panchayat. The judicial system was also to be reorganized so as to be in line with the decentralized form of polity which allowed the largest measure of local autonomy at every level and the minimum necessary functions for national government. It was a concept of grassroots democracy in the remotest villages linked to higher units at regional and national levels.

Later on, the Sarvodaya movement had also drawn on this philosophy of diffused democracy and decentralization. In consequence, "the movement for Panchayati Raj achieved both an intellectual respectability and sentimental appeal emphasizing that in such a state the best savants of the village should form the Panchayat,

---

1 Jawaharlal Nehru, *Glimpses of World History* (Bombay, 1962) p 114 and *The Discovery of India* (Bombay, 1964) p 261

being elected unanimously, and from the village level there should be indirect election to sub-districts, districts, provincial and central administrations."[2]

While Panchayati Raj was always close to the hearts of Indians, the British rulers for the first time thought of reversing the trend of centralisation only in 1882 when the Government of Lord Rippon issued a resolution proposing steps in the direction of local self-government. It was deemed desirable not for providing better government but as 'an instrument of political and popular education'. The resolution called upon the provincial governments to establish a network of local boards charged with definite duties and entrusted with definite funds throughout the country. These boards were to have preponderance of non-official members chosen by election wherever possible. The control exercised by provincial governments was to be only from outside and only supervisory. The Collector was no longer to be the *ex officio* chairman of the Board. But, despite the very progressive and comprehensive nature of these Rippon reform proposals, precious little was done in the matter of implementation. The local boards continued to be wholly nominated. The Collectors continued to be *ex officio* Presidents. The boards practically became sort of departments of government administration subject to excessive outside control.

The Decentralization Commission which reported in 1909 made some far reaching suggestions to remove some of the defects in the working of local boards. In 1915, a government resolution endorsed the Commission proposals. But, again no concrete steps in the matter were taken by the provincial governments and in practice the *status quo ante* continued.

Following the Montagu declaration of 1917 regarding introduction of responsible government in gradual stages beginning with the local bodies, a resolution was issued by the Government of India in 1918 and,

---

2 Henry Maddick: *Panchayati Raj — A Study of Rural Local Government in India* (London, 1970) p 24

under the scheme of provincial dyarchy, by 1919, rural self-government was put under the charge of the Indian ministers. Some progress was made. Besides Municipal and Local Boards Acts, laws were also passed in almost all the provinces to introduce panchayats in villages. The whole purpose of improving local government under the British was, however still the need for 'improved finance and a higher standard of administration' and not self-government. "In the case of the villages, the official policy in the inter-war period had generally been described as one of rural uplift, a policy to which the states adhered, the Punjab as early as 1923 and other states by the 1930s. Village development schemes were officially sponsored and small grants were made available to the villages on condition that the local community matched these with equal sums in contributions. Some of these schemes were outstandingly successful, but the number of villages affected was probably less than 10 per cent and the general impact upon the rural life was small."[3] There was thus no uniform pattern of local self-government in the country.

Under the Government of India Act, 1935 Provincial Autonomy started functioning in the provinces from April 1937. Congress Governments took office in eight of the 11 provinces. Considerable progress in the direction of Panchayati Raj was made during the period of the Congress rule. Specially because of the Gandhian influence and direction, constitution of village panchayats had become as important item in the programme of the Congress.

According to the January 1948 Plan of Gandhiji, each village panchayat would constitute a working party with an elected leader; 50 such leaders would elect a second-grade leader who would coordinate their efforts and who would also be available for national service. Second-grade leaders could elect a national chief to "regulate and command all the groups".[4] Above the village panchayat came the

3 Ibid, p 20
4 NV Raj Kumar, *Development of the Congress Constitution*, (Delhi, 1948), pp 145-146 as cited by Austin, op cit, pp 28-29

hierarchy of indirectly elected bodies—*taluka* and district panchayats—each of which comprised of the *sarpanchs* of the next lower panchayats. Members from the district and municipal panchayats would make up the provincial panchayat. Presidents of provincial panchayats would comprise the All India Panchayat whose president will also be the Head of the State and of the Government. Among the responsibilities of the provincial panchayats would be transport, irrigation, natural resources and cooperative banks. The national panchayat would be responsible for defence, currency, customs, running of key industries of national importance and the coordination of provincial economic development plans.[5]

It was only natural that demands would be made in the Constituent Assembly for the revival of the Panchayat system of government at local level. The ideal of a revived village life with the Panchayats bringing democracy to the grassroots had a special appeal for the Congress members of the Constituent Assembly. Yet, when it came to putting it down in the Constitution, it seems, they felt that in the context of the needs of a welfare state of the modern age, it would be difficult and improper to take India back to the era of village republics. They opted for a system of parliamentary government both at the Union and state levels with the popular Houses of the Union Parliament and the state legislatures being directly elected on the basis of universal adult franchise. In the Objectives Resolution drafted and moved by Nehru there was no reference to panchayats. The Constituent Assembly also did not deal with the subject in any detail. When the reports of the Union and Provincial Constitution Committees were debated in the Assembly, there were only a few references to panchayats. A lone member voiced sentiments favouring the village being accepted as the primary unit of political organization with the government rising from the grassroots to the province and then to the Centre.[6] Later,

5 Austin, op cit, p 30
6 *CA Deb.*, Vol V, p 92

in a letter to BN Rau, the President of the Assembly, Dr Rajendra Prasad expressed himself strongly in favour of the idea of 'making the Constitution begin with the village and go up to the Centre' with the adult franchise being utilized only for the village panchayats which could in turn act as the electoral college for electing representatives to the provinces and the Centre.[7]

Dr Ambedkar did not have much admiration for the panchayat system and he did not feel it necessary that it be given any place in the Constitution. In fact, while introducing the Draft Constitution and referring to criticism thereof, Ambedkar had expressed himself strongly against the system of village panchayats. He had described village Panchayats as institutions surviving on a 'low' and 'selfish level'. Characterizing the village as a 'sink of localism, a den of ignorance, narrow-mindedness and communalism', he had observed, "I am glad that the Draft Constitution has discarded the village and adopted the individual as its unit." These views, of course, evoked sharp protests. A large number of Members, including Shibban Lal Saxena, HV Kamath, PS Deshmukh, AC Guha, T Prakasam, K Santhanam and NG Ranga argued forcibly in favour of Panchayat system and against the position taken by Ambedkar.[8]

The Panchayat supporters reminded the Assembly that Gandhiji had always advocated Panchayat Raj and *Ram Rajya*. He stood for government from the bottom-up while the Draft Constitution visualized a Government from the top-down. Alladi Krishnaswami Ayyar, participating in a debate tried to clarify that though "the Constitution does not give sufficient importance to village communities… there is nothing to prevent the provincial legislatures from constituting the villages as administrative units for the discharge of various functions vested in the state government". Ananthasayanam Ayyangar had made a suggestion "that in the directives, a clause must

7 Austin, op cit, p 35
8 *C A Deb.*, Vol VII, pp 38-39

be added, which would insist upon the various Governments that may come into existence in future to establish village panchayats, give them political autonomy, and also economic independence in their own way to manage their own affairs".[9] As a result of the general consensus in the debate in favour of decentralization of power and panchayat institutions an amendment was moved by K Santhanam, proposing to insert an article in the chapter on Directive Principles of State Policy. All those others who spoke on the subject at this stage, emphasized the need to establish such institutions in the villages. Dr Ambedkar accepted the amendment without any comment. The Assembly also readily adopted it, presumably, as a homage to Gandhiji's views and to the long cherished Congress ideals during the national struggle for independence. The amendment which became article 40 under Directive Principles of the Constitution, reads:

> "The State shall take steps to organise village panchayats and endow them with such powers and authority as may be necessary to enable them to function as units of self-government."

Soon after Independence some of the provinces had passed Panchayati Raj Acts and taken practical steps to organise village panchayats as units of rural self-government and endow them with certain powers and authority of administration. The village panchayats gained further impetus with the beginning of the First Five Year Plan in 1951. In 1952, several States launched community development and rural development plans with the help of local Five Year Plan introduced in 1956. It was proposed to cover the entire countryside with National Extension Service Blocks though the institution of Block Development Committees manned by Block Development Officers, Village Level Workers, etc., in addition to the nominated representatives of the village panchayats of that area and some other popular organizations like cooperative societies.

9 Ibid, pp 285, 316, 336 and 352

However, all these steps proved unsatisfactory and despite the constitutional directive of article 40 and the Five Year Plans, it was disappointing and discouraging that no major steps were taken in reorganizing village panchayats in such a way as to make them the instruments of transforming society with popular participation. Of course, there were new enactments or amendments to existing Acts passed by various state legislatures increasing the number of panchayats and their elected members. The range of powers and functions were also widened. But the power of taxation given to the panchayats was subject to specific conditions imposed by the government concerned. Often, rather than meeting the stringent conditions, the panchayats preferred to raise no additional revenue by new taxation resulting in lack of funds for meeting even the essential and obligatory expenses. In short, the village panchayats continued to be more or less in the same conditions as in the pre-Independence era.

The need for popular participation in development tasks under the Five Year Plans prompted the Congress leaders now in government to look in the direction of strengthening the panchayat system. Accordingly, Balwantrai Mehta Committee was appointed to enquire into, among other things, the lack of initiative, apathy and indifference on the part of the rural population. The Committee, officially designated as the 'team for the study of Community Projects and National Extension Service', visited all the states and held extensive discussions with all those concerned. It examined whether the existing local bodies could be entrusted with the job of undertaking the administrative and development work. In its opinion, there was need for an intermediary agency between the district board and the village panchayat, as the former covered a vast area and possibly could not do justice to the role assigned to it. According to the Committee, there was to be a panchayat samiti at the block level which was to be indirectly elected by the village panchayats, some representation being given also to municipalities and cooperative organizations in the block area. The samiti was to be assigned specific functions and specific items of revenue. At the district level there was to be a coordinating body called the zila parishad consisting of the presidents of the panchayats samities, members of State Legislatures and Parliament and all district level officers of the development departments as members and, with the Collector as the chairman.

The village panchayat was to be constituted by direct election on the basis of adult franchise with a special provision to co-opt two women members and one member each from scheduled castes and scheduled tribes. The panchayat was to have specific items of revenue like a share in land revenue and certain obligatory duties like acting as the agents of the panchayat samiti for executing schemes. Thus the plan envisaged a three-tier system of decentralization, namely the village panchayat, the panchayat samiti and the zila parishad. The above scheme recommended by the Committee was endorsed by the National Development Council on 12 January 1958. It was also decided at the national level that while the broad pattern and the fundamentals of the new system may be uniform throughout the country, there should not be any rigidity. What was important was the genuine transfer of power to the people, not the details of the pattern adopted.

It was in this context that Nehru described panchayats as the 'foundations of democracy' in India. Speaking on the occasion of the inauguration of Panchayati Raj in Rajasthan on 2 October 1959, he expressed his faith in the capability of the people in managing their affairs in the manner considered best by them. He said:

> "It is only by providing opportunity to the people that they can be trained to shoulder responsibilities. It became imperative that a bold step be taken whereby more and more responsibility could be transferred to the people. People were not merely to be consulted but effective power was to be entrusted to them. Therefore, we decided that in every village there should be a village panchayat with more powers as also a cooperative society which will help its economic efforts."[10]

10 *Jawaharlal Nehru's Speeches*, Vol IV, (September 1957-April 1963), (New Delhi, 1964), p 93

Nehru was of the opinion that India would make real progress only when people living in villages became politically conscious. "Progress of our country", he said, "is bound up with the progress in our villages". If they made progress, the nation ultimately was bound to be prosperous, strong and united. Nehru was of the view that panchayats should not be allowed to be officialized; that they should be controlled and run by the people themselves and the role of officials should be strictly advisory in nature. "Let them make mistakes", he said, " a mistake is often better than the helplessness and powerlessness which comes from somebody sitting on top and carrying on the business of the panchayats". Such was his faith in the people's ability to shoulder the responsibility given to them. Speaking at a meeting held in the Indian Institute of Public Administration on 25 April 1959, he said:

> "We want to give far greater powers to panchayats and to the village cooperatives than they have today, knowing full well that they may misuse it, make mistakes and the like. The mistakes of the panchayats will not endanger the security of the country. We can survive it. But they will suffer for it, they will learn from it and the public will learn from it too."[11]

Except for Kerala and Jammu and Kashmir all the States had then adopted the three-tier Panchayati Raj system. In these two States, the lowest level organization of panchayat was established while the other two levels of panchayat samiti and zila parishad remained to be formed. A village or a group of villages, formed a panchayat of elected representatives, a few panchayats formed a panchayat samiti and the various panchayat samities of a district were governed by a zila parishad and these three institutions had a threefold purpose:

- to be autonomous and self-governing to some extent;
- to play an effective role in drawing up the Five Year Plans; and

11 *Jawaharlal Nehru and Public Administration*, op cit, pp 80-81

- to have scope for initiative and readjustment in implementing the plans to suit local needs.

It would be of interest to note that throughout the period 1950 to 1964, the government headed by Nehru was all along keenly interested in the decentralization of governmental authority and in the establishment of village panchayats. The Congress Working Committee in a resolution had stated:

> "The Working Committee have noted with appreciation the progressive introduction of the panchayat system in various parts of India. This is not only in keeping with the ancient tradition of India but is suited to present day conditions. A modern state tends inevitably to become more and more centralized. This tendency should be balanced by the growth of self-governing institutions, so that the mass of the people should themselves participate in this business of administration and in other aspects of community life, social, economic and judicial. This can best be done by the development of panchayats in the villages of India. These panchayats should have an administrative function as well as a judicial function. The CWC particularly welcome the establishment of *Nyaya* or judicial panchayats which should reduce the burden on the regular courts and make justice available on the spot in a considerable number of relatively petty matters and thus make it both speedy and inexpensive. Such panchayats should be developed throughout the country in accordance with local conditions and traditions and represent the entire community in the area concerned, irrespective of caste or creed."[12]

After the Balwantrai Mehta Committee report was presented and implementation of its various recommendations had begun in right earnest, the 1961 Bhavnagar session of the Indian National Congress

---

12 Zaidi, op cit, Vol 14, p 548

again took up the subject of Panchayati Raj for consideration. The Resolution on 'Panchayati Raj' was moved by Balwantrai Mehta himself, who said that a welfare state would never be achieved in reality so long as local self-government did not function at the district, taluka and village levels with elective elements. According to him, panchayats and the cooperatives were the two institutions through which the people could be trained for leadership. He called upon the Congressmen to take direct interest in the working of panchayats to see that the new venture really achieved its object. SK Dey, the Minister of Community Development and Cooperation, Raghubir Sahay, who was the leader of the Study Team of Congress MPs on Panchayati Raj, and Smt Ram Dulari Sinha also spoke strongly in support of the Panchayati Raj. Jawaharlal Nehru, participating in the discussion said that Panchayati Raj had immense possibilities. He allayed the fear that if at one stroke a lot of power was given to the *Sarpanches* or *Panches* it would be harmful. On the other hand, he felt, they would learn from mistakes and improve their performance. The real meaning of democracy lay in enabling the people to go forward. Panchayats could form the strong foundations of democracy and only on strong foundations could solid structure be built. The general opinion on the issue of participation of political parties in the elections ot Panchayati Raj bodies was that preferably the elections should be on non-political basis. The Resolution which was adopted at the session, *inter alia*, welcomed the Panchayati Raj movement and congratulated the states which had already adopted it and expressed to hope that other States and Union Territories would also establish Panchayati Raj bodies in the course of the year and transfer responsibility to them in as large a measure as possible.[13]

By the year 1962, Panchayati Raj had come to be accepted as a national programme. It was felt necessary that Panchayati Raj got the widest support of the people and therefore the need for avoiding

---

13 *Ibid*, Vol 17, pp 263-269 and 307-308

party-politics in the election to village panchayats was emphasized. It was hoped that the political parties would also avoid setting up candidates on party-lines for panchayat elections. Speaking on the occasion of Third Annual General Body Meeting of the IIPA, on 6 April 1957, Nehru said:

> "There are hundreds and thousands of panchayats in this country. They form the real base of our democracy. If that base in unsound, then we are not cent percent stable democratically, even with the second base of our Parliament. We are told that panchayats have not succeeded because there are squabbles, there are parties, there is corruption and all that. It is true, I think, that our experience of panchayats has been distressing. But real democracy cannot be at the top, it can be only at the base; and in India, this is not something alien; it is something natural to this soil. The fact remains that the panchayat is the primary base of our democracy and we have to improve it."[14]

Whenever Nehru found that the functioning of the system was hampered by some impediments—financial, administrative or others—the government took remedial measures. Thus, another Committee was appointed by him in 1961, under the Chairmanship of K Santhanam, Member Rajya Sabha, to make a study of the resources and finances of Panchayati Raj. Many of the recommendations of the Committee suggesting the strengthening of resource base of panchayats by additional powers of taxation were accepted and implemented. In a message to the Hyderabad journal *Panchayat* on 16 March 1963, a year before his death, Nehru remarked that community development and Panchayati Raj were among the most helpful developments in the country, together constituting a revolutionary movement which, even if it had only yielded a fourth of the expected results, yet had proved 'an amazing success', strengthening India at the very roots

14 *Jawaharlal Nehru and Public Administration*, op cit, p 68

and preparing millions of men and women to shoulder responsibility and to be self-reliant. Still later, on 22 June 1963, Nehru said, "I have full confidence in its success because I have full confidence in the Indian people". He repeatedly urged officials to exercise their leadership not to suppress others but to encourage them to develop powers of initiative in their own spheres. If self-government at the village level were fostered, he believed, democratic institutions of the upper structure would function better more easily. Speaking to the Conference of Ministers of Community Development at Delhi on 1 August 1963, he said:

> "We must give power to the people, even though it leads us to hell. We will certainly come out of the hell if we get there."[15]

The 64th and 65th Amendment Bills which later became the 73rd and 74th Amendments were the first major constitutional efforts with the stated objective of transferring power to the grassroots people. It was a great initiative by Rajiv Gandhi as Prime Minister. But, the basic question was, from whom was the power being taken to be given away to the new local tiers of governance? The facts are that the powers that were proposed to be transferred, were hitherto those vesting in State Governments. No wonder, the 64th and 65th Amendment Bills were lost in the Rajya Sabha by three votes.

With the 1991 economic crisis and process of globalization, it became imperative that the democratic process percolate to the lowest level. It has been globally observed that economic development based on market forces draws strength from deepening democratic values and Rule of Law. Narasimha Rao as Prime Minister succeeded in seeing through Parliament the two Bills in a somewhat diluted form. The 73rd and 74th Amendments laid down the framework and guidelines in regard to the obligation to holding regular elections, restricting the period of supersession, providing for reservation for

---

15 Sarvepalli Gopal, *Jawaharlal Nehru—A Biography*, Vol 3: 1956-64 (Delhi, 1984), p 242

SC/ST and women, etc. It was perhaps very unfortunate that instead of relying on the Election Commission, a parallel and separate State election machinery was provided. It should be possible to somehow integrate the two and avoid duplication and frittering away of national resources—both financial and man-power.

The 73rd and 74th Amendments left a great deal for implementation by State governments through State laws to be passed by their legislatures. Whether as institutions or as individuals, no one ever surrenders power voluntarily. The result has been that most grudgingly and reluctantly and at the last minute, different States have passed laws which are at considerable variance with each other and in varying degrees try to deny the substance of functional and more particularly financial powers to the directly elected representatives in the PRIs. The local MPs and MLAs consider the new emerging leadership in the panchayats and nagar palikas as their rivals in the power structure who threaten to take away a share of the cake. It is, therefore, necessary to clearly define, delimit and demarcate the different rules of representatives at the Union, State and local government levels.

Despite all the imperfections and loopholes which need to be plugged it must be agreed that the 73rd and 74th Amendments have the potential of bringing about revolutionary changes in the political power structure and system of governance. But, if we are really serious about providing multi-level governance and taking power to the doorsteps of the people at the grassroots, the Constitution should clearly provide for distribution of powers between the Union, the States and the local governments of panchayats and nagar palikas by suitably amending articles 245, 246 and other relevant articles and the Seventh Schedule. It would certainly do no violence to the basic structure or features of the Constitution or to the parliamentary system. It has the potential to powerfully contribute to the needs of good governance and development.

The 73rd and 74th Amendments left the question of association of MPs and MLAs to be tackled at the level of States. Accepted at that time as a political compromise, this needs to be looked at afresh from the angle of constitutional propriety and clean and people friendly governance. If the aim of PRIs was to reduce the unhealthy role of MPs and MLAs as power brokers, the decision of some of the States to include them in PRIs with or without votes does not seem to be justified. MPs and MLAs must appreciate that their role is that of law makers and policy setters at the Union level for the whole of India and at the State level for the State as a whole. Local matters must be left to be handled at local levels by the representatives of the people elected to the local bodies. Also, executive functions have to be left to executive agencies at concerned levels. Schemes like the MP and MLA LADS—Local Area Development Schemes with some Rs 3,000 crore of public money involved each year—are an affront to the constitutional principles of distribution of powers between the Union and the States and separation of executive and legislative functions. Also, these schemes make the financially bankrupt PRIs look insignificant and powerless with each MP and MLA having large funds at his disposal for spending on local area schemes which are most legitimately the concern of PRIs under the 73rd and 74th Amendments. Even if largely suggestive and illustrative, the 11th and 12th Schedules to the Constitution become irrelevant if members of the Union Parliament and of State legislatures exercise executive powers in matters of local development otherwise supposedly reserved for panchayats and nagar palikas.

One can delve deep into the functional details of PRIs. Much can be said about the contradictions and infirmities in different State laws, the working of State Finance Commissions, State Election Commissioners, District and Metropolitan Planning Committees, etc. But, all the shortcomings notwithstanding, grassroots democracy unleashed by the 73rd and 74th Amendments has come to stay and as time passes, its financial and functional domains will get extended. It can only get more assertive and strengthened till sovereign power really comes to belong to the people and the Gandhian dream of building from below can be fulfilled.

There is every case for a wholesale decentrailzation of political power in a four-tier system of governance down to the grassroot levels. With a large number of smaller States and a four-tier system of governance, it may be possible to involve various groups in governance more closely and this may make the Union stronger and the nation more integrated, emotionally and culturally. Distribution of powers should be so designed that only the most essential or minimum necessary powers are assigned to each higher level. For example, whatever can be done by the local grassroot institutions like the village panchayats or municipalities should be left entirely in their hands. Government at a higher tier should have no power to remove or supersede a duly elected government at a lower tier. Efficient bureaucracy cannot be a substitute for democratic decentralised government. Also, 11th and 12th schedules should be made mandatory and merged into a common list. Decentralization of law and order functions to the local elected bodies would be most desirable. Powers of Gram Sabha and Gram Panchayats need to be classified. Local staffing is most desirable for local bodies.

In the North-East States, local traditional institutions of Government need to be modernized with gender justice for women and used as institutions of governance. Overlapping jurisdiction of State Government, Autonomous District Councils (ADCs) and traditional system of governance and the problems thereof must be removed and jurisdictions of each clearly defined. Greater autonomy should be provided to ADCs by amending the Sixth Schedule. Problems with regard to participation of non-tribals in ADCs need to be addressed. Problems in judicial administration due to multiple overlapping jurisdictions of the traditional institutions, ADCs and the subordinate judiciary should be resolved and the emerging conflict between human rights and tribal rights and between conservation laws and tribal rights to be analysed and resolved.

To preserve 'India, that is Bharat' as a 'Union of States' it is necessary to work for building it as a 'federal union' or what Aurobindo referred to as a union of 'autonomies' with multiple tiers of government and sharing of powers from the lowest grassroot level of panchayats to the Parliament and the Government of the Union. This would also be close to Gandhiji's model polity of concentric circles instead of the present pyramidical structure. Distribution of powers should be so designed that only the most essential or minimum necessary powers are assigned to each higher level. This would be in keeping with what is now called the subsidiarity principle. Incidentally, this would be the most rational and practical way of operationalizing the Gandhian vision of a Constitution for India which recognizes the sovereign power vesting in the people at the grassroots. Ultimately policies and power must flow like magnetic lines of force between the people and government at all levels forming an inviolable bond resulting in a powerful nation of empowered people.

PART II

Making and Working of the Constitution

9

Making and Working of the Constitution

Role of Jawaharlal Nehru

Nehru was the Assembly's philosopher and its prime constitutional thinker. He paid the most meticulous personal attention to the fundamentals. The President of the Constituent Assembly, Dr Rajendra Prasad also gave credit to Nehru [and Patel] 'for the fundamentals of the Constitution'.

Nehru laid down these fundamentals through the Objectives Resolution and as the Chairman of some of the most important committees like the States Committee, the Union Powers Committee and the Union Constitution Committee. Also, he played a crucial rule in settling many controversial issues in the Constituent Assembly, in its committees and in the informal, behind-the-scene discussions.

Once he was himself constrained to assert that he "was one of those humble individuals who had something to do with the making of the Constitution". While others fashioned its structure and shape, most significantly Nehru provided to the Constitution philosophy and vision. In fact, he envisioned a total system for national regeneration standing on the value pillars of secularism, socialism, parliamentary democracy and integrity and unity of the nation—the four foundational norms of India's Constitution and polity. It is a pity that not enough has been done in the academia or elsewhere in the direction of assessing the unique contribution of Nehru to the making and working of the Constitution.

Nehru took very active part in the debates on fundamental rights provisions of the Constitution and more particularly while speaking on the First and Fourth Constitution Amendment Bills. He supported provision of adequate safeguards for minorities, tribal areas and backward classes but warned that the various safeguards were not to be confused with fundamental rights. For, the ultimate national objective was to build a united organic nation based on the rich variety and unity of Indian culture and not to perpetuate separatist tendencies and privileges or class discriminations.

Nehru dwelt at length and repeatedly on the changing concept of property in the history of mankind. In the Congress Party meetings, he spoke rather strongly against the inclusion of the right to property as a fundamental right.

Nehru intervened effectively in the debate on nominated as against elected Governors and in this connection referred to the high cost of elections in terms of time, energy and money, to many elections not being good for democracy and to the greater desirability of a nominated Governor from outside the State. He felt that having elected Governors might encourage separatist provincial tendencies and reduce the common links with the Union.

Nehru spoke at length on the respective roles of and relationship between the Legislature and the Judiciary. Within the terms of the Constitution, he felt, the will of Parliament was supreme and the Judiciary could not be allowed to function as a third chamber to thwart social reform measures.

Nehru strongly pleaded for a parliamentary system as opposed to the Presidential and other systems. C Rajagopalachari would have favoured what may be termed 'a state of national democratic government on Gandhian lines'. The system of parliamentary democracy was finally adopted by deliberate choice, in Nehru's words, "not only because, to some extent we had always thought on those lines previously, but because we thought it was in keeping with our own old traditions also".

Nehru recommended some parliamentary reforms as early as in February 1956. He referred to the paucity of time with the Legislatures and suggested appointment of committees to deal with legislation in depth. Parliamentary democracy, he felt was inevitably going in the direction of economic democracy and whatever form it might take, 'only in the measure that it solves the economic problems does it succeed even in the political field'. Nehru believed that the parliamentary form of Government was 'more likely to do so than the other forms which lead to some measure of authoritarianism'. The Parliamentary system with all its failings, had 'the virtue that it can fit in with the changing pattern of life'.

But, the Constitution is not merely an inert document. It is a dynamic process. A living Constitution is always in the making through its actual working. It gets its real meaning and content only by the manner in which it is worked. Nehru's role in building the national edifice on firm foundations and giving to the Constitution of India its life and soul by working it for the first fourteen years was most remarkable. Many loopholes were detected and he took it upon himself to plug these by bringing in the necessary amendments which clarified the real intent of the framers. While piloting the Constitution Amendment Bills and otherwise speaking on important issues, Nehru made very significant contributions to constitutional thinking on subjects like fundamental rights vs directive principles, limits to freedom of speech, rights of the individual vs interests of the society, supremacy of Parliament and jurisdiction of courts, right to property, protection to backward classes, resolution of the language problem, position of the President and the Prime Minister etc.

Nehru was the first to suggest a Constituent Assembly for India as early as in 1933 and to actively pursue the idea to its fruition. But when the Assembly came to be set up in 1946, he did not hesitate to say that it was not what was desired or what they had worked for and "some time or the other in the future we may have to summon our own proper revolutionary Constituent Assembly". Later, Nehru stressed that the Constitution then framed by the Constituent Assembly may not satisfy free India and that they could not bind future generations. Speaking on the 4th Amendment Bill, Nehru had said: "it should be remembered that however good a constitution might be at any time, after working it for some little time, flaws appear. Nothing is perfect, and then it becomes necessary to remove those flaws".

Neither the Constituent Assembly nor the Constitution framed by it could be the final goal. In the words of Nehru,

> "The Constitution is after all some kind of legal body given to the ways of Government and the life of a people. A Constitution if it is out of touch with the people's life, aims and aspirations, becomes rather empty: if it falls behind those aims, it drags the people down. It should be something ahead to keep people's eyes and minds up to certain high mark."

While Nehru wanted the Constitution to be as solid and as permanent a structure as possible, he knew very well that 'there is no permanence in constitutions'. He deprecated the Indian tendencies of deifying things that we wish to kill. If you wish to kill this Constitution, he said, make it sacred and sacrosanct. It would then be 'a dead thing, not a growing thing, a static, unwieldy, unchanging thing'. Mentioning the examples of the excellent Constitutions of the German Weimar Republic and the Spanish Republic, Nehru pointed out that any constitution that fails to deal with the real problems of life perishes. He concluded that a Constitution which is unchanging and static, it does not matter how good it is, how perfect it is, is a Constitution that has past its use. It is in its old age already and gradually approaching its death. A Constitution to be living must be growing; must be adaptable; must be flexible; must be changeable.

The Constitution adopted by the Constituent Assembly, Nehru felt rather strongly "was not a final and rigid thing which must either be accepted or broken". As society changes, as conditions change, the Constitution must also change if it is not to break down.

Nehru told the Assembly that its first task was "to free India through a new Constitution, to feed the starving people, and to clothe the naked masses, and to give to every Indian the fullest opportunity to develop himself according to his capacity." In other words, the Constitution was relevant to him only as an instrument of social change. "I trust", Nehru said, "the Constitution itself will lead us to the real freedom that we have clamoured for and that real freedom in turn will bring food to our starving people, clothing for them, housing for them and all manner of opportunities of progress." The most important question was how to solve the problem of the poor and the starving. "If we cannot solve this problem soon", he added, "all our paper Constitution will become useless and purposeless."

What Nehru said then remains as relevant today. After more than half a century of the commencement of the Constitution, Nehru would have liked us to ask ourselves whether the way in which we have worked this Constitution has helped to solve any of the fundamental problems of 'We, the people of India'.

10

The Constitution and Sardar Patel

Sardar Vallabhbhai J Patel was one of the greatest Indians who ever strode this earth. His was a multi-faceted and multi-splendoured personality. His contributions to building and enriching the nation were varied and in many diverse fields. As years and decades roll by and we are faced with newer and newer problems, Sardar Patel's vision and message become more and more relevant.

The child whom a loving father Jhaverbhai named after the great scholar-saint Vallabhacharya, the Bardoli *satyagrahi* whose able leadership won him the title of 'Sardar', has been showered with many epithets during his life time and after. He has been described as an indomitable captain of freedom fighters, India's Bismarck, modern Ashoka, Iron Man of India, Lenin of Bardoli, consolidator and builder of new India, the greatest statesman, the most remarkable son of India and much else. Dozens of scholarly volumes have been written on his life and work. His contribution to the freedom struggle, his role as an outstanding statesman, his unforgettable contribution as a unifier of the nation and integrator of states, have been ably documented. But, Sardar Patel's unique contribution as one of the most prominent founding fathers of our Constitution and as one who, along with Jawaharlal Nehru, played the most leading role in determining the nature of our polity, has neither been adequately explored nor properly evaluated.

While it was naturally the job of the draftsmen and the drafting committee consisting of professional lawyers to give shape and form to provisions of the Constitution, the spirit of our Constitution bears the imprint of Patel's vision (no less than Nehru's) and its structure is a living embodiment of his work as a nation-builder. An objective study of the Constituent Assembly by a dedicated American scholar, Granville Austin had found that the four most prominent founding fathers of the Constitution were Sardar Patel, Jawaharlal Nehru, Maulana Abul Kalam Azad and Dr Rajendra Prasad. It is obvious that of these four also, the first two stand out as having mattered the most. They really controlled the Assembly and determined the emerging edifice of the Constitution of independent India. Between them, Nehru and Patel agreed as much as they disagreed. Patel, like Prasad, was a real son of the Indian soil. He and Prasad did not have to make a *Discovery of India*. He knew his India and was every bit an Indian. He came from and knew the realities at the grassroots. He led peasants' movements and stood for zamindari abolition but he was not a Fabian socialist. While Nehru's approach to constitution-making was more idealistic and theoretical, Patel was pragmatic, down to earth, practical. While Nehru was a visionary and a dreamer, more anxious to incorporate socialistic ideals in the text of the Constitution, Patel's priority was for a Constitution that would give to the country an effective government or what in today's terminology would be called 'good governance'. He was a man of action and his vision was of a strong, stable, united and prosperous India.

Constitution of the Constituent Assembly

Patel was not only the Deputy Prime Minister and the Home Minister but the most influential leader in the Congress Party organization. His hold on the organization was unshakable. He was the most outstanding member of the AICC Elections Committee concerned with the selection of candidates for the Constituent Assembly. While seats for the Sikhs and Muslims were guaranteed, it was largely Sardar Patel's initiative that ensured fair representation to others like the Parsis, Anglo-Indians, Christians, Women, Sindhis, Scheduled Castes and Scheduled Tribes within the general category. A number of non-Congressmen were also included for their special talents and stature in law, administration and public life. As he put it:

> "In the Constituent Assembly we want men who can make a good contribution in the complicated task of constitution-making or drafting and we certainly want men of ability and experience."

A perusal of the ten heavy volumes of Patel's correspondence so ably compiled and edited by Durga Das brings out, among other things, Patel's early concern to get the best men and women in the Constituent Assembly. He was corresponding with the princes of the Indian States, premiers of provinces, Congress leaders and others all over the country—inviting suggestions, commenting on names and finally securing the election of those selected. It is recorded how Gandhiji felt pained at the Congressmen scrambling for Constituent Assembly membership as if like 'thieves and robbers' they wanted to enjoy the booty after a jail term.

Building the Union

Next to the constitution of the Constituent Assembly, or rather interlinked, was the question of integration of the princely States with the proposed Union of India. If the 500 and odd princely States spread all over the country remained outside, there could hardly be any meaningful Union of India. The question of securing the accession of princely States was therefore of prime importance to the exercise of Constitution making. In the words of Sardar Patel himself, the States' issue was the most crucial for no Constitution for the nation could be drafted while India remained divided into over 500—according to some legally and potentially independent—units.

Principles of the Constitution—beginning with the vesting of sovereignty, questions of democracy and elected representatives of the people—were all dependent on 'the resolution of States' issues and the nature of integration. Speaking on 26 May 1950, Patel said:

> "The first requirement of any progressive country is internal and external security. Therefore I started planning on the integration of the country... It is impossible to make progress unless you first restore order in the country."

Fortunately for India, thanks to Patel, vast majority of the princely States had joined the Constituent Assembly by 15 August 1947. On 12 October 1949 Patel announced in the Assembly completion of the process of integration of the princely States with the rest of the country. He said that unlike the scheme of the 1935 Act, the new constitution was 'not an alliance between democracies and dynasties, but a real Union of the Indian people, built on the basic concept of the sovereignty of the people'. What Patel had achieved was nothing short of 'a bloodless revolution' which within a remarkably short period had transformed the internal and external set up of the States. Once, he said his watch-word was 'unity and more unity'. Patel added:

> "The fact that the new Constitution specifies only nine States in Part III of Schedule I is an index to the phenomenal progress made by the policy of integration pursued by the Government of India. By integrating 500 odd States into sizable units and by the complete elimination of centuries-old autocracies, the Indian democracy has won a great victory of which the Princes and the people of India alike should be proud. This is an achievement which should redound to the credit of any nation or people at any phase of history."

On 26 November 1949 when the Constitution of India was finally adopted by the Constituent Assembly, Patel was able to declare that the Constitution had been accepted, by the ten States in Part B including Hyderabad.

Patel ensured that his promise to the princes in the matter of their privy purses, etc.,—amounting to a total liability not exceeding a paltry sum of four crore rupees a year—was duly embedded in the Constitution. He said:

> "The Privy Purse settlements are in the nature of consideration for the surrender by the rulers of all their ruling powers... Need we cavil at the small—I purposely use the word small—price we have paid for the bloodless revolution which has affected the destinies of millions of our people".

It is another matter that when Patel was not on the scene, the princes were most unceremoniously divested of their privy purses and privileges in a populist move and for political party gains.

Work in Committees

The floor of the Constituent Assembly was a forum for debates and speeches—some of them most inspiring and educative and of the highest quality. But, a man of few words and more concerned with concrete action, Patel sometimes felt disconcerted with what happened on the floor of the Assembly. Once he wrote to Nehru:

> "I try to follow the Constituent Assembly debates through the papers as much as I can, but frankly speaking, most of it seems to me to be irrelevant and beside the point. Only if we could control some of those persistent speakers, our pace would be quicker".

It is important to remember that in the matter of laying down the fundamental principles of the Constitution and the basic structure of the polity, the most substantial work was done away from the public view, behind closed doors, in committees, sub-committees or informal group meetings of senior leaders. In these fora, Sardar Patel's contribution was often the most crucial and his voice decisive. After long arguments and failure to arrive at any agreement, it would be left to the Sardar to clinch the issue with a final statement resolving the conflictual situation in such a manner that everybody would be satisfied or at least rendered speechless.

In one of the informal meetings of the top few of the Constituent Assembly held on the Raisina Hill (at what is now the Rashtrapati Bhavan) to resolve differences in regard to having second chambers, strong views were expressed both for and against. No agreement could be arrived at. At the end of it all, the man of few words, Sardal Patel is reported to have stood up and said: "An unemployed politician is a social menace. Gentlemen, we shall have the upper houses." All agreed. Subsequently, as a compromise, two chambers were provided for Union Parliament but for the States it was left to the Assembly of the State concerned to suggest the abolition or creation of the other House.

Often Patel sat in the Constituent Assembly silently presumably because he knew he had done his work well outside the Assembly and remained confident that when it came to taking decisions, the Assembly would not go against his perceptions of national interest.

Some of the most important committees of the Constituent Assembly were under the close guidance and leadership of either Patel or Nehru. Nehru was a member of three and Patel was on four committees. As Chairman, Patel headed the Provincial Constitution Committee and the most crucial Advisory Committee on Fundamental Rights, Minorities etc. He was also a member of the States Committee and the Steering Committee chaired by Nehru and Prasad respectively. Also, Patel was invariably a member of all informal groups that met to solve intractable problems or to settle basic issues.

Minorities and Reservations in Legislatures

The dexterity, astuteness and precision with which Patel handled the work of the Advisory Committee was most remarkable. A reading of the proceedings is a treat and an education in strategies of meeting management. After allowing free discussion, Patel would utter his few decisive words of conclusion which everybody would find most acceptable. Suave and soft yet firm like a rock in his convictions, selflessness and patriotism, Patel succeeded in allaying the apprehensions and fears of minorities. As a general rule he was for all legitimate minority demands of representation but not for reservation. As early as on 2 June 1946, he had written:

> "I can trust nobody who wants more representation for his community at the cost of the other community. All nationalists must accept the principle of representation on a population basis. No device to turn a majority into a minority can be accepted under any circumstances."

When the Advisory Committee on Fundamental Rights, Minorities, etc., met for its first sitting under his Chairmanship, Patel said: "Nobody can be more interested than us in India in the protection of our minorities. Our mission is to satisfy every one of them".

In the Advisory Committee and in the behind-the-scene deliberations, Patel rejected all suggestions for the continuation of communal quotas of reserved seats in legislatures. He had to work hard in favour of abolition of the communal electorates and quotas of seats. Parsi leader Homi Modi, Christian leader Dr HC Mookerjea, the Sikhs and almost all Muslims including the nationalist Muslims wanted reservations in the legislatures and in public services. Muslim members were the last to agree to give up separate electorate and reservation of seats for them. It was distressing, though not surprising for Patel to see the Muslims left in India after partition still clinging to the sinister two-nation theory and pressing for separate electorates which had led to the partition. Sometimes quietly and privately, he had to put personal pressure on the minorities to give up reservation like privileges.

The Committee resolved to have 'no reservations except for the Scheduled Castes and the Scheduled Tribes'. In view of the special position of the Anglo-Indians, the provision enabling the President and the Governors to nominate members of this community was retained. Most tactfully, the Sardar had the main resolution moved by a minority leader—HC Mukherjea—who was a prominent Christian member. The Advisory Committee recorded:

"The first question we tackled was that of separate electorates; we considered this as being of crucial importance both to the minorities themselves and to the political life of the country as a whole. By an overwhelming majority we came to the conclusion that the system of separate electorates must be abolished in the new Constitution. In our judgement, this system has in the past sharpened communal differences to a dangerous extent and has proved one of the main stumbling blocks to the development of a healthy national life. It seems specially necessary to avoid these dangers in the new political conditions that have developed in the country and from this' point of view the arguments against separate electorates seem to us absolutely decisive. We recommend accordingly that all elections to the Central and Provincial Legislatures should be held on the basis of joint electorates."

Introducing a motion for joint electorates in the Constituent Assembly on 27 August 1947, Patel said that there was unanimity of opinion "on the point that there should be no more separate electorates and we should have joint electorates hereafter." There was a strong demand from some Muslim members for continuing separate electorates. Patel iterated his uncompromising opposition to the principle of separate electorates. The introduction of the system of communal electorates was, he said, a poison which had entered into the body politic of the country. Patel attributed the partition of the country, with its attendant upheavals, directly to the issue of communal electorates.

In October 1949 replying to the demand of Muslims for reservation in services he appealed to them to drop such claims and to 'fight over issues beneficial to the whole country' in order to create an atmosphere different from 'distrust and discord'. Speaking towards the end of a very heated and communally charged debate on a draft clause which sought to bar any conversion from one religion to another, 'by coercion or undue influence' or of 'a minor under the age of 18', Sardar Patel said that it was a hard fact that in India, there were mass conversions,

conversions by force, conversions by coercion and undue influence and that children and orphans were also being converted.

Another matter of interest was also mentioned by Patel. The Constituent Assembly had always recognized that the, Scheduled Castes were a backward section of the Hindu community who were handicapped by the practice of untouchability. This evil practice of untouchability was not recognized by any other religion and the question of any Scheduled Castes belonging to a religion other than Hinduism did not therefore arise. But, the Sikhs had made a demand that some of their backward sections—Mazhabis, Ramdasias, Kabirpanthis and Sikligars—should be included in the list of Scheduled Castes. This was accepted by the Advisory Committee. Patel recognized that this was a political decision; but for the sake of securing their goodwill, he urged the Assembly to agree to this concession. Summing up, he said:

> "In the long run it would be in the interests of all to forget that there is anything like a majority or a minority in this country and that in India there is only one community."

A lengthy discussion took place on these proposals of the Advisory Committee. The majority of the speakers—and these included members from all communities, Muslims, Christians, Anglo-Indians, Scheduled Castes, as well as Hindus—offered full support to the proposal to abolish reservations on communal grounds.

Three Muslim members of the Assembly expressed their opposition to Patel's motion. Mohammad Saadulla from Assam, a member of the Drafting Committee, wanted the continuance of reservations for a period of 10 years. He also made the interesting statement that only four members of the Muslim community were present at the meeting of the Advisory Committee on 11 May and that only one of them supported the proposal for the abolition of reservations, thereby challenging Patel's claim of unanimity. Saadulla mentioned in particular that Abul Kalam Azad was neutral on this issue. Muhammad Ismail from Madras wanted a reversion to the previous position of separate electorates. ZH Lari urged the removal of reservations for all communities and suggested instead the introduction of a system of proportional representation and cumulative voting through multi-member constituencies.

These amendments were opposed by Patel in a forthright speech in which he gave a resume of what had happened at the Advisory Committee meeting. He said:

> "...It was Mr Tajamul Husain from Bihar who stood up and moved an amendment that reservations must go. He was challenged in the committee whether he had consulted the other members of the Muslim community, and he quoted chapter and verse from the representatives of the Provinces whom he had consulted. Yet he did not want a snap vote. I said that I would advise the Advisory Committee to hold over the question and ask all members of the minority communities to consult, their constituencies and find out what they really wanted. Nearly four months after that we met and unfortunately Mr Saadulla was not present or he did not appear and so the opinions that he had gathered remained with him. He did not even communicate them to us. He said that there was only an attendance of four there of whom (I do not know whether he has consulted Maulana Azad or not) he says that Maulana Azad remained neutral. He claims to know Maulana Azad's mind more than I can do. But I can tell him that Maulana Azad is not a cipher; he has a conscience. If he felt that it was against the interests of his community he would have immediately said so and protested."

The proposal of the Advisory Committee was adopted by the Assembly with an amendment that no reservation would be operative for more than ten years.

Language Problem

On the intractable language issues, the Advisory Committee was not able to arrive at any consensus and its consideration was postponed.

All references to national/official language were omitted from the Fundamental Rights provisions at the suggestion of Chairman Patel. That was on 21 April 1947. When the Provincial Constitution Committee's Report came up first for consideration, Patel suggested that the provision relating to the language to be used in the Provincial Legislatures and the Union Parliament should be considered together. Patel himself mentioned that this was a controversial matter, with the likelihood of its creating some confusion. At Patel's suggestion, therefore, the discussion was again postponed. Finally, Patel wrote to KM Munshi on 19 August 1949 that (1) Hindi in Devanagari script should be the official/national language, (2) Government should make special efforts to promote Hindi as the official language and (3) meanwhile for 10 years English may continue. This precisely was the formula finally adopted as the Munshi--Ayyangar formula in September 1949 by the Assembly with the only change being that the period of 10 years was changed to 15 years.

Fundamental Rights and Directive Principles

As between Nehru and Patel, Nehru was an advocate of unrestrained fundamental rights of the individual except in the case of property rights. Patel, on the other hand, wanted individual's rights of speech and action to be balanced by society's rights of maintenance of order and security. Patel took the initiative to arm the executive with the authority to resort to preventive detention where necessary. He noted that there was a danger of certain old type of judge misinterpreting the new process of law.

The Motilal Nehru Committee Report (1928) and the Karachi Resolution of the Congress (1931) both had spoken of 'liberty' and 'property' together. The drafts on fundamental rights presented to the Sub-committee on Fundamental Rights by Ambedkar and Munshi also spoke of right to 'life, liberty and property' , in one piece as fundamental rights. It was Sardar Patel who insisted upon right to property being separated from the right to liberty.

There was heated debate in the Advisory Committee on the question of 'just compensation' for property acquired by the state. Patel felt that if the word 'just' was retained, every case would go to the courts. It was, therefore, better to drop the word.

Patel was for abolition of zamindari but he was against acquisition of land without adequate compensation being paid. He said acquisition without compensation was 'theft' and 'dacoity'. The incorporation of the right to property in articles 19 and 31 was largely Patel's handiwork. Many drafts and reports of the property clause were attempted. Patel was closely involved. Finally, the clause reserving all property legislation for Presidential assent was at Patel's insistence. So long as he lived, Patel could block any move that seemed to him to be unjust and violative of the citizen's right to property. It is different that after his death, successive Constitution Amendment Acts went on diluting the right to property further and further till finally it was abolished from the Fundamental Rights part of the Constitution.

In his letter to the President while submitting the Advisory Committee report, Patel wrote (29 April 1947): "We attach great importance to the Constitution making these (fundamental) rights justiciable". Patel also made the point that the protection of the rights of the citizen had to be an essential feature of any democratic modern constitution.

While moving the non-discrimination clause in the Assembly, Patel rejected the suggestion to prohibit discrimination on grounds of political creed. He said, it is an 'absurd idea' to provide for non-discrimination as regards political creed. Patel was against tribals being kept apart as museum pieces and said that it was not in the interests of the tribals to "remain permanently in their present state".

About the Directive Principles of State Policy, Sardar Patel had said that though not enforceable in any court of law, these should be regarded as fundamental in the governance of the country. These very precise words formed the content of article 37 of the Constitution. In the entire Constitution the word 'governance' has been used only at one place and that is in this article. It is interesting to note that principles of governance or good governance have become the subject matter of intellectual discourse in the Political Science academia only during the last two or three decades, that is, much after the time of Sardar Patel and the framing of our Constitution. It shows Patel's farsightedness that he talked of principles of governance as early as in the first half of the last century.

It was a tribute to Patel that the report of the Advisory Committee was received most favourably and its recommendations were very largely accepted by the Constituent Assembly. What we have today in the most important parts of the Constitution under the heads 'Fundamental Rights' and 'Directive Principles of State Policy' is almost entirely the result of the work of the Advisory Committee headed by Sardar Patel.

Union-State Relations

The Provincial Constitution Committee headed by Patel submitted its Report on 21 July 1947. It contributed most substantially to the provisions of the Constitution relating to position of the Governors, relations between the Union and the states and distribution of powers between them. On the powers of the Governor, Patel was very clear that generally he was bound to act on the advice of the Council of Ministers. In the matter of grave threat to peace, Governor was proposed to be armed only with the authority to make a report to the President. Patel explained:

> "The committee in settling this question intended to convey that the Governor shall have only the authority to report to the Union President about the grave situation arising in the Province which would involve a grave menace to the peace of the Province. It was not their intention that this power or authority (to declare emergency in the State) is to be exercised by the Governor which may perhaps bring a conflict between the Ministry and the Governor. The Governor having no control over the services, the authority of the administration entirely vests in the Ministry and

therefore, although there was considerable difference of opinion on this question on account of the prevailing conditions in the country—some thought that it would be advisable under the present peculiar unsettled conditions in the country to give some limited powers to the Governor—eventually the committee came to the conclusion that it would not be workable, that it would create deadlocks, and therefore, the proper course would be to limit his powers to the extent of authorizing him to report to the President of the Union."

The final shape in which article 356 emerged followed this position although in between other alternatives were debated forcefully including the one to empower the Governor to declare an emergency on his own. The influence of Sardar Patel was visible in the post-partition move towards a stronger central authority. Personally, he had always been for a strong central authority necessary for preserving the unity and stability of the nation. Articles 354 and 356 most particularly have his imprint.

Jawaharlal Nehru was for the President being elected by the Members of the two Houses of Parliament. But here also the Sardar put his foot down and ultimately at the joint meeting of the Union Constitution and the Provincial Constitution Committees organized at his initiative, the impasse was resolved with a decision to have the President elected by an electoral college consisting of all the elected members of the two Houses of Parliament and the Legislative Assemblies of the States.

Protection to Services

Even before the Constituent Assembly met, Sardar Patel was almost single-handedly responsible for getting through the Conference of Chief Ministers (then called Prime Ministers or Premiers) of the provinces a proposal for the creation of two All India Services - the IAS and the IPS. He looked upon them as a unifying force. Again, it was

Patel's intervention that ensured the protection of terms and privileges of the Indian Civil Service Officers through the incorporation of certain provisions in articles 311 and 314 of the Constitution even though the latter was repealed in 1972 as being no more needed. Unlike Nehru who began with a strong suspicion of the Civil Services, Patel had great faith in the loyalty and patriotism of the civil services. He believed that one could not get the best out of unwilling hands. Patel endeared himself to the civil services and generated reverence as an ideal Minister who gave trust and listened patiently even where he did not agree. He earned the nickname of the 'patron saint' of the civil services. The result was that along with the Congress Party organization, Patel also controlled the permanent services and through them the entire administration. His management of the party and the bureaucracy was superb all through the years 1946-1950.

When the Draft Constitution as settled by the Drafting Committee was circulated, comments of substance were received from the Ministry of Home Affairs. The Home Ministry was very emphatic that provision in specific terms should be included in the Constitution for the setting up of the Indian Administrative Service and the Indian Police Service as all-India services. The case for such a provision was framed in the following words by Deputy Prime Minister Vallabhbhai Patel:

> "In consultation with and with the unanimous support of, Provincial Governments, we have evolved two new services to take the place of the Indian Civil Service and the Indian Police viz., the Indian Administrative Service and the Indian Police Service. An efficient, disciplined and contented service assured of its prospects as a result of diligent and honest work, is a sine qua non of sound administration under a democratic regime even more than under an authoritarian rule. The service must be above party and we should ensure that political considerations, either in its recruitment or in its discipline and control, reduced to the minimum, if not eliminated altogether... In an all-India service, it is obvious, recruitment, discipline and control, etc., have

to be tackled on a basis of uniformity and under the direction of the Central Government which is the recruiting agency... all these matters have been settled at a conference of Prime Ministers convened in 1946 and the details have been settled by correspondence with Provincial Governments.

"No criticism, therefore, can be made that either in the formation of these services or in the preparation of necessary rules and regulations provincial susceptibilities and views find no place. Indeed, there was a remarkable unanimity between the views of the Provincial Governments and those of the Central Government throughout on these questions. Any pricking of the conscience on the score of provincial autonomy or on the need for sustaining the prestige and powers of Provincial Ministers is therefore out of place. I am also convinced... that it would be a grave mistake to leave these matters to be regulated either by central or provincial legislation. Constitutional guarantees and safeguards are the best medium of providing for these services and are likely to prove more lasting.

"Any failure on the part of the Constituent Assembly to insert a provision to this effect was bound to be regarded as reflecting unwillingness to endorse these commitments solemnly given to the officers.

"It will thereby create doubts and apprehensions which, it is essential in the public interest, should not be created. On the other hand, the making of a specific provision would foster stability and an independent outlook which are essential for the efficiency and effectiveness of the service.

"We are bound in honour to carry out the undertaking and the only way that undertaking can be fully and satisfactorily discharged is by making provision in the Constitution."

The provision for the protection of All-India Service officers evoked considerable controversy. There was much criticism of the safeguards proposed and there was also bitter comment on the privileged position of these officers. Patel who defended the article vigorously was severe on the critics. He gave a resume of the history of the safeguards provided for the Secretary of State's Officers, and explained that on behalf of the new Government, these guarantees had been pledged and included in the Indian Independence Act:

> "When the Indian Independence Act was to be passed in Parliament the draft was sent here. The leaders of the nation were called for; the Cabinet was there, the Congress President was there, your President was there and your Leader today was there. Mahatma Gandhi was also present. Every section was scrutinized and the draft was approved. After (that) it was passed in the Parliament. Now, these guarantees were circulated before that to the Provinces. All Provinces agreed. It was also agreed to incorporate these into the Constituent Assembly's new Constitution. This (is) one part of the guarantee. Have you read that history? Or, you do not care for the recent history after you began to make history. If you do that, then I tell you we have a dark future. Learn to stand upon your pledged word, and, also, as a man of experience I tell you, do not quarrel with the instruments with which you want to work. It is a bad workman who quarrels with his instruments. Take work from them. Every man wants some sort of encouragement. Nobody wants to put in work when every day he is criticized and ridiculed in public. Nobody will give you work like that. So, once and for all decide whether you want this service or not. If you have done with it and decide not to have this service at all, even in spite of my pledged word, I will take the Services with me and go."

Patel took the opportunity for a word of appreciation for the civil servant. He said:

> "Today, my Secretary can write a note opposed to my views. I have given that freedom to all my Secretaries. I have told them, "If you do not give your honest opinion for fear that it will displease

your Minister, please then you had better go. I will bring another Secretary. I will never be displeased over a frank expression of opinion. Many of them with whom I have worked, I have no hesitation in saying that they are as patriotic, as loyal and as sincere as myself. These people are the instruments. Remove them and I see nothing but a picture of chaos all over the country."

All the amendments were thereafter negatived and the article adopted.

Judiciary

Patel greatly influenced the structure of judiciary provisions of the Constitution. He laid stress on fair appointments to the judiciary. Introducing the Report of the Provincial Constitution Committee, he said that the judges should be above all suspicion and should be appointed by the President. Later, when it was found difficult to resolve the 'question of judges' salaries in the cabinet, Patel suggested that in order to attract first rate stuff to the higher judiciary, salaries of the judges should be laid down in the Constitution itself. In another note to the cabinet, Patel sought to resolve the difficulty in regard to higher salary to pre-Constitution judges. Patel pleaded for keeping the 'pledged word'.

Largely thanks to Patel's foresight, unlike the United States, we do not have separate courts for handling Union and State laws. There is one unified judiciary and a single judicial hierarchy of courts. The High Courts in the States are linked to the Supreme Court and completely freed from State Government influences thereby ensuring greater independence to the Judiciary and also cementing national unity. The unified judiciary along with All India Services and a single Election Commission for elections to the Union and State Legislatures would, Sardar Patel expected, turn out to be important nation building, unifying and integrative forces.

Summing Up

To sum up Patel's role in Constitution making, it may be said that in view of Patel's position, no crucial step in the Constituent Assembly could be taken without his concurrence. When Patel and Nehru could not agree on a provision, as happened, for example, in the case of the property clause, Nehru depended on Patel and not the other way round. In fact, Patel held under some check the 'impetuous, Laski-ite socialist theoretician' in Nehru.

When during the last quarter of 1949 Nehru was on a foreign tour, Patel handled the executive work of the office of the Prime Minister as also the work of the Constituent Assembly (in session at that time). He kept Nehru fully informed through very comprehensive letters. We find Patel telling Nehru that on the issue of services some 'bad' and 'silly' speeches were made in the Constituent Assembly and he had to intervene. Provisions regarding the States were passed without much difficulty. So were the provisions regarding the Judiciary, position of J&K, Financial Emergency etc.

Sardar Patel influenced or moulded in a myriad ways the provisions of the Constitution in almost every area—Fundamental Rights, Directive Principles, Election of the President, Union-State Relations, Position and powers of the Governor, Council of Ministers, Elections to Parliament and State Legislatures, Reservation of seats for SC and ST in legislatures, All India Services, reservation of jobs in public services, minority rights, emergency provisions, integration of princely states, language clauses, independence of judiciary, appointment and salary of judges, citizenship and so on.

Sardar Patel stood for equal political rights for all citizens irrespective of religion, race, caste, gender, place of birth or the like. While conceding various linguistic religious or other minority rights, he was opposed to any political rights—like seats in legislatures—being sought on grounds of one's religion or on grounds of belonging to a minority or majority. Political rights could be claimed only as citizens of India. Every citizen—Hindu, Muslim or other—was entitled to same rights.

Patel felt proud to lay the foundations of a true secular democratic state where everybody had equal chance. The whole nation remembers with deep gratitude to Sardar Patel how he rid us of the scourge of separate communal electorates and religion-based reservations and quotas. It is particularly relevant in the national scenario when renewed demands for reservations are being made on the ground of minorities not having representation in the legislatures and services proportionate to their population.

That the Sardar is relevant today is proved also by the fact of his being remembered every time that the nation is faced with a constitutional or political crisis. His name immediately comes to mind as one who could have rid us of the problems before us. The political parties compete with each other in owning him as their icon. Important leaders both at the Union and State levels, try to emulate his style and build their profile closest to their perception of his image. Nothing can please them more than to be somehow compared to the Sardar. The legend and the legacy continues to grow and with every passing year it glows brighter and brighter.

11

The Constitution and Dr B R Ambedkar

When the Constituent Assembly was set up under the Cabinet Mission Plan, Dr B R Ambedkar was among the eminent non-Congressmen selected by the Congress High Command to be its members. Originally elected to the Assembly as a member of the Scheduled Castes Federation from Bengal, he lost his seat with the partition of Bengal. He was re-elected to the Assembly by the Bombay Congress at the request of the Congress High Command. Despite Dr Ambedkar's skirmishes with the Congress and Gandhiji going back to some 20 years, Nehru had personally invited him to become a member of his Cabinet. But, when the leadership in the Constituent Assembly selected him to be the Chairman of the Constitution Drafting Committee—a position of supreme responsibility and trust—Dr Ambedkar himself was pleasantly surprised at the choice and said:

> "I came into the Constituent Assembly with no greater aspiration than to safeguard the interests of the Scheduled Castes. I had not the remotest idea that I would be called upon to undertake more responsible functions. I was, therefore, greatly surprised when

> the Assembly elected me to the Drafting Committee. I was more than surprised when the Drafting Committee elected me to be its Chairman."

Dr Ambedkar performed the role of the Chairman of the Drafting Committee with great aplomb and efficiency. The Drafting Committee was appointed on 29 August 1947. The Committee presented the Draft Constitution to the President of the Constituent Assembly on 21 February 1948. When it came up for discussion before the Assembly, T T Krishnamachari, himself a member of the Drafting Committee, told the House that even though there were seven members in the Drafting Committee, "it happened ultimately that the burden of drafting this Constitution fell on Dr Ambedkar" and he was able to accomplish the 'task in a manner which is undoubtedly commendable'.

When the Draft Constitution as framed by the Drafting Committee was being finally adopted by the Constituent Assembly, high tributes were paid to Dr Ambedkar and his team for accomplishing a most difficult task within a very short time-schedule. Thus, Alladi Krishnaswami Ayyar expressed 'high appreciation of the skill and ability' with which Dr Ambedkar had piloted the Constitution and the untiring work that he had done as the Chairman of the Drafting Committee. Dr B Pattabhi Sitaramayya spoke of the 'Steamroller intellect' that Dr Ambedkar brought to bear upon the magnificent and tremendous task of Constitution-making. He said that whatever Dr Ambedkar felt to be right, irrespective of the consequences, he stood by it 'irresistible, indomitable, unconquerable, levelling down tall palms and short poppies'. Dr Rajendra Prasad, the President of the Constituent Assembly observed on 26 November 1949: "We could never make a decision which was or could be ever so right as when we put him on the Drafting Committee and made him its Chairman."

Quite appropriately, Dr Ambedkar has been given all the due credit for his work as the Chairman of the Drafting Committee. The coming generations would also perhaps remember him most as the chief architect of the Constitution. But, a question for further enquiry and consideration is whether it would be proper to identify him too closely with the Constitution of India as it came out of the Constituent Assembly? Should a separate and independent attempt not be made to get to the essence of his own vision of Indian polity? It may be that Dr Ambedkar's vision was substantially at variance with the views of the majority of the Constituent Assembly members and the leadership represented by Nehru, Patel and others. In fact, Dr Ambedkar was even opposed to the idea of a Constituent Assembly to frame a Constitution for India. Opposing the setting up of the Constituent Assembly, he had said in May 1945 :

> "I am wholly opposed to the proposals of a Constituent Assembly. It is absolutely superfluous. I regard it as a most dangerous project… I cannot see why Constituent Assembly is necessary to incubate a Constitution. So much of the Constitution of India has already been written out in the Government of India Act 1935 that it seems to be an act of supererogation to appoint a Constituent Assembly to the thing over again. All that is necessary is to delete those sections of the Government of India Act 1935, which are inconsistent with Dominion Status."

Later, nearly four years after the adoption of the Constitution by the Constituent Assembly, during a debate in the Rajya Sabha on 2 September 1953, Dr Ambedkar said:

> "People always keep on saying to me: oh you are the maker of the Constitution. My answer is I was a hack. What I was asked to do, I did much against my will…
>
> "I am quite prepared to say that I shall be the first person to burn it out. I do not want it. It does not suit anybody."

Explaining his statement on 19 March 1955, Dr Ambedkar said:

> "We built a temple for a god to come in and reside, but before the god could be installed, if the devil had take the possession of it, what else could we do except destroy the temple? We did

> not intend that it should be occupied by *Asuras*. We intended it to be occupied by *Devas*. That is the reason why I said I would rather like to burn it."

The fundamentals of the Constitution were settled by the Objectives Resolution moved by Jawaharlal Nehru and passed by the Constituent Assembly much before the setting up of the Drafting Committee. Speaking on the resolution, Dr Ambedkar had called it "very disappointing and replete with pedantry". Also, most of the essential details of the constitutional edifice were thrashed out at Congress Party meetings and at the most important five Committees of the Constituent Assembly like the Union Powers Committee, Union Constitution Committee, Provincial Constitution Committee, States Committee and the Advisory Committee on Fundamental Rights etc. Of these, Nehru presided over three and Patel over the remaining two. Only the Sixth Committee, viz., the Constitution Drafting Committee had Dr Ambedkar as the Chairman. The Drafting Committee was not a free agent in framing a Constitution for the country. Thus, replying to the critics of the Drafting Committee, a member of the Committee, Syed Md Sa'adulla had this to say:

> "We were only asked to dress the baby and the baby was nothing but the Objectives Resolution which this Constituent Assembly passed. We were told that the Constitution must conform and remain within the four corners of the Objectives Resolution... many of the provisions which jar against the sense of democracy, even of the members of the Drafting Committee, had to be embodied here on account of forces which were superior to that of Drafting Committee."

Sometimes, the Drafting Committee had to reconcile opposing points of view to produce a 'workable proposition which will be accepted by all'. Referring to the adoption of the parliamentary system and the limitations on fundamental rights, Dr Ambedkar once said: "they are the views of the members of the Constituent Assembly. Why blame the Drafting Committee?"

Thus, while Dr Ambedkar played an outstanding role in the framing of the Constitution and was its chief architect, those of us who had the privilege of seeing Babasaheb in flesh and blood and listen to him talk about the Constitution know it well that he was thoroughly dissatisfied with certain features of the Constitution and in private conversation even took pains to disown it quite a bit.

Even in the Constituent Assembly, he said that there were certain things which the Drafting Committee would have liked to do but it was bound by the decisions of the Assembly which in turn was bound by the agreements arrived at by the other Committees.

While moving the Draft Constitution for the consideration of the Constituent Assembly, Dr Ambedkar had said that a student of Constitutional Law, if a copy of the Constitution was placed in his hands, was bound to ask two questions. First, what was the form of Government envisaged in the Constitution and second, what was the form of the Constitution? These were the two crucial matters which every Constitution had to deal with. But, both these matters had been finally settled earlier, elsewhere and by others. And, in both these matters the scheme of the Draft Constitution did not tally with Dr Ambedkar's own views.

Fundamental Rights

Dr Ambedkar did not always have his way in the Constituent Assembly or even in the Drafting Committee. When the Fundamental Rights Sub-Committee of the Advisory Committee met for the first time on 27 February 1947, it had before it drafts of Fundamental Rights prepared by Dr BR Ambedkar, KM Munshi, BN Rau and others. Dr Ambedkar had put down and published his ideas about the essentials to be incorporated in the Constitution of free India in a monograph titled '*State and Minorities—what are their rights and how to secure them in free India*'. Dr Ambedkar's list of Fundamental Rights was 'lengthy' and 'fascinatingly detailed'. It included not only the rights proper but also general provisions in regard to the minorities, particularly the Scheduled

Castes. But, the draft articles on fundamental rights as they came before the Drafting Committee were, in several cases, based on the Drafts of Munshi, Rau and others. Dr Ambedkar was strongly in favour of the 'Due Process' clause being included in the Fundamental Rights. But, later, he was torn between his belief in due process and his official duty to uphold the decisions of the Drafting Committee. During debates in the Constituent Assembly, he remained on the fence and merely explained the pros and cons of due process and then left it 'to the House to decide in any way, it likes'. No wonder, he was to describe the Fundamental Rights as 'the most criticized part of the Constitution'.

Socialistic Programme

Dr Ambedkar believed that Social and Economic justice could not be established without embarking on a full-fledged time-bound 10-year programme of social reconstruction. The programme included nationalization of all land, industry and means of production and distribution and development of agriculture as state industry and insurance as State monopoly with every citizen covered by social security through compulsory insurance.

Dr Ambedkar was more committed a socialist than even Nehru. His proposals were, however turned down on the ground that such matters could better be left to be settled through legislation. Later, Dr Ambedkar would have liked at least the Directive Principles of State Policy to contain a 'more rigorous and justiciable' programme of social reconstruction and a clearer enunciation of the principle that 'one man one vote' was only a mechanism enabling some people to capture power. Parliamentary democracy was meaningless unless it was geared to achieving the real goal of economic democracy. Finally, he supported the Directive Principles in the form in which they were agreed to by the Assembly leadership only because he thought that half a bread was better than no bread. Also, he said 'the party in power would have to answer for them before the electorate at election time'.

Panchayati Raj

Dr Ambedkar did not have much admiration for the Panchayat system and was strongly opposed to giving them any place in the Constitution. In fact, he described village Panchayats as institutions serving on a 'low' and 'selfish level' and the village as a 'sink of localism, a den of ignorance, narrow-mindedness and communalism'. He was happy that the Draft Constitution had discarded the village and adopted the individual as its unit. The views of Dr Ambedkar were much resented and caused sharp protests. A large number of members argued forcibly in favour of Panchayat system and against the position taken by Dr Ambedkar. Finally, as a result of general consensus and against Dr Ambedkar's view, an amendment was adopted which became article 40 of the Constitution under Directive Principles enjoining upon the State the duty to take steps to organize village panchayats. Under such situations in the Constituent Assembly, Dr Ambedkar yielded to the majority and always accepted the position without comment.

Qualifications for Legislators

Dr Ambedkar did not fully subscribe to Nehru's passion for universal adult franchise inasmuch as while he could agree to every adult being a voter, he considered it most desirable that a candidate who wished to serve in the legislature should have some higher qualifications than merely being a voter. The functions that he was expected to discharge in the House required certain amount of knowledge and practical experience in the affairs of the world. Only if these additional qualifications were accepted, the legislature could hope to secure the proper sort of candidates who would be able to serve it better than mere ordinary voters. However, with regard to an amendment suggested by Prof KT Shah about literacy qualifications for being a member of state legislatures, Dr Ambedkar said: "I think that is a matter which might as well be left to the legislatures. If the legislatures at the time of prescribing qualifications feel that literacy qualification is a necessary one, I no doubt think that they will do it".

Comptroller and Auditor General

Dr Ambedkar was an ardent votary of the rule of law and of independent institutions. When draft article 124 (article 148 of the Constitution) in regard to the Comptroller and Auditor General of India (C&AG) came up for consideration in the Constituent Assembly on 30 May 1949, he protested that the C&AG had not been given the power of disciplinary control over his staff who would be appointed by the Executive. He also wanted the C&AG to be at least as independent as the Judiciary. Sentiment in the Constituent Assembly, however was apparently against investing the C&AG with such powers and Dr Ambedkar felt helpless and had to 'remain content with the sentiment as it is today'.

Union-State Relations

In the area of Union-State relations, even though Dr Ambedkar stood for a strong Centre, he was against undue interference by the Union Government in State affairs. Particularly contentious were draft articles 278 and 278A (articles 356 and 357 of the Constitution).

Dr Ambedkar admitted that there was a possibility of the articles being abused or employed for political purposes. In fact, he shared the sentiments that the proper thing would be that the articles in question were never called into operation and remained a dead letter. If at any time, they were brought into operation, he could only hope that the President, who was endowed with these powers, would take proper precautions before actually suspending the administration of the states. The first thing he would do would be to issue a mere warning to the effect that the things were not happening in the way in which they were intended to happen in the Constitution. If that warning failed, the second thing to do would be to order an election allowing the people of the State to settle matters by themselves. Only when these two remedies failed, could he resort to these articles.

Head of the State

Dr Ambedkar favoured an indirectly elected Head of State. In his monograph 'State and Minorities' he had expressed himself as clearly opposed to the traditional form of Cabinet Government. He was instead for an irremovable non-parliamentary executive both for the Union and the units.

Language Issue

Dr Ambedkar believed that primary education if it was to be of any service and if it was to be a reality, would have to be given through the medium of the mother tongue of the child. But, if national language had to have any meaning it must be compulsory for the Union and all the States to use the same national language at the official level. If the units were given the liberty to adopt another language for their official purposes, not only would the object of having a national language for India be defeated but linguistic diversity would make Indian administration impossible.

Constitutional Amendments

Nehru was strongly of the view that Parliament at least for the first few years should be able to amend the Constitution by simple majority since the indirectly elected Constituent Assembly was passing it by simple majority only. Dr Ambedkar, however, repudiated this argument. The Constitution, he said was a fundamental document. Utter chaos would result if it could be amended by simple parliamentary majority. As for those parts needing ratification by the States, he said, "We must still ensure that the basic federal structure remains unaltered". Nehru did not oppose. Perhaps he had changed his mind or found himself in a minority on this point.

Uniform Civil Code

Dr Ambedkar had very clear views in regard to the Uniform Civil Code for all citizens irrespective of religion. Speaking on draft article

35 (article 44 of the Constitution) under the Directive Principles, he pointed out that actually India already had a uniform code of laws covering almost every aspect of human relationship, for example, the Indian Penal Code (IPC), the Criminal Procedure Code (CrPC), the Law of Transfer of Property, Negotiable Instruments Act etc.

Referring to the contention of some members that Muslim Personal Law was immutable and uniform throughout India, Dr Ambedkar said that it was definitely not true inasmuch as up to 1935, NWFP (North West Frontier Province) was not subject to Shariat Law but followed Hindu Law in the matter of Succession etc. In 1939, the Central Legislature had to abrogate the application of Hindu Law to the Muslims of NWFP and to apply the Shariat Law.

Until 1937, in the rest of India, in various parts, such as United Provinces, Central Provinces and Bombay, the Muslims to a large extent were governed by the Hindu Law in the matter of Succession. In 1937, the Central Legislature intervened to uniformly apply the Shariat Law to the Muslims. In North Malabar, the Marumekkathayam Law which was matriarchal applied to all and not only to Hindus. Dr Ambedkar, however assured the Muslim Community that Uniform Civil Code was not to be enforced on any section of unwilling citizens. In the initial stage, the application of the code could be purely voluntary. This method was adopted in the Shariat Act of 1937.

While discussing draft article 13 (article 19 of the Constitution) under the Fundamental Rights also, the question of protecting personal law came up. When an amendment sought to insert a proviso to save personal law, Dr Ambedkar said if such a thing was done, social legislation would become difficult as religious conceptions in India were so vast that they covered every aspect of life. There was nothing which was not religion and if personal law was to be saved, in social matters the country would come to a standstill.

Unity of India

Dr Ambedkar had tremendous faith in the future of India, in the oneness and unity of the nation and in the development of an integrated Indian society freed completely from the scourge of castes and creeds and discrimination of various sorts. He was for dismantling the camps that divided. He looked forward to our becoming a really united people and said:

> "I have got not the slightest doubt in my mind as to the future evolution and the ultimate shape of the social, political and economic structure of this great country. I know, today we are divided politically, socially and economically. We are a group of warring camps and we may go to the extent of confessing that I am probably one of the leaders of such a camp. But, Sir, with all this, I am quite convinced that given time and circumstances nothing in the world will prevent this country from becoming one. With all our castes and creeds, I have not the slightest hesitation that we shall in some form be a united people."

The only difficulty, according to Dr Ambedkar, was "how to make the heterogeneous mass that we have today take a decision in common and march on the way which leads us to unity". He was personally opposed to the idea of grouping dictated by the Cabinet Mission Plan. He said he was for a strong united Centre—much stronger than the Centre envisaged under the Government of India Act, 1935. His constitutional vision was conditioned by the needs of unity and integrity of the nation. Whatever contributed to achieving this ideal was good and anything that came in its way deserved to be discarded. Thus, he was a great advocate of one single unified judiciary—one hierarchy of courts—as against separate State and Federal Court systems. He believed that such an integrated judicial system and a uniform Civil Code were 'essential to maintain the unity of the country'.

Quite different from the image of Dr Ambedkar in the public mind which is that of a sectional leader, what emerges from these observations is very distinctly the picture of a great patriot, a modern, progressive, liberal thinker and an enlightened intellectual with a scientific temper and a forward-looking and secular approach.

Minority Rights and Reservations

The most crucial area in which an understanding of Dr Ambedkar's real constitutional vision has the potential of throwing up new vistas and fresh perspectives, is that of minority rights.

Draft article 292 (article 330 of the Constitution) provided for reservation of seats for the Scheduled Castes and Scheduled Tribes in the Lok Sabha. Speaking on the article, Dr Ambedkar had only a cryptic remark: "This article is an exact reproduction of the decision of the Advisory Committee in this matter and I do not think any explanation is necessary". It would be difficult to gauge Dr Ambedkar's views on the subject of reservations from such observations. Also, there is evidence to show that his views in this regard were not static but kept changing. However, speaking on draft article 295 A (article 334 of the Constitution) which laid down that the reservations would cease after 10 years, he referred to some amendments which had suggested that while the period of reservation might remain 10 years only, Parliament should be given the power to alter it by further extension. Dr Ambedkar was opposed to such methods. He felt that since the matter had been provided for in the Constitution, it should not be possible for anyone to change it without amendment of the Constitution itself. While Dr Ambedkar personally would have favoured reservations for a somewhat longer period than 10 years, he was clearly opposed to reservations in perpetuity: He believed that caste distinctions were a shameful stigma on Indian society and everything needed to be done to ensure that all caste distinctions and discriminations vanished for good as soon as possible and that these did not become permanent.

Presenting the Draft Constitution to the Assembly Dr Ambedkar, *inter alia* referred to the article providing safeguards to Scheduled Castes and Scheduled Tribes and other minorities and made three points, viz one, that he or the Drafting Committee took no responsibility for the articles relating to protection of minority rights etc. Two, while initially the existence of minorities must be recognized and necessary safeguards provided to them by the majority, minorities and majorities must merge in the stream of the united Indian people and not try to perpetuate their separate identities. Three, the majority must give up the tendency to discriminate against minorities or to dominate over them and when that happened the concept of minorities would vanish.

Ambedkar's suggestions for the amelioration of the conditions of the Scheduled Castes included generous provision of funds in the budgets of the Governments of the Union and of the units for higher education, secondary and college education, and for education abroad of members of this community. He also suggested the setting up of an office of the Superintendent of Minority Affairs. Dr Ambedkar expected that if his 10-year plan of social reconstruction was implemented and the majority and the minorities both understood their appropriate roles in building a homogenous Indian nation, it would not be necessary for any, caste or class of people to depend on reservations and the like and his dream of building a casteless and classless egalitarian society and an integrated nation would be fulfilled.

Last Speech in the Constituent Assembly: Ambedkar's Testament

Dr Ambedkar was completely dedicated to his country and countrymen, fully aware of their virtues and weaknesses, proud of all that was great and glorious in their past, conscious of the demands of the present and deeply concerned about the future.

In the initial days of the Assembly, much before he became the Chairman of the Drafting Committee, Dr Ambedkar was full of hope and confidence in the future of the country. He had not the slightest doubt about our growing into a united people. This was on 17 December 1946, just eight days after the first sitting of the Constituent Assembly. But, by the time the Constituent Assembly completed its labours, Dr Ambedkar, had lost much of his zeal, hope and confidence. He was anxious and concerned about our ability to safeguard our independence, to maintain democracy and to ensure social justice. In his last speech in the Constituent Assembly on 25 November 1949—which was perhaps his greatest speech and testament—Dr Ambedkar gave expression to some of his most intimate reflections.

First, he said "however good a Constitution may be, it is sure to turn out bad because those who are called upon to work it, happen to be a bad lot."

Second, he felt disturbed about India's future and asked himself the question: "What would happen to her independence? Will she maintain 'her independence or will she lose it again?" In the past, India had lost her independence because of the treachery of some of her own people. "Will history repeat itself'?" The anxiety was deepened by the realization of the fact that in addition to the old enemies of castes and creeds, the country was going to have many political parties with diverse and opposing political creeds The question was whether Indians would place their creeds above their country. If that happened India's independence would be lost a second time and perhaps for ever.

Third, India had opted for democracy but would she be able to maintain her democratic Constitution, India had known democracy earlier. "There was a time when India was studded with republics, and even where there were monarchies, they were elected or limited." This India lost. "Will she lose it a second time?" There was every danger of democracy giving place to dictatorship or of retaining its form but otherwise becoming an autocracy. If we wanted to preserve democracy, in form and spirit, we had to hold fast to constitutional methods for achieving socio-economic objectives. Also, we had to be careful not to give too much power to anyone so as to enable him to subvert institutions.

Lastly, political democracy—one man, one vote—was not enough. Principles of Liberty, Equality and Fraternity could not be divorced from each other. Even to save political democracy, it was necessary to ensure equality in our social and economic life at the earliest possible. Fraternity meant a sense of common brotherhood of all Indians—of our being one people. It was this principle which gave unity and solidarity to social life. Dr Ambedkar was emphatic that people divided into several thousands of castes could not be a nation. The castes were anti-national as they brought separation in social life and generated jealousy and antipathy between castes. The urge among the down-trodden classes for self-realization must not be allowed to develop into a caste struggle or class war. If it did, it would be a sad day and a day of disaster.

These were Dr Ambedkar's thoughts just a day before the Constituent Assembly adopted the Constitution. And, they have tremendous contemporary relevance today. Dr Ambedkar's constitutional vision, in short, was that of building for India a democratic polity wedded to the principles of social and economic justice, non-discrimination, liberty, equality and fraternity. He would have been against perpetuating a separate Scheduled Caste status for a particular group of Indian citizens for all times. In fact, he once said, he was born a Scheduled Caste Hindu but he was determined not to die as one with the caste stigma.

Since in his life time, Dr Ambedkar found, he could not rid the Hindu society of the scourge of caste distinctions, he became a Buddhist. But, it is a strange irony that—thanks to our wretched ingenuity, political chicanery and wickedness—the pernicious castes have since infiltrated even into Buddhism. Dr Ambedkar would have surely protested. Also, he could not have appreciated the idea of further fragmentation of society on caste lines. Actually, he dreamt of an egalitarian, casteless and classless society, integrated people and a strong, independent, united India. He left it to the succeeding generations to answer the question whether his dream would come true and whether his vision would be realized?

12

National Commission on the Constitution

A National Commission to Review the Working of the Constitution (also referred to as the Constitution Commission or NCRWC) was appointed by the President on 23 February 2000. Completion of 50 years of the working of the Constitution was considered an appropriate occasion to take stock of the situation, of its successes and failures.

The setting up of the high level 11-member Commission was a unique example of sustained civil society pressure (1990-2000), successfully impacting policy makers and leading to concrete action. The Commission itself said that its appointment was preceded by 'a persistent demand in the civil society' that 'the working of the Constitution be subjected to a comprehensive review'. Civil society research institutions and think-tanks like the Citizenship Development Society (CDS), Centre for Policy Research (CPR), India International Centre (IIC) and Rashtriya Jagriti Sansthan (RJS) were particularly involved. The ball was set rolling by two articles by the present writer in *The Times of India* in December 1990 and June 1991 *inter alia* suggesting the appointment of a Constitution Commission. It was followed by his 1992 book *Reforming the Constitution*[1] again pressing the demand for a Commission. A national committee of the IIC chaired by Dr Karan Singh, a seminar jointly organized by 15 all India organizations, an India International Centre project on the Working of the Constitution again headed by the present writer and his edited work *Perspectives on the Constitution*[2] also recommended setting up of a Review Commission. The report of the national committee was presented to the President of India. An important Workshop on Rethinking on the Constitution resulted in a study volume on *Reviewing the Constitution* (2000)[3]. This coincided with the appointment of the Commission.

As its name indicated, the brief of NCRWC was to review the working of the Constitution and not to rewrite or review the provisions of the Constitution. A great deal of misunderstanding was caused simply by the Commission being wrongly called by the media 'Constitution Review Commission'. The Commission's terms of reference excluded any tinkering with the parliamentary system or what it called the basic structure of the Constitution.

To assess whether the objectives of the great founding fathers, as enshrined in the Constitution, had been fulfilled during the half century (1950-2000), the Commission was expected to act independently and objectively, without fear or favour and in the spirit of serving the best interests of the country and thereby helping the Government and Parliament to consider desirable reforms. The composition of the 11-member Commission was heavily weighted in favour of the judiciary with as many as four retired judges and four advocates as members. The sitting and a retired Attorney-General were

---

1 Subhash C Kashyap (ed), *Reforming the Constitution*, UBS, New Delhi 1992; 2nd ed. 2004, Radha, New Delhi

2 Subhash C Kashyap (ed), *Perspectives on the Constitution*, Shipra, 1993

3 Subhash C Kashyap (ed), *Reviewing the Constitution*, Shipra, Delhi, 2000

also members. A journalist, a former Lok Sabha Speaker and sitting MP, two retired IAS officers—one of them also a former ambassador and the other a former MP—and the former Secretary-General Lok Sabha who was also a Supreme Court Advocate and a known constitutional expert completed the picture.[4]

The task of drafting the report was entrusted to the Drafting and Editorial Committee[5] who submitted the full two-volume report on 15 February 2002. The final report of the Commission very largely remained the same as it was in the Draft Report. A number of very significant suggestions were approved unanimously by the Commission and important recommendations made even though a few of them got diluted in the final report.

Report of the Commission

The final Report submitted to the Government on 31 March 2002 contained nearly 250 recommendations[6]—some of them of vital importance for the survival of democratic polity and free institutions and for ushering in an era of good citizen-friendly governance. Some of these may be recalled and commented upon.

Fundamental Rights: Some of the positive and welcome recommendations in regard to Fundamental Rights were for the inclusion of (i) the freedom of the press and other media and of information, (ii) defence of justification by truth in contempt of court cases, (iii) right to rural wage employment for a minimum of 80 days in a year, (iv) right to reasonably speedy and effective justice, (v) right to safe drinking water, prevention of pollution, conservation of ecology

4 For composition of the Commission and its Report, see Subhash C Kashyap, *Constitutional Law of India*, Universal, New Delhi, 2008, Vol 2

5 The Committee consisted of Dr Subhash C Kashyap (Chairman), Shri K Parasaran and Dr Abid Hussain (Members)

6 For recommendations, see *Constitutional Law of India*, op cit

and sustainable development, and (vi) right to free education for all children up to the age 14.

Directive Principles: Under Directive Principles, the Commission recommended (i) a strategic plan of action for creating large employment opportunities, (ii) setting up of a National Education Commission every five years, (iii) population control through education and small family norms, (iv) inter-faith and inter-religious harmony and social solidarity (v) machinery for periodical review of the implementation of directive principles both by the Union and the States.

Stability and Good Governance: The Commission noted that the last few decades had seen a great deal of political instability. During one ten year period, there were seven governments and these were unable to provide stable administration and stable policies. The reasons were not far to seek. We adopted the Westminster FPTP model of elections but forgot that it presupposed for its success a two major party system. In a pluralistic society such as ours, some political parties had a vested interest in progressively appealing to narrower and narrowing loyalties. Clearly, if a candidate could win on less than one-fourth or one-fifth share of the votes polled, he did not need to generate a wider appeal. By making caste and community a factor in political power play, we made the divide even wider and deeper in the Indian society and rendered it nearly impossible for Babasaheb Dr Ambedkar's vision of a casteless and classless society ever coming true.

The Commission felt that the increasing instability of elected governments was attributable to unprincipled, opportunistic political realignments from time to time and defections and re-defections. The administrative and economic costs of political instability and short-lived governments were enormous and unaffordable. The need for political stability became more pronounced because 'in administering any economy in the global context, a reasonable degree of stability of government and strong government is important'.

The Anti-defection Law in the 10th Schedule of the Constitution was supposed to prevent defections but, in effect, it had become an enabling law for larger defections. As the Commission said, "*en bloc* defections are permitted". Defectors are usually lured with ministerships or other political offices and perquisites "so openly that it really makes a mockery of our democracy". The Commission recommended that all defectors—whether individual or groups—must resign and contest fresh election. They should be debarred from holding any public office of a minister or any other remunerative political post without winning at a fresh election. Also, votes cast by them to topple a government should be treated as invalid.

A significant suggestion repeatedly made since 1968, that is, from before the Chavan Committee Report[7] and endorsed by the Commission was in regard to the size of Councils of Ministers. The Commission recommended that the practice of having oversized Councils of Ministers must be prohibited by law. A ceiling on the number of ministers in any state or the Union government be fixed at the maximum of 10 per cent of the total strength of the popular house of the legislature as provided in article 239AA applicable to Delhi. Also, the practice of creating a number of political offices with the position, perks and privileges of a minister should be discouraged and their number should be limited to two per cent of the total strength of the lower house.

The nature of our political system and the resultant politicization of caste and communal identities had proved to be very divisive of society and disruptive of the national ethos. To cobble up a workable majority to form government, compromises had to be made and ideology or notions of quality of governance took a back seat. It became difficult to take strong measures to curb corruption and provide clean and quality governance. In the end, the citizen was the victim of all the misgovernance.

---

7 Subhash C Kashyap, *Politics of Defection*, New Delhi, 1969; *Anti-Defection Law and Parliamentary Privileges*, Universal, New Delhi, 2nd ed. 2003

The Commission found that most of the independent candidates were dummies and only vitiated the sanctity of the electoral process. Only a few—six out of 1,900 in 1998 and nine out of over 10,000 in 1996—got elected. Such independent candidates should be discouraged and only those who have a track record of having won any local election or who are nominated by at least 20 elected members of panchayats, municipalities or other local bodies spread out in majority of electoral districts in their constituency should be allowed to contest for Assembly or Parliament.

Hung houses come because the electoral system is divisive and generates communal and caste-based vote-bank politics. Also, the real cause of instability is concentration of power in the present top-down model of polity. The bottom-up Gandhian model envisaged decentralization of power with village at the centre and power flowing upward from the grassroots to concentric circles of multi-tier governance and direct elections only at the panchayat and nagar palika levels. The Gandhian model came very close to the subsidiarity principle and advocated that what could not be done at the lower tier alone should be assigned to the next higher tier. NCRWC carefully considered the strong presentations and representations made in support of this Gandhian model but the model was not found feasible in the present situation.

Another suggestion that was being pressed for more than a decade and which most directly impacted on the problems of hung legislatures and instability of governments related to the election of the Leader of the House by the Lok Sabha/State Assembly, appointment by the President/ Governor of the person so elected as the Prime Minister/Chief Minister and his removal only by a constructive vote of no-confidence. The Commission after due consideration favoured this suggestion.

The suggestion meant that if no party or pre-election alliance of parties secures a clear majority of seats in Lok Sabha or in any of the State Assemblies and the largest single party is unable to promise a stable government, the President or Governor as the case may be, should ask the House to elect its leader just as it elects its Speaker. The person so elected may be appointed the Prime Minister/Chief Minister. This can be done by the President/Governor sending a message to the House under the existing article 86(2)/175(2).

When the simple question is that of determining the majority, the safest and the simplest course would be to hold an election on the floor of the House. It would also not be necessary then to seek a vote of confidence as, in effect, it would have been obtained in advance of appointment through the process of election by the House itself. This would require neither an amendment of the Constitution nor of any law.

To ensure that Government so constituted would last for a reasonable period and would not always be on its toes fighting a grim battle for its survival all the time and having no time or interest left for the service of the people, certain steps may be suggested. Unless a motion of no-confidence is passed, the government must be deemed invariably to command the confidence of the House irrespective of party splits, mergers, defections etc. The existing rules of procedure may be amended to say that a fresh no-confidence motion cannot be discussed before the expiry of one year or more than, say, twice during the five-year term of the House.

Once the Prime Minister/ Chief Minister is appointed and the Government (Council of Ministers) duly constituted, it should be removable only by a constructive vote of no-confidence passed by a special majority. All that would be essential to do so would be amending Rule 198 of the Rules of Procedure that lays down the form and procedure of a no-confidence motion. Under this scheme, the same motion which expresses lack of confidence in the Council of Ministers headed by 'A', would also contain, the name of the proposed successor, 'B'. This would mean that there would be continuity in Government and if the motion is passed, another leader would immediately take over. This would greatly reduce, if not completely eliminate, chances of getting into a situation where some forces join to bring down a government but are unable to provide an alternative thereby necessitating frequent elections.

We must stop the practice that has developed of members rushing to the President/Governor during intersession periods with letters of withdrawal of support or representations regarding the Government of the day losing majority support as unhealthy, pernicious and against the scheme and spirit of the Constitution. The founding fathers never visualized the Head of State acting as a policing agent counting heads on a day-to-day basis to examine if on any day the government has lost the backing of the majority. It is such an approach that causes horse-trading and instability and the Government all the time remains busy fighting to save itself and survive through whatever means. Development work and interests of the people naturally suffer.

While any effort to provide that the Lok Sabha/State Assembly should not be subject to dissolution before expiry of its fixed term or that the Council of Ministers should have a fixed term, would be deemed most undemocratic, the above recommendation of the Commission for the election of the Prime Minister/Chief Minister by the House and his removal only on a constructive vote of no-confidence has tremendous potential to lend the much needed stability to Government without any formal constitutional amendment.

Whatever the Constitution Commission may have done or not done, it did succeed in removing some of the constitutional illiteracy and creating some Constitution consciousness among the people. The Constitution became topical, something that was newsworthy and was being talked about as being relevant to citizen's concerns.

On the overall assessment of the 50 years working of the Constitution, the Commission said:

> "There are more failures than successes making the inference inescapable that the 50 years of the Working of the Constitution is substantially a saga of missed opportunities."

That there has been a steep fall in the standards of conduct in public life and in administration is widely accepted. There is a crisis of character and values in politics and public administration, is stating the obvious. Growth of a certain cynicism towards normal democratic processes and an erosion in the respect for political parties, politicians, legislators and civil servants, present a disturbing scenario.

The source of many of the maladies is in the disregard of the interests of the citizens and in the absence of good governance. The citizens have to realise their citizenship obligations and come forward to be active participants. Every citizen, in whatever position has certain responsibilities towards fellow citizens. Good governance is citizen-friendly governance.

The only hope for building a united and integrated nation with dignity of the individual lies in the growth of institutions of civil society and the citizens rising above petty self-interests, identifying the hard core of citizenship values enjoined by the Constitution and making a determined bid to work together to protect and promote them by contributing their utmost.

The citizen needs to be restored to a position of pre-eminence at the centre of all State objectives and activities. The State must cease all unnecessary interference or exercise of political and administrative controls over the daily lives of citizens. Ways and means have to be found for reasserting the will of 'We, the People' over the organs of the State—Legislature, Executive and Judiciary—and restoring power to the citizen where it belongs. This would call for respect for citizenship values and emergence and strengthening of a civil society with an aware, awake, responsible and participant citizenry.

It is only when we fulfill the basic duty of politics of restoring the power of the Constitution and its institutions back to their legitimate owners—the people—that things will begin to change. Really, no reforms shall succeed and nothing can change unless the sovereign power is exercised by the people and they use it to discharge their citizenship responsibilities.

Nations are made only when people rise above their narrow self interests and are prepared to make sacrifices for their fellow citizens. Unless the citizens of India at large, are vigilant and conscious of their obligations as citizens, there is no likelihood of any constitutional reform agenda being implemented because there are powerful vested interests which want the *status quo* to continue.

Corruption

Suggesting methods for removal of corruption as part of the political reforms agenda, is not difficult but the problem is to moot suggestions that would not hurt powerful vested interests and which would be acceptable and implementable.

According to the Constitution Commission, "Unless public office is regarded as a trust that a public servant holds for public good, even the most enlightened policies for promoting the welfare of the society will not work. How to restore this ethical and moral dimension to public life in India is one of the most crucial issues of governance at present". There should be a way to block some of the routes that the dishonest find to advantage in the existing laws. The Commission felt that graft and corruption thrived in secrecy. The Freedom of Information Legislation may go some way to ensure that transparency in administration was promoted and greater accountability ensured.

The Commission made suggestions for (i) Public Interest Disclosure or Whistle Blower Acts to protect informers of wrong-doing, (ii) confiscation of *benami* property, illegally acquired assets, and property disproportionate to known sources of income and (iii) making public servants liable to pay damages and compensation for *mala fide* acts.

Action on the Report

After circulating the report for public information and generating a national debate, the Government was expected to place it before Parliament with a report on the action taken or proposed to be taken.

While some action has been taken in an *ad hoc* manner on some of the recommendations most often without a reference to the report of the Commission, an integrated view has yet to be taken. According to a letter written by the Government (Minister of Law & Justice) to political party Presidents, certain recommendations which addressed key issues like funding of elections, Anti-defection Law and the size of Council of Ministers were 'at various stages of consideration' and some Bills had already been introduced in Parliament. But, after all the human and material national resources that went into the Commission Report, the people are still completely in the dark about what has been done or is proposed to be done to consider the recommendations of the Commission.

Thus, for example, claiming and appearing to accept the recommendations of the Commission, the 91st Constitution Amendment diluted their impact potential and left several loopholes and escape routes. The suggested ceiling of 10 per cent of the strength of the popular house on the number of ministers was enhanced to 15 per cent thereby creating a situation whereunder at the Union level and in some of the States instead of reducing the number of Ministers, appointing a few more assumed legitimacy. Also, what was worse and more sinister was that no regulation or control at all was proposed over the practice of creating any number of other posts of Cabinet rank or of Minister of State category. Such posts were created and continued to be created at the sweet will of the powers that be. There was no accountability to anyone and there was no transparency inasmuch as the people never got to know the number of posts created from time to time or those existing at any point of time. According to the Commission (NCRWC), the magnitude of the harm thereby caused to public interest, to the efficiency of administration and to the exchequer was, indeed, incalculable.

The 91st Amendment took away the protection that was provided to group defections on the ground of party splits and one-third of the members of the party defecting. But, the other group defection under the merger clause still continues to be protected under the amended law, that is, if a group of two-third of the members of a legislature party decide to defect to topple a government, to get a share in the Ministry or in return for other material benefits, they can be saved from disqualification by claiming to have decided to merge their party with some other party. Thus, the principle that group defections are as bad as individual defections or that a crime is a crime whether committed by one person or by a group of persons has not been accepted fully. A group can still get away with it only if its size is bigger, viz., two-third instead of one-third of the strength of the party in the House.

If we were convinced that all defections were bad, what was recommended by the Commission (NCRWC) and was needed was an unambiguous provision without any provisos and exceptions. It should have been clearly and categorically laid down that all those who defect from their party shall stand disqualified from membership forthwith and shall remain so until they get reelected.

The decision in matters of disqualification on grounds of defection is still left in the hands of the Presiding Officers even though the experience thus far has been largely disastrous. Certain provisions of the 10th Schedule have been given entirely different interpretations by different Presiding Officers creating terrible uncertainty and fluidity in the application of the law. Despite all this, it seems there is no will to depoliticize the disqualifying process or to give up the power vested in the Presiding Officers.

Lastly, the latest amendment does not say anything about the validity of the vote of defectors. In a scenario where the purpose of defection is to destabilize a government and a group of defectors is used or succeeds in toppling the government and the house has to be dissolved and fresh elections held because an alternative government cannot be formed, the possible punishment or disqualification from membership until fresh election would constitute no deterrent to defectors inasmuch as all the other members also would have to go with them to face fresh elections.

It is necessary that reform measures should not seek *ad hoc* patch-work solutions or to merely create illusions of reform without holistically tackling the basic problem. Half-measures producing a smokescreen of change are worse than no change.[8]

When the Commission was appointed and also when it was at work, doubts were expressed in certain quarters of opposition parties and in the media about some 'hidden agenda' of the Government. But, when the report came, neither the opposition nor the media could find anything to find fault with the recommendations of the Commission. Unfortunately, the interest in the Report faded away thereafter.

It seems necessary that public debate on the Commission's Report is initiated and activated with a view to prevailing upon the Government to consider the recommendations and making their plan of action for implementation of accepted recommendations known to the people.

What is most important is that the recommendations made by the National Commission are analysed and widely debated by the people and a national consensus emerges in favour of implementing the acceptable recommendations.

It may be possible for political parties to project the more important recommendations as election issues during the elections. Also, armed with adequate awareness of the recommendations of the Commission, the civil society and the voters can effectively confront the parties and candidates with questions seeking their reactions and plan of action for implementing the basic recommendations directed to good governance and citizen-friendly administration.

Though some half-hearted efforts have been made to regulate a few of the matters through ordinary legislation, judicial intervention or constitutional amendments, many of the problems remain unresolved and stare us in the face. It is a challenge for our judiciary, Parliament and the academic and professional community of jurists to find a legitimate and pragmatic mechanism for fundamental constitutional changes that may be considered imperative in the light of the experience of working the present system.

---

8 *South Asia Politics*, February 2004, editorial

A number of recommendations made by the Commission have impacted national policies and brought about significant even though piecemeal and somewhat half-hearted reforms. To mention a few: (1) introduction of the minimum rural wage employment guarantee scheme, (2) amending the 10th Schedule (Anti-defection Law) to disqualify group defectors who were thus far protected by the split clause, (3) making education a fundamental right for children between the age of 6 and 14, (4) limiting the size of all Councils of Ministers at the Union and State levels, (5) disqualifying all defectors from holding public office until re-election, (6) amending the Contempt of Courts Act to make truth as an admissible defence in cases of Contempt of Court, (7) passing the Right to Information Act.

Conclusion

In a democracy, the real and the ultimate masters are the people, the citizens. Not enough has been done to educate or orient them to their responsibilities as voters and participants in the democratic process. There is no reason, why citizens' vigilance groups and committees should not come up at every level and on a wide scale. The citizens need to be educated in and for democracy and constitutionalism and in the matter of their own citizenship obligations in a representative, participatory democratic polity. For, ultimately the responsibility to save freedom and democracy is that of 'We, the People of India'.

13

Constitution Commission Controversy

Addresses by the President and Prime Minister

In fulfilment of the commitment made in the NDA Agenda for Good Governance and President Narayanan's opening address to the Houses of Parliament, the Government notified the appointment of an11-member Constitution Review Commission. While issuing the formal notification on 22 February 2000, the name was appropriately modified to read as 'National Commission to Review the Working of the Constitution'.

The Gazette notification clearly mentioned that the Commission would examine, in the light of the experience of 50 years, as to how best the Constitution could respond to the changing needs of efficient, smooth and effective system of governance and socio-economic development of modern India with framework of parliamentary democracy and to recommend changes, if any, that were required in the provisions of the Constitution without interfering with its basic structure or features.

Even before the Commission commenced working, considerable controversy had been generated on the issue. We were confronted with differences in perception between political parties and interests. In fact, it showed up our special penchant for creating a controversy even where none needed to exist. Both politics and media thrived on it. This was most unfortunate because the purpose of the Commission could not be to create controversies. Presumably, it was expected to resolve conflicts and scout for the widest possible nation-wide consensus between all sections of our people and all parties and interests. Once it got going, it should have been possible for the Commission to dispel all doubts and suspicions of any 'hidden agenda' influencing it.

In the very nature of things, the Commission could not but act entirely objectively, remain independent of the government and free from any political party pressures. It should also be crystal clear that the Commission could have no authority to change even a comma in the text of the Constitution or any law of the land. It could only try to identify the crucial problems and present the results of its review and analysis in the light of the 50 years' experience of working the Constitution. The Commission could only make recommendations. The government itself might or might not accept them and even if the government found some of the recommendations acceptable, the proposals as formulated by the government would have to be examined and placed before the Parliament and the people at large for free and full debate and deliberation. Parliament and Parliament alone could bring about any modification in the provisions of the Constitution. Therefore, but for some failure of communication and consultation, there was perhaps not much justification for a Cartesian reaction of *cogito ergo sum* at that stage.

Our founding fathers gave us a Constitution which has stood the test of time. Its basic features, objectives and values were most unexceptionable. The Constitution deserved respect from all of us. It was a symbol of our national unity and integrity. It should be kept above the marsh and mire of party-politics. Also, the highest constitutional office of the President must not be dragged into political controversy. It was not fair to the President to make him look opposed to his own government.

Much was being of the alleged differences between the President and the Prime Minister on the issue of the Review Commission. A great deal had been written and spoken about the so-called clash of opinions between them. It all started with a misreading of the addresses delivered by the President and the Prime Minister in the Central Hall of Parliament House on 27 January 2000 at the function held to celebrate the 50 years of the Republic and the Constitution of India. The two addresses were both prepared separately and in advance of the function. Neither was a response or reaction to the other. Also, when the two texts were examined closely, it became obvious that the controversy was unwarranted. The priorities and concerns of the President and the Prime Minister were not at all at variance. They were both in effect saying the same thing.

The President said that, "We have to consider whether it is the Constitution that has failed us or it is we who have failed the Constitution." The Prime Minister said the same thing in different words when he expressed the apprehension that the institutions were not working as the Constitution intended, that the conduct of those running the institutions was not in keeping with what their proper functioning required.

The President expressed himself against discarding the parliamentary system. The Prime Minister talked only of repairing the parapet and leaving the Parliament and State legislatures in better condition. Later, he categorically stated that there was no question of discarding the parliamentary system.

The President said that we had a right to bring about necessary changes in the political and economic system but the basic philosophy and soul of the Constitution must remain sacrosanct. The Prime Minister also emphasized the need for faster socio-economic development and benefitting the poorest and the weakest. He said the Constitution had provided a robust structure and flexibility. Later, the Prime Minister clearly said that the basic structure and basic features of the Constitution must remain inviolate.

It would thus be obvious that the President and his Prime Minister were essentially expressing very same of similar views on the subject. Under our Constitution, the President was the head of the State, all the executive power vested in him, all executive action was taken in his name and in the discharge of all his functions, he acted on the advice of his Council of Ministers. In other words, Government of India had to be viewed as the 'President acting on the advice of the Council of Ministers' or 'the President-in-the-Council-of-Ministers'. The advice tendered by the Council of Ministers to the President was confidential between the two and it could not be questioned even in a court of law as to what, if any, advice was tendered. The President and the Prime Minister were not and could not be seen to be separate centres of power in our parliamentary polity. The centre of power—the executive—was only one and that was the President as advised by the Council of Ministers. Any effort to project a wedge between the President and his Ministers would be highly improper.

Constitution was being reviewed and made all the time. A review should mean a review of the working of all the institutions and functionaries of the State and through them of the, working of the Constitution. Those who suggested that amendments were acceptable but there was no case for review of the working, forgot that amending the Constitution was a far more serious proposition than reviewing its working and that every amendment involved a review while review did not necessary lead to amendment.

The Commission hopefully was to do precisely what the President and the Prime Minister both had suggested, that is, consider who had failed—the Constitution or those institutions, the Executive, Legislature and the Judiciary, working it. It could suggest for the consideration of the government, the Parliament and the people, legal or other possible reform options, without altering the basic features or the parliamentary system.

Also, it was felt that most of the desirable reforms in areas like the electoral laws, anti-defection laws, misuse of article 356, universalization of elementary education, decentralization of power, etc., could be brought about by ordinary legislative measures, that is, without any basic changes in the text of Constitution. The people wanted faster economic development and clean, efficient and citizen-friendly governance.

We have to stop the fruitless and largely irrelevant debates on various western paradigms: presidential vs parliamentary, accountability versus stability, and the like. We need to look at our own historical and cultural background and our experience of working various institutions. In short, the focus of the review was expected to be on seeing to what extent the objectives of the Constitution had been fulfilled and the dreams of the founding fathers realized in practice. If there were shortfalls and failures, who or what was responsible for them and what should be done to meet the needs, urges and aspirations of the people.

14

Debate on Constitutional Reforms

Presidential System for India

The debate on constitutional reforms is as old as the Constitution. In fact, it started in the Constituent Assembly among the founding fathers themselves and has continued since. In 1956, Nehru himself expressed his doubts whether the parliamentary system could meet the needs of the times and complexities of modern administration. Again, in the 60s the desirability of a switch-over to the Presidential system was actually discussed. Several eminent men including a person like JRD Tata advocated a Presidential system for India. When after the 1967 General Elections, the Congress monopoly of power began to be eroded at the level of States, prominent Congress leaders came forward to prescribe the Presidential model as the remedy for all of India's ills.

The debate in favour of a Presidential system was resumed with the most pronounced vigour during Mrs Gandhi's times, again by Congressmen like Vasant Sathe and others. In fairness, Sathe has to this day stood steadfastly and consistently for a Presidential system or for a strong, directly elected executive head—may be the Prime Minister—with real powers. Also, in the academia, the theme of Constitutional Reforms has been discussed repeatedly almost all over the country during the last several years. Quite a few book length studies have appeared besides the topic having become a hot favourite at seminars and symposia and in the columns of prestigious national dailies.

On completion of 50 years of the working of the Constitution in 2000, the President appointed a National Commission to Review the Working of the Constitution (NCRWC). The Commission submitted its Report in 2002. The debate on Constitutional reforms, however, continues.

Unfortunately, the moment a re-look at the Constitution is suggested, we immediately jump to presume that a change over to the Presidential System is being proposed. It arises from the mistaken belief that we in India ever adopted the Westminster type of parliamentary democracy or that the choice was between the British Parliamentary System and the American Presidential System. Many of the essential pre-requisites of the Westminster system did not exist in India nor do they exist today. If one goes by the text of the Constitution as it came out of the Constituent Assembly, it had at least as many features of the American Presidential System as of the British Parliamentary System. As against Britain and like the United States, India is a republic with a federal structure and an elected head of state. The President is the Supreme Commander of the armed forces, is elected by an electoral college and the executive power vests in him.

The suggestion for a review of the Constitution should not therefore be perceived as being based on some preconceived notions of preference for a Presidential system. In any case, there is nothing like the Presidential system. It has many variants. Besides the US system, there are the Latin American, Sri Lankan, Philippine, Bangladeshi, Pakistani, French and other Presidential models. They are all different, some are hybrid. Those over-simplifying the issue and talking in favour of or against the Presidential model have first to clarify which Presidential model they are talking about. Even while talking of the US model, very often the commentators are under the illusion that the US President is directly elected by the people. In fact, he is also elected by an electoral college only.

As for the merits of the issue, it would be desirable to go back to the perception of the founding fathers. The Constituent Assembly had some strong advocates of the Presidential system as well. Dr. Ambedkar finally explained why they preferred the parliamentary over the Presidential model. Both were democratic. The stress in the parliamentary model was more on accountability. In the Presidential model, stability—both of the executive and of the legislature—was better assured. With their experience of the arbitrary colonial rule of the British, the framers of the Constitution prized accountability more than stability.

Nobody seriously disputes the fact that Indian polity is passing through a very critical phase. All would agree that there is enough in the national scenario that is disturbing and distressing and calls for introspection on where did we go wrong. Is the system to blame or the people who have been operating it have proved to be vile?

The case for a review has become unassailable. Those who are opposed to constitutional review say that there is nothing wrong with the Constitution or the political system, the fault lies with the people. However, they are ignoring the fact that these people are largely the products of the system. Also, the system is for the people, and not the other way round; it has to be adjusted to the needs of the people. We cannot keep waiting for angels to descend, our people cannot be changed or others imported to work this 'excellent' system.

Even after 94 amendments why has our Constitution failed to deliver? Why have there been nearly 120 occasions when the constitutional machinery has been declared to have failed in one State or the other? Why do the basic problems of poverty, illiteracy, overpopulation, shortage of food and drinking water remain? Why have unemployment, criminalization, casteism, communalism and consumerism become more acute problems than ever before? Our Constitution, in the words of Jawaharlal Nehru, 'was purloined' by lawyers. It became their paradise and failed to fulfil the hopes, aspirations and objectives of the founding fathers. In fact, we reduced their dreams to a heap of debris.

Review of the Constitution should mean a holistic, integrated approach to see what, if any, amendments are necessary in the light of 58 years' experience of working the Constitution. Political or constitutional reforms need not necessarily mean changing the polity from parliamentary to presidential Also, not all the needed changes may call for constitutional amendments as such.

The essential prerequisites are that the system should be suited to the needs, background, ethos and experience of the people, even their weaknesses and shortcomings. It should also throw up the right kind of leadership, competent men and women of character and integrity.

Tyranny of models can be terrible. We would have to get over the fruitless and irrelevant debates on various western models - presidential, parliamentary or others. We have to identify our problems, needs and aspirations and then objectively consider what systemic changes, if any, are necessary to resolve our problems, meet our needs and fulfill our aspirations. We have to evolve a constitutional culture and a political superstructure that is in consonance with our historical and cultural past, and in conformity with the needs of the present and the future.

Areas requiring immediate attention seem to be those of Union-State relations, decentralization of powers including financial powers to the states and down to the lower grassroot levels, ensuring greater probity, integrity and transparency in public life and making the administration clean, efficient, less costly and more citizen friendly.

What precise reforms finally emerge should depend upon an institutional, non-partisan expert review and on developing a consensual approach which takes into account all the viewpoints, alternatives and options including the recommendations of the National Commission on the Constitution (2002).

Stability of ministerial chairs (called the stability of government) or of ensuring a fixed five year term for members (in the name of preventing frequent elections and colossal expenditure thereon) cannot be our only concerns.

PART III

Parliament and Law Makers

15

Not Public Servants

For a democratic polity, nothing can be sadder than the representatives of the people losing their credibility and respect. It is even more unfortunate if they refuse to see the writing on the wall. For quite some time now, people have been wary of the public faces of the Members of Parliament and State legislatures claiming to be wedded to service and sacrifice. It is felt that the cost of maintaining the large army of politicians and the position of prestige and honour accorded to them are quite disproportionate to the service, if any, that they render to society.

At the time of seeking election to Lok Sabha and to State Assemblies, every politician goes round with folded hands bowing to the public and begging their support. He talks of the democratic ideals and of the people being the ultimate masters and vows to being the most devoted servant of the public. But, having seen behind their public service masks, people by now know only too well that these worthies—honourable exceptions, if any, apart—are only for themselves and interested only in acquiring power and getting rich quick. In their scheme of things, service to the public has the lowest priority, if any at all.

It can hardly be said that the present day tribe of politicians and their hangers-on are devoid of ingenuity when it comes to defending their interests or misdeeds. Faced with the newer and newer disclosures and exposures of scams and scandals involving corruption and misappropriation of staggering amounts of public money, all sorts of novel arguments, legal quibbling and hair-splitting interpretations of statutes are advanced every day to side-track the substantive issue of guilt of corruption and to stress the escape routes to prove that under the law as it stands, they cannot be proceeded against or prosecuted. They go a step further to say that if the law is not clear on the point or if the courts' interpretation goes against them, the law should be suitably amended; after all, they are themselves the law makers.

One of the developments in our public life is most bizarre; today Members of Parliament and State legislatures themselves are asking for not being regarded as public servants. In fact, every politician of every hue seems to be united in wanting immunity from criminal law under some pretext or the other. Articles 105(2) and 194(2) of the Constitution are cited to assert that no member of a legislature is "liable to any proceedings in any court in respect of anything said or any vote given" in the House or in a Committee thereof. Under this provision, immunity even in matters of bribery, blackmail and the like is sought for Members on the ground that they are protected by parliamentary privileges as if giving and accepting bribes or committing more heinous crimes do not constitute any offence when intended to influence voting in the House or as if bribing etc., can be considered part of the proceedings of the House.

Public memory is proverbially short, but we have not forgotten that the JMM bribery case was first raised in Lok Sabha as one of breach of privilege and contempt of the House inasmuch as the alleged bribe givers and takers were all members of the House and the bribe was alleged to have been given for unduly influencing the business of the House and vote by its members. But, after being discussed for five hours, ironically enough, the question of breach of privilege was not allowed to be raised. So much for the respect of the constitutional provision of article 105.

As for laws, almost the only provisions with regard to corruption among public servants are in the Indian Penal Code (Sections 161-165) and the Prevention of Corruption Act. The Indian Penal Code which is inherited from the hoary past of the colonial regime, while defining public servants does not specify ministers or members among them. The Commission of Public Enquiries Act, 1952 refers to matters of public importance but, again, does not specifically mention ministers or members. So far as the ministers are concerned, it has since been held by the courts that they hold public office. The law by now is pretty well settled that they are covered by terms like 'public service' or public servants. In Tamil Nadu, the Publicmen (Criminal Misconduct) Act, 1973 specifically defines publicmen as including the Chief Minister, Ministers and Members of the State Legislature. Several of the State Lokayukt Acts similarly extend to persons occupying offices in public life.

Whether members of Parliament and of State legislatures are public servants for purposes of the Prevention of Corruption Act has been settled by the highest court. The Supreme Court has held that Members of Parliament are also public servants for purposes of offences under the Prevention of Corruption Act. Earlier, the two High Courts which had occasion to pronounce on the matter differed. While the Bombay High Court ruled that they were not public servants, the Orissa High Court said that they were. It would be seen that the facts and circumstances of the cases before the two courts were very different. In the case before the Bombay High Court, in order to proceed against the alleged culprit, it was perhaps deemed necessary, in the best interests of justice, to hold that he was not a public servant. This case, therefore, could not be legitimately cited as providing an escape to the politicians being proceeded against on charges of corruption. With the Supreme Court decision, politicians were feeling very uncomfortable.

In any case, if the law is not clear and needs to be modified, it may be so modified in the light of the Supreme Court decision, as to make it clear that all members of Parliament and State legislatures shall be deemed to be holding public office and covered under the definition of public servants, that no permission would be needed to proceed against them and that the punishment for offences of corruption in their case would be twice more severe than what can be awarded to other offenders of the same crime. For, responsibility must be deemed to rise with holding of elective offices of high prestige.

Quite interstingly, the Lokpal Bill 1996 used the term 'public functionary' and specifically included present or past Prime Ministers, other ministers and members of Parliament. Also it covered cases of corruption as defined in the Prevention of Corruption Act, 1988. If the intentions of the Lokpal law were honest, whatever its defects otherwise, it should have tried to settle the question of legislators being public servants for purposes of the Prevention of Corruption Act. The 1996 Bill, however, never became law and setting up the institution of Lokpal still remains a pious promise and a dream.

If persons in public life were not to be regarded as servants of the public, one wondered what else were they? Masters? The Father of the nation, much before his assassination but after the nation became free, had recorded in his diary that whether he was alive or not, he could say so on the basis of his life-long experience of serving this nation that instead of remaining servants of the people, if they tended to become their masters, a revolution would sweep the country and the people would catch hold of them one by one and finish them on the streets.

No wonder, our representatives today are so concerned about their personal security that crores of public money are spent every day on protecting them from the very people whom they ostensibly represent.

16

Judicial Custody and Right of an MP to Attend House

The observations of the designated TADA court of Additional Sessions Judge SN Dhingra on 26 February 1996 made an excellent press copy particularly in the context of the then political scenario. Much was made of it by the media and by members in the two Houses of Parliament. Even though HKL Bhagat was prompt to distribute copies of the order in the Central Hall of Parliament House, unless an authentic copy became available, Parliament had only the newspaper reports to go by. Nevertheless, the uproar in both the Houses could hardly be ignored.

Since the objectionable remarks about the Houses of Parliament and their members were ordered by the High Court to be removed from the records of the TADA Court and the dust raised by the controversy could be said to have settled down, it would be appropriate to consider the ramifications of the issues involved.

The Court was pronouncing its orders on Kalpnath Rai's appeal seeking permission to attend Parliament. Rai, a sitting member of Parliament and a former minister, was in judicial custody charged under TADA. A question of lasting relevance that was being asked in the portals of Parliament was whether members of Parliament enjoyed any privilege that allowed them to attend House proceedings even while they were in judicial custody.

Where detention was without trial and under an executive order, there could be some argument whether on the merits of each case, the concerned court could use its discretion and allow a member under detention to attend the House. In fact, there had been some instances of such permissions being given. However, the judge was entirely within his rights and realms of the law of the land and *lex parliamenti* in turning down Rai's request for being allowed to attend Parliament inasmuch as (i) member's privilege of freedom from detention during the session of the House did not apply at all when the member concerned had been charged 'with an indictable offence'. (ii) in a criminal case, even when a member was released on parole, he could not attend the sittings of the House, (iii) in cases of preventive detention also, a member could claim no privilege or special right to be allowed to attend the sittings of the House of which he happened to be a member.

The Privileges Committee of Lok Sabha has held that "no substantial distinction can be drawn on the ground that preventive detention may proceed merely on suspicion". A member of the Madras Legislative Assembly in detention prayed to the High Court for issue of mandamus or other appropriate writ to declare and enforce his right to attend the sittings of the Assembly. The Court categorically held that the member could claim no such privilege and once a member is lawfully arrested and detained, he "cannot be permitted to attend the sittings of the House". The Supreme Court has also held that in such a case "a member of Parliament can claim no special status higher than that of an ordinary citizen."

The TADA court of ASJ Dhingra, however, did not stop at pronouncing the law as it stood and refusing the permission sought by Rai, but it allowed itself to make certain remarks about Houses of Parliament and members in general which were unnecessary and unwarranted in the context of the matter required to be adjudicated.

The TADA Court had exceeded its jurisdiction and the High Court showed great sagacity in defusing the difficult situation by saying that the ASJ had shown lack of 'judicial restraint' and ordering the removal of objectionable remarks from the records.

In matters of Judiciary-Legislature interface, the Constitution clearly lays down the position in articles 121-122. Parliament is not empowered to discuss the conduct of any judge of the Supreme Court or of a High Court. in the discharge of his duties except in the case of a motion for presenting an address to the President for the removal of a judge. There is a corresponding restraint on the courts inasmuch as the validity of any proceedings in either House of Parliament cannot be questioned before a Court of law on the ground of any alleged irregularity of procedure. The courts have no jurisdiction to issue a writ, direction or order which affects the internal affairs of the House.

The precedent which came nearest to the controversy created by the observations of the TADA Court arose in 1981 when the then Chief Justice of India, Justice Chandrachud and another judge, Justice Tulzapurkar, during proceedings on a case in the Supreme Court allegedly said that members of Parliament must speak with a 'sense of responsibility' and 'just because they are in Parliament' they cannot 'say anything they like because they are immune'. When the matter was raised as a breach of parliamentary privilege on the floor of the Lok Sabha, the Speaker called for the records and found that a member had made uncalled-for remarks on the performance of the Supreme Court. He reminded the members of the constitutional position under which conduct of a judge could not be discussed on the floor of the House. He added that specific roles had been assigned to the courts and legislatures and the two were expected 'to have mutual respect for each other'.

Two wrongs do not make one right. It was patently wrong for the ASJ to throw judicial restraint to the winds and to say the type of things that men on the streets and academics unencumbered by any constraints of office have been saying about the politicians. But, the

Houses of Parliament also did not consult their dignity when they stooped to making a big issue of the remarks of the ASJ's court. For the badly beleagured Rao government, perhaps, it came as God-sent to divert attention from scandals like those of *Hawala* and alleged purchase of support of some MPs to a issue on which all sections of the House could feel equally pricked.

We cannot forget that if politicians in general lose their credibility with the people at large, if there is a steep erosion in the respect for the executive and the legislature as institutions of good and neat governance and they seem to have become dysfunctional and, if the people are constrained to turn more and more only to the judiciary for everything from garbage removal to protection of human rights, one cannot blame the Courts much for giving vent to popular perceptions. After all, judges cannot be expected to remain entirely cloistered from the social realities and political temperature around them.

The case had all the potential of developing into a full-fledged question of breach of privilege and contempt of the Houses of Parliament. However, an ugly situation of conflict and confrontation was avoided by the Presiding Officers exercising caution and restraint. The High Court also soon enough came forward to provide the necessary corrective and save a situation in which after being battered by the judiciary for some time, the politicians could find some justification to take up cudgels against it.

17

Fixed Term Legislators

Simultaneous Polls to Lok Sabha and State Assemblies

I

The Agenda for Governance issued by the BJP-led National Democratic Alliance (NDA) as part of its manifesto for the 1999 general elections to the Lok Sabha had *inter alia* spoken of its resolve to appoint a commission to review the Constitution. In the same breath it spoke of 'measures for ensuring a fixed term (five years) for all elected bodies including legislatures'.

The Law Commission in its comprehensive report on the 'Reform of the Electoral Laws' in the words of its Chairman, Justice Jeevan Reddy "stressed the necessity of having one election once in five years for Lok Sabha as well as State Assemblies". This was widely interpreted by the media to mean advocacy of a fixed five year term for Lok Sabha and State Assemblies. The Chairman was later at pains to emphasize that the Commission made no such recommendation. Simultaneous election both for Lok Sabha and all the State Assemblies only once in five years was a goal suggested for gradual achievement over the years. The Commission had said, "Maybe a constitutional amendment can solve the problem". While it was unfortunate that the Law Commission thought it fit to release its report during the process of elections, it must be said in fairness to the Commission that it had also categorically stated that the question of assuring 'a fixed, unalterable, term to Lok Sabha and the Legislative Assemblies' was 'a major issue' which could be 'considered if and when a review of the Constitution' was undertaken.

However, in his opening Address to the two Houses of Parliament on 25 October 1999, the President reiterated the intentions of the Vajpayee Government to bring forward necessary measures for providing a fixed five-year term for Lok Sabha and State Assemblies. The matter was too serious and had too many constitutional and systemic ramifications to be decided in a casual manner and in isolation with other allied issues. Perhaps, the purpose could have been achieved easily without raising any controversy on this issue.

Quite naturally, in the context of several successive 'hung' legislatures and frequent elections, members irrespective of party affiliations were unanimous in demanding for themselves a fixed five-year term. Whatever happened to the nation, governments might come and go but members must be assured full security of a five-year term. Once the fear of dissolution of the House was removed, their bargaining power and potential to topple governments would improve and they could demand their pound of flesh with impunity. Once again, some unscrupulous small parties could get into the business of playing their games of brinkmanship, bluff and blackmail.

While the nation could hardly afford too frequent general elections and no body really wanted them as annual features that they had tended to become, the problem must be looked at from the citizens' perspective and not as one of providing a safe haven and a guaranteed five-year security to every Lok Sabha member, MLA and so on.

Unless sooner dissolved, the Lok Sabha and State Assemblies under article 83(2) and 172(1) already had a fixed five year term. Under the existing scheme of things, the power of the House to pass a vote of no-confidence in the Council of Ministers was counterbalanced by the power of the Government to seek dissolution of the House. What was, therefore proposed to be taken away was the provision of possible earlier dissolution.

A member is elected as a representative of the people. He must represent their aspirations all the time and must remain continuously responsive, and accountable to them. Also, in the scheme of our polity, the cardinal function of elected members of Lok Sabha and State Assemblies is to provide a responsible government. If a House fails to do so, it loses all legitimacy and relevance.

In some countries, members must regularly report to the electorate about their personal performance and the work of the elected body of which they are members. Some constitutions or representation laws provide procedures under which a member may be recalled by his electors if he betrays their trust and loses their respect. Loknayak Jayaprakash Narayan had strongly pleaded for a similar provision of recall for our legislators.

Ancient Indian polity (for example see *Mahabharata*, *Anushashan Parva* and the *Manusmriti*) recognized the concept of sovereignty in perpetuity vesting in the people. If the ruler indulged in injustice, lied, made false promises or otherwise defaulted in the discharge of his duties, he could be removed by the people. In certain cases, it was considered a right and a duty of the people to kill such a person 'as a mad dog'.

Ordinary citizens today were not guaranteed any security of life. Vast majorities suffered from lack of food and drinking water. Unemployment, illiteracy and malnutrition were rampant. But, crores of rupees were being spent on the personal security and foreign medical treatment of persons many of whom should actually have been behind the bars for their criminal deeds. Most unfortunately, there had been a tremendous erosion in people's esteem and respect for their `representatives'. With majority of them being elected by minority of votes and with more votes cast against them than for them, even their representative credentials under the present system had come to be of doubtful validity. In this climate, to come up with proposals to provide them secured tenures irrespective of the conduct they indulged in and of what they did or did not hardly spoke of much political wisdom. It was not even in the interests of the MPs and MLAs whom it might have been intended to placate. To say the least, it was an ill conceived, badly formulated and sadly timed move. It seems the NDA advisers and the Law Commission believed that the nation belonged to the politicians and not to the people and that if MPs and MLAs were provided with high perks, security and stability of tenure, lucrative pensions for life and kept happy, the rest could take care of itself.

Practically no educational, public service or character qualifications are prescribed for contesting elections. It was well-known that persons with criminal records—with charges of smuggling, rape, murder, dacoity, etc.,—could also contest elections, get elected and even occupy high offices of ministers etc. Once elected, a member got payments and perks which were fabulous by any standards. In fact, if the costs of all the perks in cash and kind were counted, it would be more economical for the public exchequer to pay rupees two or three lakh per month as salary to each member. Also, rupees two crore now placed at the disposal of each member every year for the so-called 'Area Development Scheme' was another scandal about which the less said the better.

A fixed five-year term for members would not only provide guaranteed security and stability with all the benefits for five years but also assure a pension and certain perks like free railway pass for life. Could any one devise a more alluring bait, a greater security bonanza and a better insurance policy?

The prime need and a matter of highest priority for the Vajpayee Government should have been to provide a feeling of security to every ordinary citizen, some reasonable stability to society and the system and some assurance of good governance and a quality of life to average man and woman. To do this, we needed a holistic review of the party system, the electoral process, the judicial system and the public administration. Also, the provision of a fixed term for legislators would have necessarily required a major constitutional amendment and it would have been imperative to examine whether it did not militate against democratic principles and basic features of the Constitution or structure of our polity.

The issue deserved to be examined and debated with an open mind along with all the other suggestions and options *inter alia* for ensuring greater political stability without sacrificing the higher democratic value of accountability.

II

The debate on having a fixed term for legislators and/or synchronizing Lok Sabha and State Assembly elections only once in five years, was resumed in the year 2003.

Believed to have started with a suggestion made by Vice President Shekhawat, it gained momentum and a controversy started immediately after the Deputy Prime Minister Advani said that such a proposal was under consideration. It was later clarified that a decision would be taken only after wide consultations. The intention obviously was to first have a national debate and hopefully evolve some consensus.

Actually, much before the current debate, the National Commission to Review the Working of the Constitution (NCRWC) Report submitted early in 2002 *inter alia* recommended, "With a view to reduce costs and strain on human and other resources, state and Parliamentary level elections, to the extent possible, should be held at the same time." The spirit of the recommendation was that it would be ideal if elections could be held simultaneously but that the progress towards the goal had to be slow. The crucial words were "to the extent possible" which could mean 'wherever or whenever possible'.

The questions that arose and needed to be examined were (i) whether the Constitution and the election law permitted simultaneous elections to Lok Sabha and State Assemblies, (ii) what were the precise contents of the proposal, (iii) did it seek to revive through the back door the earlier wish of having fixed terms for members and houses of legislatures and outlawing dissolution of any House before completing its full term, (iv) what were the likely benefits and dangers of the proposed simultaneous polls?

Among the arguments that were being advanced against the proposal of simultaneous elections, the strangest was the one that it would be violative of the basic features of the Constitution and hence unconstitutional. It was being forgotten that violation of the Constitution was not permissible even before the basic features doctrine. And, who under the sun knew what precisely were all the basic features of the Constitution and what parts of the Constitution did not constitute basic law of the land? In any case, where did any judge ever declare that holding separate polls for Lok Sabha and State Assemblies was part of the basic features of the Constitution? In fact, it was not even mentioned anywhere in the Constitution. The founding fathers of our Constitution visualized simultaneous elections. Before 1971, as many as four general elections for the Lok Sabha and State Assemblies were conducted together and accepted as perfectly constitutional. It was so in 1951-52, 1957 and 1962. In the fourth general election in 1967 also 16 State Assemblies went to polls along with the Lok Sabha. In the scheme of the Constitution and the laws of the land, nothing had changed since. The problems were elsewhere. These started with premature dissolution of some State Assemblies and later of Lok Sabha itself thereby necessitating different time schedules for Lok Sabha and State Assembly elections.

Under the Representation of the People Act, elections to a House could be held anytime within six months preceding the date of the scheduled dissolution on completion of the five year term. It might be stated quite categorically that if premature dissolution of the Houses of Legislatures was prevented, elections to Lok Sabha and State Assemblies could again be synchronized within a span of few years. These would be constitutional and valid. The job of the CEC was to conduct elections, to superintend, direct and control elections and ensure that these were free and fair and held efficiently and honestly.

It was not his function to pronounce on the constitutionality or legality of simultaneous elections or to outright dismiss by a diktat any possibility thereof. It was of the utmost importance that holders of high constitutional offices did not rush to make unwarranted statements, exercise self-restraint and resist the temptation to hog media headlines.

Considered most positively, simultaneous elections would drastically reduce the total cost of elections for the Government, the political parties and the candidates, save valuable human and other resources, promote national perspective as against local or regional perspectives, strengthen national parties, prevent disintegration of parties and mushroom growth of splinter groups based on narrow vote bank politics, ensure relatively greater stability of governments making it possible for them to concentrate on taking harsh decisions in the interest of development and good governance. As against this, some of the regional and small parties smelt a rat in the proposal because it was likely to hurt their minority and caste vote banks.

It was not clear from the proposal mentioned by the Deputy Prime Minister whether simultaneous elections were to be viewed as a long term objective and we had to consciously try to gradually reach the goal. If so, this was unassailable and unexceptionable. Also it was fully in keeping with the well-considered recommendations of the Constitution Commission. If however, the purpose was to guarantee a five year term to all Members of Parliament and Legislative Assemblies more or less in the same manner as a six-year term was assured to Rajya Sabha members or if the proposal contained any element of compulsion or of amending the Constitution to hold all elections together in one go, it would certainly be undemocratic, impermissible and not possible either constitutionally or politically.

The life of any Legislative House could not be arbitrarily cut short so long as it provided a government that was responsible to it and commanded its confidence. Also, it would be most undemocratic if attempt was made to provide by law a guaranteed five-year tenure to all legislators.

Dissolution becomes inevitable usually only in circumstances when one government loses the confidence of the House and another cannot be formed by any party or combination of parties. To meet this situation, prevent the high costs of frequent and separate elections to different Houses and provide greater stability to governments, the Constitution Commission made two other important and inter-related suggestions viz (i) that of the election of the Prime Minister or Chief Minister by the House in case no single party or coalition of parties enjoyed clear majority support in Lok Sabha/Vidhan Sabha and (ii) that of the Council of Ministers once appointed being removable only by a constructive vote of no-confidence. Thus, a legitimate government commanding the confidence of the House would always be in position and it would not be necessary to dissolve the House and hold fresh election before completion of its five-year term. Acceptance of these NCRWC recommendations would not involve any constitutional amendment or legislative action. And, taken together, these would lead to the fulfilment of the objective of simultaneous elections within a few years.

18

Parliamentary Privileges

The Law and the Farce

By articles 105 and 194 of the Constitution, 'we the people of India' entrusted to our representative institutions—the Houses of Parliament and State legislatures, their committees and members—certain power, privileges and immunities in order to enable them to function freely and to serve and represent us fearlessly.

'Privilege' means a special or exceptional right or freedom or an immunity enjoyed by a particular class of persons or some individuals. It is 'special' in the sense that it is a right or freedom which is not available to the rest of the people. In its legal sense it means an exemption from some duty, burden, attendance or liability to which others are subject. Privilege can also be defined as a right which others do not have. Parliamentary privileges are not the privileges of Parliament as such inasmuch as the Parliament consists of the President and the two Houses while Parliamentary privileges belong only to Houses of Parliament, their members and Committees.

The privileges, in practice, give rise to certain powers, immunities and exemptions. It does not, however, imply that the privileges belonging to members place them on a footing different from that of an ordinary citizen in the eyes of law, unless there are good reasons in the interest of the Parliament itself to do so.

According to the Preamble, the most fundamental objective of the Constitution was that of promoting the dignity of the individual. But, the Constitution was soon hijacked by various vested interests. Our elected representatives, instead of being the protectors and promoters of our interests and dignity, became power-merchants and enemies of public weal. They placed self before service and got involved in furthering their own self-interests at the cost of the people.

Parliamentary Privilege Law becomes a farce if legislators begin to consider themselves to be very much apart, distant and above the people—a new high caste, a new elite, a landed aristocracy or what Dr Lohia used to call a new *biradari* and if parliamentary privileges come to be viewed as their birthright and inherited property. They must not forget that the privileges were entrusted to them only for representing the people and to protect their interests.

Sometimes, in the new political culture, the parliamentary privileges become a multi-headed monster, a giant of unfathomable dimensions. The law of parliamentary privileges becomes a weapon in the hands of the ruling parties, misused by them in many ways for personal, party and partisan ends through their majorities in the Houses and Committees. Our legislators seem to presume that their privileges stand higher than the interests of the people at large and the fundamental freedoms of the individual and of the media.

Institutional definitions and jurisdictional delimitations of various organs of the State are getting blurred. More than once a stage of confrontation between the Legislature, the Judiciary and the Press has been reached and every time we seemed to have got to the brink of the precipice.

All persons including members, ministers and Presiding Officers are equal in the eyes of law. Parliamentary privileges are intended only for protection of the functional freedom of the Houses, their members and Committees so that they can discharge their parliamentary duties as representative of the people without let or hindrance, in a free and forthright manner. Inasmuch as the privileges are extended to them only as representatives of the people and in the interests of their functioning as such, it may be said that actually the privileges are in the interests of the people and defensible only so long as they remain so.

Parliamentary privileges do not place members on a footing different from that of an ordinary citizen in the eyes of law. Members, apart from being representatives of the people, are ordinary citizens except when they perform their duties in Parliament or a State legislature. The privileges are available to the members only when and to the extent that they are functioning as representatives of the people and discharging their parliamentary responsibilities. The privileges do not, in any way, exempt the members from their normal obligation to society which apply to them as such and perhaps more closely in that capacity, as they apply to others.

Thus, the privilege against assault or molestation is available to a member only when he is obstructed or in any way molested while discharging his duties as a member, In cases, when members were assaulted while not performing any parliamentary duty, it was held that no breach of privilege or contempt of the House was committed. Similarly, parliamentary privilege is not attracted if a libel or a reflection upon a member does not concern his character or conduct in his capacity as a member of the House and is not based on matters arising in the actual transaction of the business of the House. Further, a member does not enjoy any special privilege in regard to the censoring of mail and tapping of telephone authorised by law and equally applicable to all citizens.

In India, we do not have to trace our parliamentary privileges to old history in another country. We do not have to suffer from the hang-over of the British background. Here, the parliamentary privileges were neither granted to the House nor wrested from any King as in England. These privileges do not belong to any feudal body like the one time House of Commons; they belong to representatives of the people elected to the Houses of Legislatures. These are not and should not be seen as something antagonistic to the rights and interests of the people, because the privileges fundamentally belong to and emanate from the people, through the Constitution which has been adopted, enacted and given to the nation by the people themselves. The people of, India, in this way, have conferred these rights on members to be exercised by them collectively and individually in their capacity as representatives of the people in the wider interests of the people. It was the deliberate act of our Constitution-makers to invest our members with these privileges, powers and immunities. If these privileges are understood as the privileges of the people and for the people, much of the confusion and the resistance against them would disappear. The trouble arises only when these are viewed as privileges of members or Houses available against the people and the press.

Courts of law in India have recognized that a House of Parliament (or of a State legislature) is the sole authority to judge as to whether or not there has been a breach of privilege or contempt of the House in a particular case. According to judicial pronouncements on the subject, the courts may look into the existence and extent of privilege even though the exercise thereof is entirely and solely the domain of the concerned House of the Legislature.

It is of the utmost importance that the penal powers of the House are used only in extreme cases. The committee of privileges have held that in the ardour of political contest and in the heat of the moment sometimes strong words may be used but the law of parliamentary privilege should not be administered in a way which would fetter or discourage the free expression of opinion or criticism, however, prejudiced or exaggerated such opinions or criticisms may be.

A reference is sometimes made to the so-called 'judgment of the Supreme Court' as reported in AIR 1965 SC 745. It may be mentioned that this was not a judgement, but an opinion of the Supreme Court on a special reference made by the President of India under article 143 of the Constitution on 26 March 1964. This related to the committal to prison of Keshav Singh by the UP Vidhan Sabha for committing a breach of privilege and contempt of the House and his writ petition to the Allahabad High Court for setting him free, which led to a chain of events giving rise to important and complicated questions of law regarding the powers and jurisdiction of High Court and its judges in relation to the powers and privileges of the state legislature and its members.

In 1959, the Supreme Court held in the *Searchlight* case that the provisions of clause(2) of article 194 indicate that the freedom of speech referred to in clause(I), is different from the freedom of speech and expression guaranteed under article 19(1)(a)and cannot be cut down in any way by law contemplated by clause(2) of article 19.

The provisions of articles 105(2) and 194(2) are constitutional laws and not ordinary laws made by Parliament or the State legislatures and that, therefore, they are as supreme as the provisions of Part III (articles relating to Fundamental Rights).

The principle of harmonious construction must be adopted and so construed, that the provisions of article 19(1)(a), which are general, must yield to article 194(1) and the latter part of its clause (3) which are special.

In 1965, the Supreme Court in its advisory opinion in the above mentioned Special Reference Case of 1964 (Keshav Singh Case), observed as follows:

It would not be correct to read the majority decision in the *Searchlight* case as laying down a general proposition that whenever there is a conflict between the provisions of the latter part of article 194(3) and any of the provisions of the fundamental rights guaranteed by Part III, the latter must yield to the former. The majority decision, therefore, must be taken to have settled that article 19(1)(a) would not apply, and article 21 would.

In dealing with the effect of the provisions contained in clause (3) of article 194, whenever it appears that there is a conflict between the said provisions and the provisions pertaining to fundamental rights, an attempt will have to be made to resolve the said conflict by the adoption of the rule of harmonious construction.

It may be stated that the judgement of the Supreme Court in the *Searchlight* case is the definitive one and the guiding principles as set out by the Supreme Court in that case are held to apply in such matters.

The opinion of the Supreme Court was discussed by the Conference of Presiding Officers of Legislative Bodies in India held at Bombay on 11 and 12 January 1965. The Conference unanimously adopted a resolution expressing its view that suitable amendments to articles 105 and 194 should be made in order to make the intention of Constitution makers clear beyond doubt so that the powers, privileges and immunities of Legislatures, their members and Committees could not, in any case, be construed as being subject or subordinate to any other articles of the Constitution.

The Allahabad High Court, in their judgement in *Keshav Singh* case dated 10 March 1965 (that is delivered after the advisory opinion of the Supreme Court), observed as follows:

- In our opinion, both upon authority and upon a consideration of the relevant provisions of the Constitution, it must be held that the Legislative Assembly has, by virtue of article 194(3), the same power to commit for its contempt as the House of Commons.
- In our opinion, the provisions of article 22(2) of the Constitution cannot apply to detention in pursuance of a conviction and imposition of a sentence of imprisonment by competent authority.
- Since we have already held that the Legislative Assembly has the power to commit the petitioner for its contempt and since the Legislative Assembly has framed rules for the procedure and conduct of its business under article 208(1), the commitment and deprivation of the personal liberty of the petitioner cannot

but be held to be according to the procedure laid down by law within the meaning of article 21 of the Constitution.

- Once we come to the conclusion that the Legislative Assembly has the power and jurisdiction to commit for its contempt and to impose the sentence passed on the petitioner, we cannot go into the question of the correctness, propriety or legality of the commitment. This Court cannot, in a petition under article 226 of the Constitution, sit in appeal over the decision of the Legislative Assembly committing the petitioner for its contempt. The Legislative Assembly is the master of its own procedure and is the sole judge of the question whether its contempt has been committed or not.

The Government, therefore, decided that an amendment of the Constitution was not necessary. It was of the opinion that the Legislatures and the Judiciary would develop their own conventions in the light of the opinion given by the Supreme Court and the judgement pronounced by the Allahabad High Court.

It may, therefore, be seen that the judgement of the Supreme Court in the *Searchlight* case is final till today insofar as matters of privilege are concerned.

The Press is often called an extension of Parliament. It conveys to the people the substance of parliamentary legislation and discussion and keeps the people informed of what is happening in Parliament. The duty of the Press is to report faithfully and not to distort the events in Parliament.

19

Freedom of the Press and Parliamentary Privileges

When Jawaharlal Nehru visited New York for the first time as the Prime Minister of India, a Press Correspondent asked him at the Airport, "Mr Prime Minister, do you have in India the same kind of freedom of the Press as we have here in the United States." Nehru is reported to have promptly replied, "Oh, we have much worse". The moral of the story is that India right from the early years of her Independence has valued the fullest freedom of the press even at the risk of its being sometimes misused. For, ultimately freedom of the press is only an aspect of the freedom of expression of the people. In a democracy, the people are supreme repositories of the sovereign will and power of the State. They would like that their freedom to express themselves through the medium of the press is protected at all costs.

We are a free country. We are proud of the freedoms we enjoy. Freedom of speech and of expression are the foremost among these and include the freedom of the Press. In a democratic country, freedom of the Press can be interfered with only at the most colossal cost to the polity. Yet, we find threats and warnings to the Press and the public being issued from the temples of democracy under what are called parliamentary privileges without anybody being told what precisely these privileges are. The Press and the people would like to know and be convinced about them as well.

The Press is often called an extension of Parliament. It conveys to the people the substance of Parliamentary legislation and discussion and keeps the people informed of what is happening in Parliament. The duty of the Press is to report faithfully and not to distort events in Parliament.

Although freedom of the press is not expressly guaranteed by the Constitution as a fundamental right, it has been held by the Supreme Court is several judgements that it is implicit in the freedom of speech and expression guaranteed under article 19 (1)(a).

Freedom of press had always been a cherished right in all democratic countries. Therefore, it has rightly been described as the Fourth Estate. The democratic credentials of a State are judged today by the extent of Freedom the press enjoys in the State.[1]

The purpose of the press is to advance the public interest by publishing facts and opinions without which democratic electorate cannot make responsible judgements. Freedom of the press is the heart of social and political intercourse. It is the primary duty of the courts to uphold the freedom of the press and invalidate all laws or administrative actions which interfere with it contrary to the constitutional mandate. The constitutional guarantee of the freedom of speech and expression is not so much for the benefit of the press as it is for the benefit of the public. The people have a right to be informed of the developments that take place in a democratic process and the press plays a vital role in disseminating this information.[2]

---

1 *Secretary, Ministry of Information & Broadcasting, Govt of India v Cricket Association of Bengal*, AIR 1995 SC 1236; *Printers (Mysore) Ltd v Asstt CTO, (1994) 2 SCC 434.*

2 *Rajendra Sail v Madhya Pradesh High Court Bar Association,* AIR 1993 SC 171

This freedom must, however, be exercised with circumspection and care must be taken not to trench on the rights of other citizens or to jeopardise public interest. It is manifest from article 19(2) that the right conferred by article 19(1)(a) is subject to imposition of reasonable restrictions in the interest of, amongst others, public order, decency or morality or in relation to defamations or incitement to an offence. It is, therefore, obvious that subject to reasonable restrictions placed under article 19(2) a citizen has a right to publish, circulate and disseminate his views and any attempt to thwart or deny the same would offend article 19(1)(a).

Another extension of the power of the people and their freedom of expression is manifested in what have come to be called parliamentary privileges. Modern democracies are usually representative. Ours is a representative parliamentary democracy where the people govern themselves through their elected representatives in Parliament (and State legislatures).[3]

Parliamentary Privileges do not exempt members from the obligations to the society which apply to other citizens. Privileges of Parliament do not place a member of Parliament on a footing different from that of an ordinary citizen in the matter of the applications of the laws of the land unless there are good and sufficient reasons in the interest of Parliament itself to do so. The fundamental principle is that all citizens including members of Parliament should be treated equally before the law. The privileges are available to members only when they are functioning in their capacity as members of Parliament and performing their parliamentary duties.

Article 105 of the Constitution defines the powers, privileges and immunities of the House of Parliament and of the members and committees of the two Houses. The more important of the privileges, namely, freedom of speech in Parliament and immunity for members

---

3 *Life Insurance Corporation of India v Prof Manubhai D Shah*, AIR 1993 SC 171

form any proceedings in any court of law in respect of anytime said or any vote given by them in Parliament, are specified in this article. In other respects, powers and privileges of each House, its Committees and its members are, in effect, identical to the power and privileges enjoyed by the British Hose of Commons as on 26 January 1950.

Absolute immunity from proceedings in any court of law has been conferred under the Constitution on all persons connected with the publication of proceedings of either Houses of Parliament, if such publication is made by of under the authority of the House [article 105(2)].) This immunity does not, however, extend to the publication of reports of parliamentary proceedings in newspapers, whether published by a member of the House or by any other person, unless such publication is expressly authorised by either House (article 361 A of the Constitution).

A question that is very often raised is whether the privileges of the legislature extend to taking action against a writer, speaker or a cartoonist who makes valid criticism of the shortcomings of the legislatures. No doubt, Parliament or any legislature for that matter is entitled to take action for any malicious writing, speech, etc., casting aspersions on its functioning or on the functioning of its Committees. No action is, however, taken if the criticism is fair and *bona fide*.

The Select Committee on parliamentary Privilege of the House of Commons (UK), 1967, made the following recommendation:

> The House should exercise its penal jurisdiction (a) in any event as sparingly as possible, and (b) only when it is satisfied that to do so is essential in order to provide reasonable protection for the House, its Members or its Officers from such improper obstruction or attempt at or threat of obstruction as is causing, or is likely to cause, substantial interference with the performance of their respective functions.

Subsequently, the Committee of Privileges of the House of Commons in their Third Report (1976-77) reiterated this recommendation and the House of Commons, UK, adopted it on 6 February 1978. The Committee of Privileges of the Second Lok Sabha, in their 13th Report had observed, *inter alia*, as follows:

> Nobody would deny the Press, or as a matter of fact, any citizen, the right of fair comment. But if the comments contain personal attacks on individual members of Parliament on account of their conduct in Parliament or if the language of the comments is vulgar or abusive, they cannot be deemed to come within the bounds of fair comment or justifiable criticism. Even the Press Commission (1954) held the view that 'comment couched in vulgar or abusive language is unfair'. Nor can 'fair comment' be stretched to include irresponsible sensationalism.

The Committee of Privileges of the Sixth Lok Sabha in their Fourth Report had observed:

> The Committee are conscious that the freedom of the press is an integral part of the fundamaental right of freedom of speech and expression guaranteed to all citizens under article 19(1) (a) of the Constitution. The Committee consider it important that in a Parliamentary system, the Press should enjoy complete freedom to report the proceedings of Parliament fairly and faithfully. If, however freedom of the Press is exercised *mala fide*, it is the duty of Parliament to intervene in such cases. At the same time, the Committee are of the view that parliamentary privilege should in no way fetter or discourage the free expression of opinion or fair comment.

The Committee of Privileges of the Seventh Lok Sabha in their First Report observed, *inter alia* as follows:

> The Committee feel that it adds to the dignity of one and all if power in a democratic system is exercised with restraint; the more powerful a body or institution is, the greater restraint is called for particularly in exercising its penal jurisdiction.

For those who revere the freedom of the Press and the prestige of parliamentary institutions with equal earnestness, it is distressing to read of the governmental assaults on the liberty of press persons and threats of confrontation between the judiciary and the legislatures and between the rights of the people and the real or not so real—existent or non-existent—privileges of legislators.

In 1956, Parliament enacted a law for the protection of *bona fide* publication of parliamentary proceedings. The Parliamentary Proceedings (Protection of Publication) Act 1956 was, however, repealed in 1976 during the Emergency of 1975-1977. After the end of the Emergency, the law was revived and finally, as a part of the efforts to provide adequate safeguards against the recurrence of the 1975-77 type emergency, the Constitution (44th Amendment) Act, 1978 inserted, in the form of article 361A, a special provision guaranteeing the right of the media to report freely and without censorship the proceedings in Parliament and the State legislatures and making it a constitutional protection. Protection extends to the publication in newspapers or broadcast by wireless telegraphy of substantially true reports of any proceedings of either House of Parliament, provided the reports are for public good and are not actuated by malice. The above protection has been accorded within the overall limitation that the House has the power to control and, if necessary, to prohibit the publication of its debates or proceedings and to punish for the violation of its orders. Normally, no restrictions are imposed on reporting the proceedings of the House. If, however, the reports are *mala fide*, there is willful misrepresentation or suppression of speeches of particular members, it is a breach of privilege and contempt of the house and the offender is liable to punishment. Further, the Press is forbidden to publish any part of the proceedings or evidence given before, or any document presented to a Parliamentary Committee before such proceedings or evidence or document has been reported to the House. It is also incumbent on the Press not to disclose the proceedings or decisions of a secret sitting of the House, until the ban on secrecy is lifted by the

House. Any such publication or disclosure is treated as a gross breach of privilege of the House. Similarly publication of such portions of the debates as have been expunged from the proceedings of the house by order of the Speaker is a breach of privilege and contempt of the House and accordingly punishable.

The Supreme Court held that under article 361A, no person can be proceeded against in any court for publication of a substantially true report of legislative proceedings unless the publication is proved to be with malice.[4]

The founding fathers envisaged vide articles 105 and 194 of the Constitution codification of parliamentary privileges by Parliament by law. But so far no law has been made and these privileges remain undefined. It is a somewhat curious situation that even after 58 years of the commencement of the Constitution, we are unable to lay down precisely by law when a Member of Parliament is not subject to the same legal obligation as any ordinary citizen is. The only idea behind parliamentary privileges is that members who represent the people and are expected to speak for the people should not be obstructed in any way in the discharge of their parliamentary duties and are able to express their views freely and fearlessly inside the Houses and Committees of Parliament without incurring any legal action on that account. Privileges of Members are intended to facilitate them in doing their work to advance the interests of the people. They are not meant to be privileges against the people or against the freedom of the press.

To prevent ugly situations appearing again and again in the name of protecting parliamentary privileges, the only honest and straightforward course would be for Parliament and State Legislatures to abide by the constitutional provision and codify their privileges by law so that the people and the press know what precisely these privileges are and what are their limits, if any. The consequences of indecision or procrastination may be disastrous for our polity.

---

4 In *CK Daphtary v OP Gupta* (AIR 1971 SC 1132)

20

Codification of Privilege Law

In its fourth report presented on 19 December 1994, the Privileges Committee of the Tenth Lok Sabha recommended rather strongly and firmly against any legislation to codify parliamentary privileges. The recommendation was said to be based on the Committee's finding that there was no evidence to show any misuse of the privileges. The committee stopped short of saying that the founding fathers of our Constitution were less than wise when they specifically envisaged enactment of legislation on parliamentary privileges. Also, the Committee conceded that there were many misapprehensions in the minds of the people in regard to the nature, purpose and extent of parliamentary privileges. Notwithstanding the findings and recommendations of the Committee, the perception of the people was likely to persist. This was so particularly in the context of the national scenario and a general erosion in the respect for the elected representatives in the eyes of the people at large.

It was difficult to accept the Lok Sabha Committee's contention that there had been no misuse of powers under the privilege law. Instances of misuse indeed were many. Whenever matters of privilege became party issues and persons were punished on grounds of political party considerations and by majorities of the moment, misuse inevitably took place. The Lok Sabha itself had gone on record to accept this when the punishment of expulsion for breach of privilege and contempt awarded to Smt Gandhi by one Lok Sabha with Janata majority, was rescinded by another Lok Sabha with Congress majority. Smt Gandhi was considered to have remained a member throughout and was retrospectively paid all the salaries/allowances as a member of the House for the entire period of 'expulsion'. Further, the resolution for the purpose passed by Lok Sabha had strongly deprecated the misuse of privilege law on party lines. There were many other instances from the Lok Sabha and from other Houses that could be cited.

Very often, when notices of breach of parliamentary privilege are received from members, these are routinely referred to the writers, newspaper editors, etc., who are alleged to have breached some privilege. Most often, no privilege is involved and such references result in extracting regrets for nothing. Not knowing much about what constitutes breach of privilege, people prefer the path of least resistance and offer regrets to satiate the pride of the masters. When some cases are contested, the Privileges Committees or the Secretariats concerned have to beat hasty retreat or ultimately have to face judicial intervention and consequent discomfiture. In one case, when the editor of a prominent daily was sought to be punished, it was found to be a difficult task to convince the Privileges Committee of the concerned House that no privilege of the kind alleged to have been breached existed and that the editor could not be punished merely for being an unrelenting critic.

Under article 361(A) of the Constitution and Parliamentary Proceedings (Protection to Publication) Act, faithful reporting was fully protected. Also, it has been held that right of fair comment cannot be denied to the Press so long as it is not in 'vulgar or abusive' language.

If a member of the Legislature obstructs the proceedings of his House and prevents other members from exercising their right to speak by creating or contributing to pandemonium or indulging in unruly or disorderly, vulgar or indecent behaviour unbecoming of an honourable member, he is guilty of unparliamentary behaviour, of lowering the prestige and honour of the House, of committing breach of parliamentary privilege and contempt of the House. It is he who should be punished. Publishing in the newspaper for the information of the people at large, a faithful and factual report of what happens in the House of a legislature cannot be said to be a breach of any parliamentary privilege by the Press.

Not codifying the law of privileges of Parliament, deliberately keeping it vague, ambiguous and inscrutable, creates problems for the Press and the citizens. All the jurisdictional problems between the legislature and the judiciary and conflict and confrontation between the rights of the citizens and the Press vis-à-vis the law of parliamentary privileges can be resolved to a very large extent, if the legislative wing gives up its obduracy on the issue of codification of privileges.

The priests and the presiding deities of the temples of democracy have, during the last 58 years, adopted a very short-sighted attitude and disfavoured legislation for codification of privileges. There can be no constitutional or moral justification for flouting the clear intentions of the founding fathers. It is no secret that codification is being avoided because a deep rooted vested interest has developed in not codifying the privileges and continuing the present state of uncertainty and vagueness. The Presiding Officers Conferences and conferences of Chairmen of Privileges Committees and other such fora have repeatedly expressed themselves against defining and delimiting their privileges by law, as that would make them subject to fundamental rights and to judicial review.

By providing for privileges being defined by law by the respective legislatures, Constitution-makers ordained that the privileges be defined by law clearly and precisely for the benefit of the Press and the public. After all, the people and the press are entitled to ask and know what the blessed privileges are before they can exercise all due care not to breach them. It is felt that with nobody really knowing what the exact parliamentary privileges are, many untended violations may be caused and newspapers and public might be put into difficulties. It is, therefore widely felt that the parliamentary privileges should be codified to make the position clear and free from ambiguity. The point has also been made that the concept or privileges in a democratic society seems to be anachronistic and therefore, if any, there should be only those privileges which may be absolutely necessary for the proper and effective functioning of legislatures and those too should be invariably defined in clear and precise terms.

In a parliamentary system with respect for rule of law, independent judiciary and constitutional government, it is only imperative that any privileges or special rights of any class of people including those of the elected legislators should be subject to Fundamental Rights of the citizens, for, situations may come up where the rights of the people may have to be safeguarded even against the legislature and legislators. There is no guarantee that all those who come to occupy high offices will always be gentlemen.

To prevent ugly situations appearing again and again in the name of protecting parliamentary privileges, the only honest and straightforward course would be for Parliament and state legislatures to abide by the constitutional provision and codify their privileges by law. The consequences of indecision and procrastination may be disastrous for our polity.

For futher study see Subhash C Kashyap, *Parliamentary Procedure, Law, Privileges, Practice & Precedents,* 2006 one vol. ed., Universal, New Delhi, Chapter 24, pp. 632-742, *Our Parliament,* N.B.T. New Delhi, 2005 Ed., Chapter 14, pp. 240-265, *Anti Defection Law and Parliamentary Privileges,* 2003 ed., Universal, New Delhi; For contemporaneous analysis and comments see Subhash C Kashyap, (Codify Privileges of Parliament) *Times of India,* 5 December 1990: (Law and Farce of Parliamentary) (Privileges) *Financial Express,* 18 May 1992; Legislators are nota privileged class. *Times of India,* 20 May, 1994; (Protecting) Privileges, *Hindustan Times,* 25 May 1994 ; (Parliamentary Privileges: Use and Misuse *Indian Express,* 20 January, 1995

PART IV

The Judiciary and the Law

21
The Doctrine of Basic Features*

Unfortunately there is a great deal of constitutional illiteracy in our country. Constitutional studies are not accorded the space they deserve in democracy. Even at law schools and the new Law Universities, too little focus is put on studying the text of the provisions of the Constitution—its background and its working—and too much attention is devoted to what is called 'case law' containing the gems of the wisdom of judges. Perhaps, it is a professional necessity. The law school has to produce lawyers who can stand in courts and cite past decisions of their exalted lordships to show how they have improved upon and embellished the provisions made by the founding fathers. There is considerable myth and misunderstanding about the Constitution and for much of it the Courts are responsible.

To really understand the Constitution, a student of India's Constitution should, as a first step read the words in the text of a constitutional provision carefully and try to understand their normal,

---

* From an address at the Guru Govind Singh Indraprastha University, Law College.

natural meaning. In the *Kesvananda Bharti case*, the Supreme Court also said that unless otherwise indicated, every word is supposed to have been used in its normal or ordinary connotation and should be given the plain common sense meaning. Surprisingly, while interpreting the Constitution and the laws, the Supreme Court itself does not always seem to do that. The purpose of interpretation is to ascertain the intent of the framers from the words used. We must go by what the Constitution says and not by what judges say it says. The need is to critically evaluate the interpretations made, including those by the judges.

The Doctrine of Basic Features of the Constitution is a relatively recent innovation in India. It is a judicial invention and a product of what is termed 'creative jurisprudence'. Naturally, it makes a difficult and delicate theme to study. Constitution of a country is its foundational law and lays down the basic features of its polity. Every provision of the Constitution is the basic law of the land. Its provisions can hardly be so divided as to make some parts of the Constitution basic and others peripheral or some more basic and others less so. The Constitution determines the basic structure of the political system, establishes the organs of the state and defines and delimits their jurisdictional realms and responsibilities and regulates their relationships with each other and with the people. All the three organs, that is, including the Judiciary, are responsible to the people who are the ultimate sovereigns. Each organ has to discharge its duties only within the domain assigned to it. Ultimately, no institution, however supreme, is above the people. Parliament is not sovereign and the Supreme Court is not supreme except in its own domain. Neither of the three—Executive, Legislature and Judiciary—can arrogate to itself a position superior to the collective sovereign will of the people to which they are and must at all times remain totally responsible and accountable for the discharge of their duties. Every act of the Executive, Legislature and the Judiciary has to be tested on the altar of the Constitution and the weal of the people for its validity and legitimacy.

In the British parliamentary system, Parliament is, by tradition, supposed to be supreme and sovereign. There are no limitations on its powers, at least in theory, inasmuch as there is no written constitution and the Judiciary has no power of judicial review of legislation. In the US system, the Supreme Court with its power of judicial review and of interpreting the Constitution has assumed supremacy; virtually no limits are recognized on the scope of judicial review and judicial pronouncements on the legality of legislation are final. In India, the Constitution has arrived at a middle course and a compromise between the British sovereignty of Parliament and American judicial supremacy. Courts in India are also endowed with powers of judicial review of legislation. But, judicial review in India, as conceived by the founding fathers, is limited. If an Act of Parliament is set aside by the judiciary as *ultra vires* or violative of the Constitution, Parliament can re-enact it after removing the defects for which it was set aside. Also, Parliament may, within the limits of its constituent powers, amend the Constitution in such a manner that the law no longer remains unconstitutional.

In the Constituent Assembly, there was considerable discussion on the desirability or otherwise of incorporating in the Constitution the 'due process of law' clause. The founding fathers, after due deliberation, decided against adopting the American precedent and opted in favour of the formulation 'in accordance with procedure established by law'. However, the Supreme Court by its verdicts has practically brought the due process clause back into the Constitution. This goes against the basic scheme of the Constitution.

The mythology of the basic features of the Constitution can be traced back to the amendment clause of the Constitution. Under article 368 of the Constitution, which is the specific provision dealing with amendment of the Constitution, Parliament is the repository of the constituent power. An amendment of the Constitution can be initiated only by the introduction of a Bill in either House of Parliament so that the initiative in the matter of constitutional amendment has been exclusively reserved for Parliament. The President cannot do it by an ordinance nor can the Supreme Court do it by a judicial diktat.

We are all well aware of the judicial history of the marches and countermarches and the varying and contradictory interpretations given by the Supreme Court regarding the parameters of the constituent power of Parliament. It is hardly necessary to refer to the *Shankari Prasad*, *Sajjan Singh* and *Golak Nath Cases.*

Until the 1967 judgement in the *Golak Nath* case, the Supreme Court had *inter alia* held that there was no limitation on the amending power, every provision of the Constitution including the fundamental rights could be amended. In the *Golak Nath* case, by a 6:5 majority it reversed the earlier decisions and held that the fundamental rights enshrined in the Constitution were transcendental and immutable, that article 368 of the Constitution laid down only the procedure for amendment and did not give to Parliament any substantive power to amend the Constitution, that a Constitution Amendment Act was also law within the meaning of article 13 and as such Parliament could not take away or abridge the fundamental rights even through a Constitution Amendment Act passed under article 368.

In 1973, in *Kesavananda Bharati vs State of Kerala* (AIR 1973 SC 1461) the Supreme Court reviewed the decision in the *Golak Nath* Case. Ten of the 13 Judges held that article 368 itself contained the power to amend the Constitution and that 'law' in article 13 (2) did not take in a constitutional amendment under article 368. The law declared in *Golak Nath* Case was accordingly overruled. On the question whether the amending power under article 368 is absolute and unlimited, seven Judges, constituting a majority, held that the amending power under article 368 was subject to an implied limitation; a limitation which arose by necessary implication from its being a power to 'amend the Constitution'. By a majority of 7:6 the Court ruled that "Article 368 does not enable Parliament to alter the 'basic structure' or framework of the Constitution". Three different terms 'basic elements', 'basic features' and 'basic structure' were used. What constituted the 'basic elements', 'features' or 'structure' was, however, not clearly made out by the majority and remained an open question.

Following this decision in the *Kesavananda* case, clauses (4) and (5) were inserted in article 368 by the Constitution (42nd Amendment) Act, 1976, to dilute the limitation of 'basic features' to the amending powers of Parliament. These clauses say that (a) "there shall be no limitation, whatever on the constituent power of Parliament to amend by way of addition, variation or repeal the provisions of this Constitution" under article 368, and that (b) a Constitution Amendment Act would not, therefore, "be called in question in any court on any ground", that is, it would not be subject to judicial review. But the applicability of the doctrine of basic structure was reaffirmed by the Supreme Court in *Indira Gandhi vs Raj Narain* (AIR 1975 SC 2299) and *Minerva Mills vs Union of India* (AIR 1980 SC 1789). In the latter case, the Court held clauses (4) and (5) as void, on the ground that this amendment sought to totally exclude judicial review, which, according to the judges, was a 'basic feature' of the Constitution. The Court further said:

> "Since the Constitution had conferred a limited amending power on the Parliament, the Parliament cannot under the exercise of that limited power enlarge that very power into an absolute power. Indeed, a limited amending power is one of the basic features of the constitution and, therefore, the limitations on that power cannot be destroyed. In other words, Parliament cannot, under article 368, expand its amending power so as to acquire for itself the right to repeal or abrogate the Constitution or to destroy its basic and essential features. The donee of a limited power cannot by the exercise of that power convert the limited power into an unlimited one."

We need to mark the words 'Constitution had conferred a limited amending power'. Where is it in the Constitution? Can it be shown to have been the intention of the founding fathers? Who says that it is a limited power? Obviously, only the Supreme Court itself. But can the Court read into the Constitution what is *non est* and in effect legislate or even make the Constitution? A presumption is taken to be a self-evident premise or axiom and the myth is built on it.

So long as the decision in the *Kesavananda* case is not overturned by another Full Bench of the Supreme Court, any amendment to the Constitution is liable to be interfered with by the Court on the ground of affecting one or other of the known or unknown basic features of the Constitution.

In the *Kesavananda* case, Justice Sikri (para 302) had tried to tabulate the basic features of the Constitution as follows:

- Supremacy of the Constitution
- Republican and democratic form of government
- Secular character of the Constitution
- Separation of powers
- Federal character of the Constitution

In the same case, Justice Hegde and Justice Mukherjee included the sovereignty and unity of India, the democratic character of our polity and individual freedom in the elements of the basic structure of the Constitution. They believed that Parliament had no power to revoke the mandate to build a welfare state and an egalitarian society (para 682). Justice Khanna also said that Parliament could not change our democratic government into a dictatorship or hereditary monarchy nor would it be permissible to abolish the Lok Sabha and the Rajya Sabha. The secular character of the State could not, likewise, be done away with (para 1437).

In *Indira Nehru Gandhi vs Raj Narain* (AIR 1975 SC 2299, paras 55 and 213) Justice Chandrachud found the following to be the fundamental elements of the basic structure of the Constitution:

- India as a sovereign democratic republic
- Equality of status and opportunity
- Secularism and the freedom of conscience
- Rule of Law

The same Judge in the *Minerva Mills* case added the 'amending powers of Parliament', 'Judicial review' and 'balance between the Fundamental Rights and the Directive Principles' to the list of elements basic to the Constitution. The concept of basic structure was further developed by the Supreme Court and the position that the basic features cannot be altered even by constitutional amendments was further confirmed and more essential features of the basic structure were added in *Waman Rao* case (AIR 1981 SC 271), *Bhim Singhji* case (AIR 1981 SC 234), *SP Gupta vs Union of India* (1st Transfer of Judges case, AIR 1982 SC 149), *Sampath Kumar's* case (AIR 1987 SC 663) and *Kihoto Hollohon vs Zachilhu* (AIR 1993 SC 412, (1992) SC 309); *L Chandrakumar vs Union of India* (AIR 1997 SC 1125). In *PV Narasimha Rao vs State* (AIR 1998 SC 2120), Justice SC Agarwal held that 'Parliamentary Democracy' is part of the basic structure of the Constitution.

In the *SR Bommai* case regarding the dismissal of BJP Governments in Madhya Pradesh, Himachal Pradesh and Rajasthan, Justice Jeevan Reddy and Justice Ramaswamy reiterated that federalism inter alia was a basic feature of the Constitution. Justice Ramaswamy held that a democratic form of Government, federal structure, unity and integrity of the nation, secularism, socialism, social justice and judicial review were among the basic features of the Constitution.

Chief Justice Ray did not find it possible to hold the concept of free and fair elections as a basic feature whereas Justice Khanna, in the same case, found this principle to be an element of the fundamental features of the Constitution (*Indira Nehru Gandhi* case, paras 55 and 213). Justice Chandrachud did not subscribe to the view that the Preamble to the Constitution holds the key to its basic structure (para 665). Justice Beg, on the other hand, found that the Court can find the test (of constitutional validity) primarily in the Preamble to the Constitution. The Preamble, he believed, furnished the yardstick to be applied even to constitutional amendments. The mythology around the great judicial invention of the doctrine of basic features continues to grow. But, it is evident that so far there has been no consensus in this regard among the Judges themselves and no majority judgment is available laying down all the features of the Constitution that may be considered 'basic'. The Court has not foreclosed the list of the basic features as suggested by different Judges in different cases. In the *Indira Nehru Gandhi* case, Justice Chandrachud *inter alia* observed that "the theory of basic structure has to be considered in each individual case, not in the abstract, but in the context of the concrete problem".

The Constitution of India does not contain any provision in regard to basic features. There is nothing to suggest that the Constitution makers wanted any provisions of the Constitution to be absolutely unamendable. It was certainly not beyond the ingenuity of the founders to provide for it if they wanted it to be so. In fact, all the evidence is to the contrary. It was repeatedly declared in the Constituent Assembly and elsewhere by Nehru, Ambedkar and others that they did not wish to bind the succeeding generations, that, to use Nehru's words, "if you make anything rigid and permanent you stop a nation's growth, the growth of a living, vital, organic people".

If the sovereign people through their representatives cannot bring about desired change, who will? Closing the doors on peaceful change through constitutional democratic means may be an invitation to anarchy and violence. For, if the people are determined to alter any part of the structure or features of the Constitution, nothing can stop them. Sovereignty vests in the people of India and not in the hands of the Supreme Court. If the sovereign will of the people can find expression in any institution, it can only be in one representing the people. Nehru very categorically held that the Court could not be allowed to become the third chamber over the Lok Sabha and the Rajya Sabha.

What the Supreme Court has done in recent years is to assume to itself a power of veto on all constitutional amendments. Instead of interpreting the amendment clause of the Constitution and declaring the law, the Court, in effect, says that it will decide in each case whether to permit Parliament to amend the Constitution. In other words, the constituent power gets transferred from the elected representatives of the people to the judges of the Supreme Court. Justice Cordozo, the favourite icon of many of our learned judges, raised the question very clearly in the first quarter of the last century when he asked whether the judicial process is creative or declaratory. My humble submission is that our Constitution is crystal clear on the point and says that the job of the Supreme Court is to 'declare' the law (article 141). To quote the first Chief Justice of India:

> "In a democratic country, the people make the laws through their legislature. It is not the function of the court to supervise or to correct the laws passed by the legislature as an overriding authority."

The Supreme Court must remember that it is not above the Constitution and laws, that it is also accountable to the ultimate sovereigns, the people of India and that just as the power to amend is said to be a limited power only to amend, the Supreme Courts's own power to interpret and declare the law cannot be extended to making or rewriting the provisions of the Constitution. To paraphrase differently the Supreme Court's own observations about Parliament's amending powers, one is tempted to say that since 'the Constitution had conferred a limited' power of judicial review and of interpreting the Constitution only for 'doing complete justice' within its 'jurisdiction', the Supreme Court cannot 'under the exercise of that limited power enlarge that very power into an absolute power'. Indeed, limited judicial review 'is one of the basic features of our Constitution and, therefore, the limitations on that power cannot be destroyed'. In other words, the Supreme Court, under article 32, 141 and 142 cannot expand its power of interpretation so as to acquire for itself the right to amend or prevent amendment to the Constitution on the ground of a self-invented 'basic features' doctrine and thereby in effect destroy the most basic feature of Indian polity, namely the primacy of the people and democracy as a Government of the people, by the people arid for the people. It is the people and the Constitution framed by their representatives that have given certain limited powers to the Supreme Court as to other organs. 'The donee of a limited power cannot by exercise of that power convert the limited power into an unlimited one'.

Rights of citizens extend to examining each decision of the Court on merits and, where necessary, criticizing it and building opinion against it. After all, even the law declared by the Supreme Court is binding only on the lower courts. It does not prevent us from critically analysing it. Well-informed public opinion must come to impact judicial decision-making and national affairs in a big way. Today's need of renaissance and resurgence make it more imperative than ever before.

22

Expanding Dimensions of Jurisprudence*

Declining Constitutional Law

Constitutional law is first and foremost the law ordained by the Constitution. Principles of constitutionalism dictate limitations on the powers of all organs including the Judiciary. Arbitrary power in any hands is bad. Under the scheme of our Constitution, Parliament is not sovereign nor is the Supreme Court supreme except in its own sphere. All the three organs derive their authority from their creator—the Constitution.

Trouble starts when instead of concentrating on their assigned roles, organs of the State or their functionaries start expanding their jurisdictions, interfering with or assuming the role of others. Unfortunately, the present scenario is such that the Executive, the Legislature and the Judiciary have all failed to deliver in their respective spheres. The Executive has failed to govern and provide security to ordinary people or ensure good citizen-friendly governance. The legislators have declining interest in law making, they refuse to codify their privileges and want to exercise executive

---

* From keynote address at the Delhi University, Faculty of Law.

powers. Obvious instances are occupation of executive offices of profit, MPLAD scheme, etc.

So far as Judiciary is concerned, it tried to step in where, it felt that the Executive and/or the Legislature had failed to perform their responsibilities. In their juridical prudence, the Supreme Court judges were attracted by doctrines of gaps or silences in the Constitution or in the performance of the Executive or the Legislature which they had to fill by not only adjudging the failure and mandating appropriate action by the concerned organ but by themselves becoming the law givers and executing agency. When judicial wisdom decides to fill up the gaps or give voice to silences through creation of law, it expands the dimensions of traditional concepts of jurisprudence or wisdom of law, proudly calling it 'creative jurisprudence'. For some decades now, with all due deference, the Judiciary may be said to be under a narcissus complex, looking at its image of a creator or artificer of law.

Creative jurisprudence thrives and assumes popular acceptability, legitimacy and respectability in the background of weak non-performing executive and legislative wings. But, as the Supreme Court itself observed in the *Aravali Gold Club* case, if the two organs of the State fail to perform their functions properly, it is for the people to provide a corrective. The remedy is not in the judiciary taking over the legislative or executive functions, because that will not only violate the delicate balance of power enshrined in the Constitution, but also the Judiciary has neither the expertise nor they resources to perform these functions.

There is nothing wrong with the Court under powers of judicial review declaring a law or executive action *ultra vires* the Constitution. Also, it is certainly the sacred duty of the Court to secure the fundamental liberties of the citizens against arbitrary exercise of power by the Executive or the Legislature. To the extent that the courts have given wider meaning and content to fundamental rights and freedoms of the individual, the trend is a happy one. But, it is one thing to do so and quite another for the Judiciary to arrogate to itself the power to make laws, to read in the Constitution what is *non est* or to exercise a veto on the express will of Parliament in exercise of its constituent power. The question is raised as to 'what is to be done if Parliament passes a law which is impossible of implementation'? An equally pertinent question would be 'what is to be done if the Supreme Court passes orders which are not implementable?'

Liberalization of *locus* in matters of public interest and emergence of the large body of Public Interest Litigation are welcome developments so long as necessary restraints are exercised and PIL does not come to stand for Private Interest or Publicity Interest Litigation. Enough has been written and spoken on the subject, but, it would be relevant to specifically refer very briefly to five articles, namely articles 21, 124, 141, 142 and 368 to illustrate the point that through the so called creative jurisprudence, the principles of Constitution, constitutional law and constitutionalism are being eroded.

Article 21

Article 21 of the Constitution guarantees that no person shall be deprived of his life or personal liberty "except according to procedure established by law".

If one looks at the debates in the Constituent Assembly and its Committees, it becomes very clear that after long and careful consideration and extensive and in-depth debate, the founding fathers took a conscious decision to discard the 'due process' clause of the American Constitution and instead adopted the phrase 'procedure established by law'. The Constitution as it came out of the Constituent Assembly and as it was interpreted by the Supreme Court in the early years of the working of the Constitution, for example in the 1950 *Gopalan* case, provided protection only against arbitrary executive action and not against legislative will of Parliament. The job of the courts was to see whether an action was in accordance with the law laid down by the Legislature and whether the law was in conformity with the Constitution. The due process of law gives much wider scope to the Supreme Court in the United States to grant protection to the rights of its citizens by declaring laws violative of these rights void not only on substantive grounds of being unlawful and *ultra vires* the Constitution, but also on procedural grounds of being unfair, unjust or unreasonable. Under 'the procedure established by law' provision, it is not for the Court to go into the question of the reasonableness, suitability, policy implications, fairness, etc., of legislation. It has only to examine the constitutionality of the law with reference to the substantive question of whether the law is within the powers of the law-making authority.

However, our Supreme Court, it would be seen, by successive judgements, has so interpreted article 21 as if there was no difference between 'due process of law' and 'the procedure established by law'. In other words, due process of law provision has been read into article 21 through 'liberal interpretation' and 'creative jurisprudence' of our Supreme Court clearly superseding the explicit intent of the Constitution. This, however, does not mean any disagreement with the Supreme Court widening the scope of the right to life to living with dignity, having a livelihood, education etc.

Article 124

Under article 124(2), Supreme Court Judges are to be appointed by the President 'after consultation with such of the judges of the Supreme Court and of the High Courts as the President may deem necessary'. The proviso to the article says that in the case of appointment of a judge other than the Chief Justice, the Chief Justice of India shall always be consulted. The only obligation for the Government was thus to consult the Chief Justice and other judges. Significantly, the appointment was not required to be made '*in* consultation' but only '*after* consultation'. There are no blanks, no gaps, no silent areas. The provision was crystal clear. There is no ambiguity or vagueness. However, in 1993, in the *Advocates-on-Record* case, the Supreme Court practically took over the power of appointment of judges in its own hands. Even after the 1998 Advisory opinion, the position remains largely unchanged. The Executive power of appointment, irrespective of a clear constitutional provision, came to be exercised by the Judiciary whereunder a collegium of Judges selects their brother judges to sit with them.

The Constitution provides for impeachment only in the case of the President of India. There is no provision for impeachment, yet thanks to judicial creativity we, including the judges, all talk of judges being subject only to impeachment like the President. The myth is widespread.

Articles 141-142

Articles 141 and 142 are often cited to support arguments in favour of judicial supremacy and the legitimacy of creative jurisprudence.

Article 141 lays down that the law declared by the Supreme Court is binding on all courts in India. The points that emerge from this simple statement are that the declaration of the Supreme Court in regard to what the law is and what it means is final, that while considering a petition or/and adjudicating a dispute between parties, the job of the Supreme Court is to 'declare' the law, that is, which law applies, what it says and means, and not to make or create the law, law-making being a function in the Legislative domain. What the Supreme Court declares as the law or how it interprets the law is binding on all courts. Thus, while the Supreme Court's interpretation of law is binding on all lower courts, the legislature is free to change the law within the limits of the constitutional mandate. The citizens and students of law also remain free to discuss, disagree and make comments in good faith. That the Supreme Court can go wrong is accepted by the Court itself having the power to review, revise, modify and alter its own decisions. Obviously, 'all courts' does not include the apex Court itself and means only the courts lower to it.

Article 142 of the Constitution is one of those articles which created a lot of uncertainty and even confusion in the matter of position and role of the Supreme Court vis-à-vis the Constitution.

Obviously the intention was that the wise men in the Supreme Court would analyse, explain and interpret the law for all to understand and, in particular, remove any existing ambiguity and vagueness and declare the precise law. Unfortunately, the way in which provisions like article 142 have been interpreted, the law of the Constitution has been made more vague and unclear. In fact, the Court has gone so far as to extol vagueness as a virtue when it said that it was advisable to leave its own powers under article 142 'undefined', 'uncatalogued', 'elastic' and not subject to limitation under any statutory law.

It seems the Supreme Court has failed to decisively declare the law under article 142 inasmuch as

- the view taken by the Supreme Court in 1963 was overruled as not being good law in 1995;
- a judgement in 1996 (DDA case) made a case for keeping the power under article 142 'undefined' and 'elastic', in other words, not declaring the law and leaving it 'to be moulded' to suit different situations by the individual judges from time to time;
- what was established by the 1995 judgement was overturned in 1998 by another judgement.

The result is that the law is kept vague, undefined and elastic with the Court keeping to itself the power to interpret it and decide in its discretion as it deems fit in each case.

The marginal heading to article 142 is clearly indicative of the fact that the main focus of the article is on providing for the 'enforcement' of decrees and orders of the Supreme Court. It is not on any special powers of the Supreme Court. Article 142 was not envisaged as an independent and separate source of substantive power to the Supreme Court. A dispassionate reading of the text of the article makes it clear that under clause(1) the Supreme Court may issue a decree or order only 'in exercise of its jurisdiction', that is, it cannot exceed its assigned jurisdiction. The manner in which a decree or order of the court shall be enforceable shall be as 'prescribed by or under any law made by Parliament' and in the interim as prescribed by the President. Article 142(2) opens with the words "Subject to the provisions of any law made in this behalf by Parliament".

In the face of such clear and specific assertion of the primacy and supremacy of Parliamentary law in both the clauses of article 142, it is surprising how it could be held that the powers under article 142 cannot be controlled by any statutes passed by Parliament when the manner of enforcement of orders and decrees of the Court is under the authority of the Legislature and the Executive vide article 142(1) and when all the powers regarding calling for persons and papers and punishing for contempt of itself are subject to parliamentary law vide article 142(2).

The middle path adopted and the view propounded in *Vineet Narain vs Union of India* (AIR 1998 SC 889) and *Vishakha vs State of Rajasthan* (AIR 1997 SC 3011) seems relatively more judicious when the Supreme Court concedes that its job is only to fill the vacuum by its orders till the executive or the legislature step in to perform their role.

The astounding statement of the Supreme Court in the 1991 *Veeraswamy* case to the effect that 'it is well-recognized and established that this court has always been a law-maker' is the clearest example of the Court exceeding its jurisdictional limits and assuming the law-making powers of the Legislature. If the Court is recognized as the law-maker, what remains of the functions of Parliament as a law-making body and as the supreme representative institution of the people?

Again, to draw plenary powers from article 142 as a source of substantive powers, in particular, to ensure the observance of the *due process of law*, is an affront to the founding fathers who spent long hours deliberating and discussing the matter and finally deciding very categorically not to incorporate in the Constitution this U.S. doctrine. More attuned to American judicial thinking and perhaps not so respectful to the clear words of the Constitution, it may be iterated, our Supreme Court seems to bring by the back door, the due process clause rejected by the founding fathers.

Article 368

Under article 368 of the Constitution, which is the specific provision dealing with amendment of the Constitution, Parliament is the repository of the constituent power of the Union. The procedure for Constitution amendment, as spelt out in this article, has certain -distinctive features which clearly mark out Parliament's constituent capacity from its ordinary role as a legislature. On a Constitution Amendment Bill, as duly passed/ratified, being presented to the President, the President's assent is mandatory and, unlike in the case of ordinary legislative Bills, he has no option to withhold his assent or return the Bill to the House for reconsideration. It is significant that none of the provisions of the Constitution is unamendable inasmuch as Parliament can in any way amend, alter or repeal any provision of the Constitution and such amendments cannot be questioned in any court of law on any ground whatsoever unless they tend to alter or violate what may now be considered as the basic features of the Constitution.

So far as the Constitution is concerned, the 'basic features doctrine' remains the most potent illustration of judicial overreach, of creative jurisprudence and of an affront to constitutionalism as it is against the principle of limitation of powers.

23

Justice for Judges

Justice Ramaswami Case

I

Towards the end of the ninth Lok Sabha, the national scenario was getting murkier and increasingly depressing. A new controversy that had come to the fore concerned those who manned the highest judiciary in the land. Often hushed but some times also loud voices were being heard in regard to the constitutional and statutory provisions, rules and procedures for considering cases of judicial corruption and for removal of the judges of the Supreme Court and the High Courts. In a case which was before a seven-judge Bench since 1976, involving a former Chief Justice of the Madras High Court, the Supreme Court had reserved its judgement on the issue whether the judges of the Supreme Court and High Courts were subject to the Prevention of Corruption Act.

The Supreme Court was also reported to 'have been thinking of laying down a guideline' that complaints against the judges of the High Court and the Supreme Court under the Prevention of Corruption Act should be first seen by a Committee comprising a Supreme Court judge, an eminent jurist and Chief Justice of a High Court. In another matter concerning a former Chief Justice of the Punjab and Haryana High Court and then a sitting judge of the Supreme Court, Justice V Ramaswani, serious allegations and charges were bandied about.

Judges are also human and not infallible. Also they come from the same social milieu as other citizens. They are subject to the same pressures and tensions as other professionals. There may be some very genuine allegations against a judge. Grave improprieties and more may have been committed. But, one has to proceed in accordance with the law of the land and not start a witch-hunt or a campaign of vilification or character assassination through the Press and otherwise and condemn someone without even giving him the benefit of being heard. The due process of law that is available to every citizen cannot be denied to a judge. He has also to be dealt with under the rule of law.

Facts

The facts of the case agitating the bar and straining the relations between the Bench and the Bar, in brief, were that a sitting judge of the Supreme Court, Justice V Ramaswami was reported to have been responsible for some serious administrative lapses, financial irregularities and extravagant expenditure on matters like furniture, travel, telephones, etc., while he was Chief Justice of the Punjab and Haryana High Court. The allegations/findings were contained in an audit report of 15 March 1990.

The advocates in Delhi launched an agitation against the judge. The agitation continued for some three months. The judge concerned proceeded on leave on the advice of the Chief Justice. Even after return from leave, he was not allotted judicial work. Meanwhile, the Chief Justice of the Supreme Court appointed a Committee of three judges to inquire into the allegations. The Committee made an interim report on December 1, 1990, that there was no lapse in the judicial conduct of the judge, that *prima facie* no 'moral turpitude' could be ascribed to the judge, that nothing could be said with 'finality and certainty' till the audit proceedings against the judge and the criminal trials against the registry officials 'become final' and that there was, therefore, no justification to deny him judicial work.

Justice Ramaswami resumed his judicial duties on 20 December 1990—after a break of some five months. The report of the three Judge Committee was made public by the Chief Justice on 21 December. The Supreme Court Bar Association demanded that the judge should resign or that the Chief Justice should stop assigning him judicial work. Since nothing of the kind happened, the Association finally decided to boycott the court in which Justice Ramaswami sat on the Bench. After some earlier postponements, the threatened boycott was finally put down to take effect from 22 February, fortunately the last working day of the Court before the Holi holidays ending on 4 March. The Chief Justice, in a bold move, had in the meanwhile taken the judge on his own Bench.

To add to the difficult situation created by a decision of the Supreme Court Bar Association which was divided with 300 plus votes on either side, the Supreme Court Advocates-on-Record Association resolved on 21 February to disassociate themselves from the proposed boycott thereby giving further evidence of strong difference of views among the members of the Bar themselves. Another body of advocates, the All India Vigilant Advocates Front, also opposed the boycott on the ground that it would result in boycotting other judges on the Bench.

Some of the issues thrown up by the controversy were:

- Whether or not it was within the jurisdiction of C & AG to audit the accounts of the Supreme Court and the High Courts? To what extent could the contention be upheld that after specified budget allocation was made to a High Court it was entirely up to the Chief Justice of that High Court to spend that amount more or less as he liked?
- To what extent could the Bar assume the responsibility of instilling morality in the conduct of Judges? Could it be left to the majority vote of the Bar Association members to decide whether

a judge should continue or resign or be removed or whether a judge should or should not be given judicial work? What would happen if the Bar was almost evenly divided between those for and against a judge? Did the professional ethics of the advocates not forbid them from boycotting courts and undermining the prestige and independence of the judiciary?

- To what extent were the advocates or a section thereof justified in launching a concerted drive against a judge and trying to build public opinion against him? Were the judges also to adopt populist postures and try to curry favour with the advocates in a struggle for survival? Would a group of advocates not be guilty of contempt of the court if they openly flaunted charges of corruption and lack of integrity against a judge of the High Court or the Supreme Court thereby lowering the prestige of the Bench and the Bar in the estimation of the people?
- To what extent did the Bar Council standards of professional conduct and etiquette require an advocate to bear a respectful attitude towards the dignity of the institution of judges and to do nothing to lower them or the judiciary in public esteem? Would an advocate indulging in making allegations of misconduct against a judge, campaigning for his removal or resignation etc, not be guilty of bringing the judiciary to disrepute?
- To what extent were the advocates protected by their right and duty not to be servile, to function as officers of the court and not hesitate to complain to appropriate authorities whenever there was proper ground for serious complaint against a judicial officer?

All these questions had to be very carefully considered in all their ramifications particularly because what happened at the level of the Supreme Court Bar was bound to affect the atmosphere in the courts all over the country. We were already witness to the spectacle of frequent strikes by lawyers in district and other courts. On one pretext or the other, some lawyers tend to forget their professional duties, their obligations to their clients and their responsibilities vis-à-vis justice and the law of the land. Only some years earlier strike or boycott of courts or of judges by the lawyers would have sounded strange but not any more. If advocates resort to threatening the courts and stop work, where shall the common man go for justice?

All this was nevertheless not a brief for delinquent or corrupt judges. That they were there was no secret anymore. The simple point was whether members of the Bar were justified in regarding themselves as a constituency of judges with rights of passing votes of no-confidence against defiant judges and whether they could legitimately discuss in public and through the media matters like misconduct of judges and pass resolutions while even the Houses of Parliament were prohibited from doing so. Under article 121 of the Constitution no discussion could take place in Parliament with respect to the conduct of any judge of the Supreme Court or of a High Court 'in the discharge of his duties' except upon a motion for presenting an address to the President praying for the removal of the judge in accordance with the procedure laid down in article 124.

The Constitution makers were anxious to ensure the independence of the judiciary and the prestige of the judges. They, therefore, guaranteed to them security of tenure. They had the highest respect for and faith in the judiciary. There could be no doubt that during the last decades, that faith was largely borne out in the exemplary conduct and record of our judiciary as the last bastion of democracy and the sheet-anchor of the rights of the citizens, and most of the judges were known to be above board.

The question however remained whether the machinery provided by the Constitution was adequate whether, there could be found some way—short of constitutional remedy for removal of a judge—to discuss and deal with the conduct of a judge. According to some, the constitutional provisions laid down a very cumbersome procedure. A former Chief Justice of the Supreme Court was reported to have called it "practically impossible". In the interest of maintaining the highest reputation of the judiciary in our country, it would be most desirable to develop some appropriate mechanisms and institutional devices for going into *bona fide* complaints and allegations against the judges. Perhaps this should emerge from some initiative from the judiciary itself.

II

History of sorts was perhaps made on 10 May 1993, when for the first time ever a sitting judge of the highest court of the land, Justice V Ramaswami was arraigned for trial before the Lok Sabha on charges of misuse of funds for purchase of 25 silver maces for brother judges and furniture, furnishings, carpets and electrical appliances, including air conditioners, in excess of the permissible limit of Rs 38,500, use of the staff car for private trips and paying from the public exchequer heavy telephone bills without separating private calls.

Those who were familiar with the culture and life style of the senior bureaucrats and politicians in positions of power irrespective of their cadre or party affiliations, would tend to feel amused at the list of charges. For, it would be difficult to find a VIP in whose case the permissible limits of furniture etc are not exceeded and staff cars and telephones are not used for private work. Also, in public mind, the few lakhs of Ramaswami paled into insignificance in the context of the scandals involving hundreds and thousands of crores of public funds. One wondered whether our public men would agree to an inquiry by a Supreme Court judge to find out how many of them were guilty of such irregularities. It needed to be recalled that the Lokpal Bill in its various incarnations was repeatedly scuttled in the Houses of Parliament and not allowed to become law despite all the debates, committees and the like. Why?

It was to be hoped that someone had the moral courage to stand up and say that the first salvo against Justice Ramaswami should be fired by one who, while in office, was above such conduct. Those living in fragile glass houses were not expected to throw stones at others.

What happened in the Lok Sabha on 10 May was part of the proceedings for the removal of a judge on grounds of 'proved misbehaviour' under article 124 of the Constitution. It needed to be reiterated categorically that notwithstanding what was being repeated in the media every day, there was no provision in the Constitution for the 'impeachment' of a judge.

The Ramaswami story, it is said, actually started in late 1989. As the then Chief Justice of Punjab and Haryana High Court, he was elevated to the Supreme Court in the face of competition and in preference to others. One learns of how the Bench, the Bar and the political party forces were sharply divided between the supporters and detractors of Justice Ramaswami.

While some of the charges against Justice Ramaswami emanated from the audit report of March 1990, it cannot be disputed that the case was deeply politicized from day one. The Delhi advocates started an agitation demanding that no work be allotted to Justice Ramaswami. When he continued to hear cases, the advocates decided to boycott his court. The agitation continued for several months. The Bench, the Bar and the political parties again stood badly divided. A public campaign of vilification and character assassination through the press, public platforms, etc., was carried out by the section of the advocates opposed to him. In a way, he stood condemned before the public eye without due process of law, without even getting an opportunity to be heard. It was only later in February 1991 that the prescribed procedure for the removal of a judge was initiated when 108 members of Lok Sabha gave notice of a motion in that regard. On the last day of the last session of the ninth Lok Sabha, Speaker Rabi Ray admitted the motion and announced a three-member committee. Soon after the announcement, the House was adjourned in the midst of grave disorder.

The Congress Party reacted strongly and dubbed the action of Speaker Ray, 'politically motivated' and unbecoming of a person holding the office of Speaker.

When Lok Sabha was dissolved on 13 March 1991, a question arose whether the Inquiry Committee appointed by Speaker Ray continued or ceased to exist. By its ruling, the Supreme Court held that the motion did not lapse with the dissolution of Lok Sabha. But, the court in effect held that even after the President had passed orders for the removal of a judge, he would still have the option to appeal to the Supreme Court and seek judicial review of the orders.

The three-member committee found that certain charges in regard to misuse of funds etc stood established. Justice Ramaswami did not appear before the Committee and seemed prepared to fight it out to the bitter end. On the other hand, the media, some sections of political parties and a section of lawyer-politicians again mounted an offensive in order to bring moral pressure and force Justice Ramaswami to resign without facing Parliament. However, Justice Ramaswami was not the type to break down, having withstood all the threats and pressures that far. By inviting full exposure and trial before open Houses of Parliament, he had shown his consistency, stamina and fibre. He refused to adopt the softer and safer option to resign and run away from the proceedings.

Even though the Inquiry Committee held Justice Ramaswami guilty of misconduct, when the matter came up before the Lok Sabha on 10 May 1993, the motion for presenting an address to the President for his removal was lost for want of the requisite number of votes. It was said that the matter had become highly politicized between the Congress and others, and between the north and the south. The Congress members absented themselves from voting. Justice Ramaswami retired on his normal scheduled date of retirement—15 February 1994.

24

How to Discipline Judges?*

The Union cabinet is reported to have decided to introduce a new version of the Judges (Inquiry) Amendment Bill. The 2008 Bill is believed to provide for establishing a National Judicial Council to inquire into allegations of 'misbehaviour' or 'incapacity'—the two grounds laid down for the removal of a judge of the Supreme Court or a High Court.

Action for initiating impeachment proceedings against a judge is being talked about and questions are being asked in regard to the provisions and procedures. Actually, the first thing to be remembered is that despite the widespread myth and use of the term in the media and elsewhere, there is no provision in the Indian Constitution for 'impeachment' of a judge of the Supreme Court or a High Court. 'Impeachment' proceedings are provided for only in the case of the president of India and for none else.

Also, there is a fundamental difference between procedure for removal and impeachment procedure and between the impact of the

---

* *The Times of India*, 21 November 2008

adoption of a motion for impeachment and the passing of a motion for presenting an address to the president seeking orders for the removal of a judge. The grounds for the impeachment of the president have to concern 'violation of the Constitution' while an address for removal of a judge has to be on the ground of 'misbehaviour or incapacity'. In case of impeachment, the moment the motion is passed by the two Houses, the President ceases to hold office. But in case of the motion for removal, it is for the President to consider issuing necessary orders.

Article 124 of the Constitution in effect provides that a Supreme Court judge can be removed from his office by a presidential order passed after an address by each House of Parliament supported by a majority of not less than two-thirds of the members of the House present and voting is presented to the President in the same session for such removal on the ground of proved misbehaviour or incapacity. Article 124(5) specifically lays down that Parliament may by law regulate the procedure for the presentation of an address and for the investigation and proof of the misbehaviour or incapacity.

In pursuance of article 124 (5), Parliament passed the Judges (Inquiry) Act, 1968. The Judges (Inquiry) Rules, 1969 lay down the details of procedure for investigation and inquiry into the allegations against a judge. If not less than 100 members of Lok Sabha or 50 members of Rajya Sabha give notice of a motion for the removal of a judge on grounds of some definite allegations of misbehavior or incapacity, the Speaker/Chairman of Lok Sabha/Rajya Sabha, would decide the admissibility of the motion. If the motion is admitted, a committee would be appointed for holding the necessary investigations.

The judge concerned would be provided with reasonable opportunity for defence. If the committee found the judge not guilty of 'any misbehaviour', and not suffering from 'any incapacity', then the whole matter would be dropped forthwith. If, however, a verdict of guilty of misbehavior or of incapacity was returned by the committee, the House would proceed to consider the motion. If the motion was passed by majority of the total membership of each House and more than two-thirds of those present and voting in either case, misbehavior or incapacity of the judge shall be deemed to have been proved and an address shall be presented to the president during the same session of Parliament for the removal of the judge.

History of sorts was perhaps made on 10 May 1993. It was the last day of the last session of the ninth Lok Sabha when for the first time ever a sitting judge of the highest court of the land, Justice V Ramaswami, was arraigned for trial before the Lok Sabha on charges of misuse of funds for purchase of 25 silver maces for brother judges and furniture, furnishings, carpets and electrical appliances, including air conditioners, in excess of the permissible limit of Rs 38,500, use of the staff car for private trips and paying from the public exchequer heavy telephone bills without separating private calls.

Speaker Rabi Ray admitted the motion and announced a three-member committee. Soon after the announcement, the House was adjourned in the midst of pandemonium. The three-member committee found that certain charges in regard to misuse of funds stood established. Even through the committee held Justice Ramaswami guilty of misconduct, when the matter came up before the Lok Sabha, the motion for presenting an address to the President for his removal was lost for want of the requisite number of votes. It was said that the matter had become highly politicized. The Congress members absented themselves from voting. Justice Ramaswami retired only on his normal scheduled date of retirement on 15 February 1994.

It is to be seen whether investigation and inquiry by the now proposed National Judicial Council composed of only persons from the judiciary will prove to be an improvement over, the existing procedure of investigation and inquiry by an *ad hoc* committee appointed by the Lok Sabha or Rajya Sabha.

25

Issue of Shankaracharya's Arrest

Position Under the Constitution

In whatever manner you look at it, the arrest of His Holiness the Kanchi Shankaracharya in November 2004 was a great national shame. That it did not generate much of a spontaneous public reaction on a non-party basis could be some evidence of our general tolerance, insensitivity or apathy.

While the veracity of the serious allegations was naturally to be adjudged by the courts, the manner and timing of the police action in Tamil Nadu and Andhra Pradesh were most deplorable.

Several versions were in circulation about the possible motives behind the action. One wondered whether it was only the seriousness of the charge or

- was it the anxiety of a non-Tamilian Brahmin chief minister to try to outsmart her DMK rival and establish her credentials with the anti-Brahmin Tamil vote banks? or,
- was it meant to humiliate the person of one of the highest Dharma gurus and to denigrate and, if possible, destroy the Shankaracharya institution? or,

- was it to punish the elder Swami for his reported remark regarding the chief minister's 'arrogance'? or,
- was it to settle scores in the matter of the take-over of a sick hospital by the *Muth*? or,
- was it to avenge the refusal of the Shankaracharya to issue an appeal to the people to support AIADMK?

The justification for the Deepavali midnight haste was stated to be some information with the police that he was likely to flee to Nepal in a private helicopter that was kept in readiness. It is difficult to believe the bizarre story. Travel from the extreme south all the way up to Nepal by a private helicopter hardly made sense. Also, despite all the decline in the quality of governance and security arrangements, are we to understand that the entire machinery of the government could not foil such an escape bid? Even if preemptive steps were desirable, could the helicopter not be impounded or the security alerted to ensure that His Holiness, the Shankaracharya, did not cross the Indian borders?

Ever since the arrest, the *netas* and the intellectuals kept repeating parrot-like that all were equal before the law, that processes of law must not be interfered with and that law must be allowed to take its own course. Are all really ever treated as equals or equally before the law? Is law really allowed to take its own course without interference? We all know the course it takes. Many cases in recent years involving politicians and industrialists come to mind where the law proved to be less then equally applicable in practice.

None of the accused involved in those cases could be said to be of a status and stature higher to that of the Shankaracharya. Also, they were accused of some of the most heinous crimes including murder, rape, subverting democratic processes and rule of law by swindling public money to the tune of thousands of crores and for bribing elected representatives for survival in power thereby polluting the entire Indian polity. Irrespective of the public perception about their guilt, many of them roam free as not enough clinching evidence was found or there were loopholes in the law. Less said about the law being allowed to take its course, the better.

At long last, on 25 November the Prime Minister broke his silence on the issue and condescended to depart from his studied stance of unconcern, indifference and total disavowal of all responsibility in the matter. The only and somewhat cryptic remark made by him earlier was to the effect that the Centre has no role in the affair.

It is most astonishing that it took 13 days for the PM to realize that "His Holiness enjoys a high religious status and position in society", that "investigations involving a person of his eminence need to be conducted with extreme care and consideration" and that his "indifferent health" also needed to be taken care of.

Only if the PM was better advised and without fearing the reaction of the comrades had said this earlier perhaps it would not have become so politicized or become a *Hindutva* issue appearing to be the concern of BJP, RSS and VHP alone.

In reality, it could not be said that it was purely an internal matter of the state of Tamil Nadu. The institution of Shankaracharya was venerated all over the country and anything done to Shankaracharya was bound to have all India ramifications. When we brag about India being one with one Constitution, one people one citizenship, how can the PM wash his hands of a grave matter like this by simply saying that Centre had no role.

It was not an issue of secular-*Hindutva* divide or majority-minority issue. The Shahi Imam of Jama Masjid—even if for his owns reasons—was among the first few to deprecate the action of the Tamil Nadu Government. Even Karunanidhi was quick to revise his views and openly declared that the police action smacked revengefulness on behalf of the CM.

Also, when some of the most distinguished persons of the eminence of the most respected former President of India, Shri R Venkataraman, former PM, Shri Chandra Shekhar and former long-time Deputy Chairperson of Rajya Sabha, Smt Najma Heptullah—whose secular credentials could not be doubted even by Congressmen—sat in protest, there must be really something of national concern.

It was high time that the 'Progressive' Government realized that the only agenda of their leftist supporters from outside was destabilization to smoothen their ultimate aim of capturing power at the Centre. Dr Manmohan Singh must also not be unaware of the fact that in his cabinet there was some 'progressive' and 'secular' ministers who had no hesitation in prostrating before the Shankaracharya and seeking his blessings for return to positions of power. He must also be knowing that privately some of them are really appalled at what had happened.

Lastly, it needed to be appreciated that there was no conflict between secularism and true Hinduism. In fact, the two stood for each other. Respect for all the different ways was the basic tenet of Hinduism. This Hindu sentiment was offended. Even if not so visible on the surface, it was bound to find expression. After all, even the Congress could not for long depend entirely on the outside support of the Communists and the votes of the Muslim League and other communal elements. It would need Hindu votes.

In terms of the Constitution and the laws also:

- The Union Government cannot absolve itself of responsibility in matters having all India ramifications
- Ordinarily law and order is a state subject but the executive powers of the State are to be so exercised as to ensure compliance with Union Laws.
- The Union executive can give to the State Government necessary directions.
- All the executive powers of the State are vested in the Governor who is appointed by the Union and represents it in the State. While ordinarily he acts on the advice of his ministers, he (unlike the President) has an area of discretionary powers, parameters of which are also left to be defined by him in his discretion only.

- The Supreme Court has laid down certain norms and guidelines to be followed in the matter of arrests and treatment of the accused under article 20. Under article 21, right to life has been interpreted to include right to life with human dignity. Even in the process of arresting an accused, human dignity has got to be respected.
- Under article 355, it is the duty of the Union Government to *inter alia* ensure internal security and constitutional government in the States.

The Government of India could not have been a helpless spectator.

PART V

Constitutional Conflicts and Controversies

26

Politics of Defection and Anti-Defection Law

The Fourth General Elections held in February 1967 constituted a watershed in the post-independence political history of India. The monolithic Congress regime and its haloed leadership had concealed both the many operational weaknesses and the basic inner strength and resilience of the Indian system. While strongly reaffirming the people's deep involvement in the democratic process, the electoral verdict shattered the Congress Party's virtual monopoly of political power. It also exposed the artificiality of the political stability, democratic maturity and parliamentary sophistication at which the system had appeared to be operating. Results of the fresh elections held in five States in February 1969 only carried the process a stage further.

Spate of Defections (1967-69)

The most important developments in the post-1967 political and parliamentary scene in India were the formation of coalition governments of widely heterogenous elements in several States and the numerous defections on the floor of the State legislatures which affected the fate of ministries and the course of politics. The phenomenon, the politics of defection as it came to be called, had several psychological and socionomic dimensions and was closely related to the dynamics of human relations and leadership processes.

Of the sixteen States of the Union that went to the polls in 1967 (there were no elections in Nagaland) the Congress Party did not gain an absolute majority in eight and failed to form the government in seven. Even in those States in which the Congress retained control, its strength was much depleted and in several cases defection by a few members changed the Party's legislative majority into a minority. In seven of the eight states where Congress failed to win an absolute majority, no single party took its place. The general contours of the political power structure in the states were obviously undergoing basic changes. The highly fragmented opposition saw in the situation an opportunity to seize power; there began a process under which non-Congress parties, including those of the extreme right and the extreme left, ignored their ideological differences and joined together on the basis of what were called 'minimum common programmes'. United Fronts were forged and coalition governments emerged in several States—initially in Kerala, Orissa, Bihar, Punjab and West Bengal. But soon, Congress governments were ousted from three other States —Uttar Pradesh (UP), Haryana and Madhya Pradesh—and replaced by United Front governments, so that at one time the majority of the States (9 out of 17) and the majority of the population were for the first time governed by non-Congress coalition ministries at the State level.

The next phase involved the ouster of the United Front governments in UP, Bihar, West Bengal, Punjab and Madhya Pradesh by the Congress-led opposition, and the formation of Congress-supported governments by defectors from the United Fronts in West Bengal, Punjab and Bihar. This led to the imposition of President's Rule in Haryana, West Bengal, UP, Bihar and Punjab. Fresh Assembly elections were held in Haryana in May 1968 and in the other four states in February 1969. Congress governments in coalition with or with the support of defectors were formed subsequently in Madhya

Pradesh, Haryana, Bihar and UP, while non-Congress coalitions came to power in West Bengal and Punjab. The Congress coalition in Bihar did not last even four months and was succeeded by a non-Congress United Front Government which in its turn survived only nine days. Finally, President's Rule was once again imposed in Bihar.

The political defection phenomenon, thus, was responsible for the collapse of seventeen governments in a period of almost as many months. Significantly, each of these cases was the direct result of defections by legislators, most of whom hoped to gain ministerial office or other personal benefit and were prepared to assist in the toppling of existing governments and formation of others in their place to attain their objective. Several other states where governments managed to stay in office were also affected, to a greater or lesser degree, by defections. While this was by no means merely a North Indian phenomenon, the states most affected were in the north, all of whom faced a constitutional crisis or near crisis at one time or the other after the 1967 General Election.

Approximately 3,500 members of the legislative assemblies of the States and the Union Territories were elected in 1967; of these some 550 changed their political affiliations, that is, indulged in the politics of defection. Several legislators did so more than once and in terms of acts of defection the number actually exceeded the 1,000 mark. In effect, some 16 per cent of the total membership of State Assemblies had been involved, and the percentage would be even higher, perhaps 25 per cent, if we included the legislatures in such States as Tamil Nadu, Assam, Jammu and Kashmir, Nagaland, Orissa, and Maharashtra where the governments, whether Congress or non-Congress, had been more stable and defections infrequent.

During the 10 years prior to 1967, there had been a total of 542 defections; in the year following the February 1967 election there were 438 such cases. In strictly numerical terms, the overall advantage had accrued to the Congress. During the 1957-1967 period, when it had a virtual monopoly of power, the Congress party netted most of the gains from defections by legislators. After the fourth general elections, however, defections became more of a two-way traffic and, in fact, during the first year (1967-68), the Congress lost more legislators than it gained. Interestingly, during the same period, all the other organized political parties also suffered a net loss, as many of the defectors did not join another party but instead formed a separate pressure group or party of defectors with a view to seizing or sharing power.

The presence of a large number of independent legislators further accelerated the pace of defection. There were 375 independents in the State legislatures, many of whom had won election by defeating the official candidates of the parties which they had deserted on being denied party tickets. Not being 'independents' by principle, they were prepared to trade their label and offer their votes to the highest bidder. Indeed the largest number of defectors to various political parties—primarily to the Congress—came from the independents category. Of the 174 independents elected to the assemblies in Bihar, Haryana, Madhya Pradesh, Manipur, Punjab, Rajasthan, UP and West Bengal, 90 joined various political parties after the election. It was natural, therefore, under conditions of general instability and marginal-majority, governments that the independent legislators frequently were in a position to tilt the balance and play a decisive role in toppling existing governments and installing new ones.

Political defections were, of course, neither new nor unique to India. What was new, however, in the situation, was the magnitude, range and character of defections and above all the fact that the direction of defection had been reversed since the fourth general election, with the Congress suffering a net loss of 175 legislators in the first year alone. In most of the pre-1967 cases of defection, it was obvious that the dominant Congress party had been playing with the human weaknesses of members of the opposition. It was alleged by the opposition leaders, and not entirely without foundation, that the Congress was responsible for the non—emergence of a real democratic alternative to the Congress. If defections from the ruling party were bad, then inducing the members of the opposition to defect to the Congress was equally bad. In a parliamentary democracy, a stable opposition was as essential as a stable government, for both the government and the opposition had to work on the basis of some agreed norms. The first and the foremost of these norms was that the opposition was also loyal and responsible and that it was respected and recognized as a part of the government in the wider sense of the term.

Reasons for Defections

Legislative defections in India have been the product of the various socio-political complexes under which the system operates and must be accepted as hard sociological reality. The causes are historical, institutional and motivational, and often a combination of all three. The root cause perhaps lies in the history and nature of our political parties. Before independence, the Indian National Congress had been something much more and much less than a political party. It was essentially a freedom movement under which men and women of diverse beliefs, outlook and background were brought together with the all-embracing single aim of achieving emancipation from foreign rule. It is pertinent to recall here the 1942 Quit-India Resolution, in which the Congress declared that "it has no intention of gaining power" which "when it comes will belong to the whole people of India".

The pledge was not fulfilled, for after independence Congress rushed to grab power. Everything changed, Congress ceased to be the all-embracing and unifying national movement, and instead became something of a political party and the government of the country. Congress politics began to appeal to many as a gateway to a better career and high public status, as also frequently considerable material gain.

In 1948, shortly before his assassination, Gandhiji had proposed the dissolution of the Congress as a political party and its transformation into a social service organization to be called the Lok Seva Sangh which would be devoted to the task of social regeneration and economic uplift of the masses through a programme of voluntary constructive work. Gandhiji wanted Congressmen to leave politics, government administration and electioneering to others. Those interested in the game of politics could, of course, leave the Lok Seva Sangh and join or form political parties of their choice. In a rather strongly worded comment Gandhiji had said:

> "The Congress has gained the trust of the people on account of its many sacrifices and penances but if at this moment it were to let the people down by becoming their overlord instead of their servant and arrogate to itself a position of master, I venture to prophesy on the strength of my experience of long years that though I may be alive or not, a revolution will sweep over the country and that the people will pick out the white capped ones individually and finish them and that a third power will stand to gain by this."

But the Congress leaders, including Nehru and Sardar Patel, strongly disagreed. Perhaps they thought the Congress was essential for running the government and that there was no other alternative, or that it was after all a going concern and the season of harvest had arrived. Those who claimed to have suffered during the national struggle looked for conformable berths in the new power structure.

After the third General Elections, the Central Parliamentary Board of the Congress party adopted a resolution which stipulated that a legislator belonging to another party should not be admitted to the Congress unless he first resigned his seat in the legislature and agreed to contest the election on the Congress ticket. But the party bosses in the states did not favour the resolution which was never implemented. No defector from another party admitted to the Congress was made to resign his seat and contest a bye-election on the Congress ticket. Every admission was made under an exception clause in the 1963 resolution. Indeed, even groups from the opposition, including the Asoka Mehta faction of the Praja Socialist Party, were admitted to the Congress unconditionally.

Factions had always existed inside the Congress of course, and the leadership of the party not only accepted dissidence but even encouraged and rewarded it at times. With the assumption of power by the Congress at the Union and State levels, personal ambitions, fights over the fruits of office, in-group rivalries, and caste, communal, regional and linguistic pulls within the organization assumed more importance than and actual differences of ideology. Factionalism reached serious and threatening proportions, and defections were, to a certain extent, an outgrowth of these long-standing internal rifts which got accentuated in the post-1967 period because Congressmen could then try to gain their objectives outside the party if they failed to get them from the party. What provided the major and immediate incentive for the large-scale defections in various State legislatures was the somewhat unexpected and phenomenal success of the opposition parties at the polls and their emergence in such strength as to be able to form, alone or in combination, alternative governments to the Congress in several states. Human nature being what it is, some Congress legislators rallied to the party which was in position to distribute office and patronage. The myth of the invincibility of the Congress had been exploded and new gates to the citadels of power opened. Disgruntled back-benchers in the party were filled with new hopes and ambitions. With the strength of the Congress and of the combined opposition parties near evenly balanced in several States, every single legislator became what may be called a 'marginal legislator' with the opportunity to become a 'fence-sitter' or to play the game of brinkmanship in which he would quote his price for crossing the floor in one direction or the other.

There was moreover, no personality in the Congress or in the opposition capable of calling a halt to this practice. The fight was among equals—a free for all with no holds barred and no ethical inhibitions left. The dissident Congressmen suffered no qualms of conscience in indulging in the game of defection politics. They knew very well that it was largely the desire to share power that had kept the party together since independence, and that they had little affinity with the dominant faction in the party and little role in formulating its policies and programmes. After the fourth General Elections, the Central parliamentary Board of the Congress party formally changed its policy with regard to the admission of defectors from other parties. It was decided to waive all restrictions on the defection of non-Congress legislators to the Congress and to leave this matter to the discretion of the State units of the party. In some States several defectors from other parties were admitted to the Congress fold, and a number of former Congressmen were also welcomed back. At the Hyderabad session, the All-India Congress Committee (AICC) authorized the Congress State legislators to form coalition governments with defectors from other parties. Also, Congress President, S Najalingappa, openly appealed to those who had left the Congress to return to its fold. Commenting on this statement editorially, *The Statesman* observed: "Ratting on a party after taking electoral advantage of it is bad enough; ratting again on another which has given refuge is much more sordid."

It was indeed most unfortunate that while the erstwhile have-nots—that is non-Congress party legislators—looked upon the situation as a golden opportunity, the Congress itself, badly battered and demoralized at the polls, seemed to go by the logic of despair that everything was fair in a battle for survival. What happened in West Bengal, Punjab, Bihar, Haryana, Manipur and Madhya Pradesh did little credit to the Congress Party, which had not lagged behind the other parties in encouraging defections. In Punjab, Bihar and West Bengal, defectors were rewarded with ministerial positions and several minority ministries composed of defectors from the opposition were installed in office with Congress support.

The developments in West Bengal, Bihar, Punjab, UP, Haryana, Madhya Pradesh and Manipur highlighted another aspect of the situation. The tempo of unprincipled defections might not have reached such proportions but for the unwillingness of the Congress party to share power by entering into coalitions with like-minded democratic parties. For examples, through coalition with parties such as the PSP, the Jan Sangh and the Swatantra, Congress could have formed more stable governments in several States where it was still the single majority party. Such coalitions under the prevailing circumstances would not only have been possible but would have brought stability and discouraged defections by small groups of backbenchers eager to gain ministerial office. But, used to a monopoly of power, Congress was unprepared to share it, presumably on the grounds that the United Front governments would fall apart due to their inner contradictions and that power would inevitably revert to the Congress. Speaking in that vein at Indore in March 1968, Congress President Nijalingappa said that the time would soon come when all these 'anti-democratic (United Front) governments will be entirely liquidated because of their own sins' and the Congress would once again rule the entire country.

The problem of large-scale defections could be looked at from several other angles. Individual legislators and all the political parties condemned them, but none of them hesitated to indulge in the game when the opportunity presented itself. Those who themselves resorted to defections, were the loudest in condemning the practice. Some of them, however, made a distinction between defections on grounds of ideology or principle and those resorted to merely for personal benefit. But, the ease with which legislators left one party to join another made it obvious that they did not take political principles or party ideology seriously.

In practice, it was almost impossible to draw a fine line between defections on grounds of conscience and those for personal gain. Also, since there was no real ideological polarization among the parties and differences were not of black and white but of shades of grey, no real change of ideology was involved when a person left one party and joined another. He could still assert his loyalty to the principles and argue that he was defecting only to implement them better. This almost total absence of ideology as a force in competitive politics contributed to the growth of defection politics. Sometimes conflicts of personalities and temperamental incompatibilities between a legislator and his party bosses could lead the former to repudiate the party. Not infrequently, senior and trusted party workers were denied tickets for contesting the election merely on grounds of their affiliation with a dissident group in the party.

Viewed in the light of a study of concrete instances and quantitative analysis thereof, it would seem that most of the defections were directed towards individual or group interests. Their most dominant characteristic had been their proximity in point of time to the rise and fall of governments and undoubtedly the most important motivational force had been the prospect of power and the lure of ministerial office. It is significant that during the first year after the fourth General Election, as many as 115 defectors were rewarded with ministerial posts in non-Congress governments or in Congress-supported and Congress governments. Seven of them became chief ministers; one was rewarded with a Speakership and several others with less important offices such as parliamentary secretaries.

It was, however, obvious that many more legislators entertained ministerial ambitions than could really expect office; the rest had to serve as back-benchers with occasional ad hoc assignments on committees, commissions, delegations, etc. Even during the height of Congress rule under Nehru, the legislators who were most insistent and most capable of causing embarrassment had to be placated with office, not only at the state level but also at the Union level. The one ready device found was to keep the size of the ministries elastic and make additions as and when required. The proliferation of ministers at the centre had progressed at such a rate that at the end of 1969 there were 53 ministers in comparison to the 14 serving in that position in the first Nehru cabinet. The business of politics and of politicians had thus become by necessity, basically power-oriented.

Viewing the problem from the angle of the legislator, it had to be remembered that he was made of the same stuff as his fellow men and was subject to the same hopes and fears, the same ambitions and quests for significance, the same foibles and frailties and the same craving for identity. If anything, indeed, he was trying to live under precarious conditions of survival. A politician's job hardly permitted him to be consistently scrupulous. Often, moral values had to be compromised with pragmatic considerations, for failure in politics was inexcusable. Defection from a party was only one example of such a compromise. But, accustomed to extol near-perfect heroes and conditioned by the background of the long struggle for independence during which involvement in politics was seen as one of great sacrifice and devotion to high ideals, Indians very often applied special and impossible standards to their legislators and leaders. On the other hand, ministerial office with its substantial patronage and influence, tended to have more than a natural attraction for the Indian legislator.

The reasons for the initial emergence of the phenomenon of large-scale political defections could be summed up as follows: (1) the history and nature of political parties in India, and particularly the Indian National Congress; (2) the aging leadership, bossism and the growth of establishments with vested lack of ideological orientation and polarization among the parties; (4) the low level of popular involvement in the membership, objects and activities of political parties and the virtual indifference of the people to acts of defection by their representatives; (5) in-fighting and factionalism in the parties which lead to group-defections when, for example, party tickets were denied to members of a dissident faction; (6) the marginal and unstable majorities in State legislative assemblies after the 1967 Elections and the prospect of non-Congress parties being in a position to capture power; (7) conflict of personalities and temperamental incompatibilities between a legislator and his party bosses: (8) the temptations of office and money, status and the like or denial of the same; (9) the tremendous gap between the emoluments, status and other benefits attached to the office of a minister and that of an ordinary legislator; (10) the existence of powerful lobbies and pressure groups that commanded loyalties that were far more intense than loyalties to political parties; and (11) the unwillingness of the Congress party to share power and enter into workable coalitions with like-minded parties.

Committee on Defections

Under a non-official resolution moved on 11 August 1967, and finally adopted by the Lok Sabha on 8 December 1967, a Committee of constitutional experts and representatives of political parties was set up in March 1968 under the Chairmanship of YB Chavan, then Union Home Minister. (Ironically enough, the man who moved the resolution himself changed his party allegiance twice—first he crossed the floor to sit in the Opposition as a member of Congress (O) and then made a return journey to the ruling Congress). The Report of the Chavan Committee was placed on the table of the House on 18 February 1969. Trusting that action on its recommendations would be taken 'as early as possible', the Committee *inter alia* suggested: (1) barring appointment as Prime Minister/Chief Minister of a person who was not a member of the Lower House; (2) barring appointment as minister of a defecting legislator for a period of one year or till such time as he resigned his seat and got himself re-elected; and (3) limiting the size of the Council of Ministers at the Union and State levels.

It would appear that on other significant suggestions, members of the Committee could not reach any agreement. According to some expert assessments, the labours of the Committee turned out to be an exercise in evasion, if not hypocrisy. Still, for whatever they were worth, it could be legitimately expected that being the recommendations of a high-level all-party Committee, they would find wide acceptance and would be implemented forthwith. However, this did not happen.

The Report was discussed and referred to *ad infinitum* both inside and outside the legislatures. It came up for consideration in Rajya Sabha on 12 August 1969 and Members of all sections of the House, as expected, expressed serious concern over the malady of defections. All the usual things on the subject were iterated. The debate continued even thereafter, with the Government expressing its seriousness about implementing the report and bringing about measures to curb defections and the Opposition groups disagreeing and doubting. In the meantime, defections continued unchecked, parties split, large groups crossed floors, Houses of Legislatures stood dissolved, governments were toppled, huge sums of money changed hands under the table and ministerships and other prices were freely distributed among actual or potential defectors by almost all parties.

Suggestions for Reform

Besides the All-Party Chavan Committee on Defections, several academic and public bodies, independent scholars and concerned citizens made valuable suggestions for tackling the problem of large-scale unprincipled defections. These included (1) the evolution of a code of conduct by the political parties; (2) greater emphasis by the parties on the choice of candidates for election; (3) using the pressure of public opinion; (4) granting the Chief Ministers the power to dissolve the legislature; (5) elimination of independents; (6) debarring defectors from appointment as ministers; (7) disqualifying defectors from membership in the legislature and/or contesting elections, (8) recognition or registration of parties and list system of voting, (9) provision for recall, (10) limiting the size of ministries. However, most of these suggestions were not found to be feasible legally and constitutionally nor acceptable politically. Even if they were otherwise acceptable, they could have only a minimal impact due to the in-built resistance of the parliamentary system as it operated in the context of the Indian political culture. Thus, in order to cater to the needs of political stability consistent with the country's democratic ethos, even as early as in the late 60s, some rethinking on the operation of India's Constitution seemed necessary as for example, to include a few elements of the Presidential system like the irremovability of the Executive. Fortunately, this could be accomplished without any major amendments in the text of the Constitution as it stood then. What was required was merely a reinterpretation and a desire to work it anew. In the ultimate analysis, however, it was for the people to assert themselves. Ideals of freedom and democracy given to themselves by the people of India required constant vigilance, enlightened public opinion and a competent leadership endowed with integrity and an understanding of the sophisticated operational mechanics of the system. It was not generally realized that any worthwhile democratic experiment in order to be successful needed a good deal of investment in political education. Little attention was paid to this aspect of politics and an organized effort in this direction was never made.

Congress Split and After

Towards the end of 1969—the Gandhi Centenary Year—politics took a new turn at the all-India level. The Congress 'split' was followed by waves after waves of fresh group defections. Many members of Parliament changed their loyalties, party disciplines were shattered, voices were raised against the 'Syndicate' and the party bosses; questions of conflict between discipline and conscience cropped up; and for the first time in Indian politics, conscience was politicized. And all this occurred on such a vast scale, particularly within the dominant Congress party, that the term 'defection' lost its meaning, and it became well-nigh impossible for anyone to determine who defected and who remained loyal to the party or, in fact, which was the real Congress and which merely a pack of defectors.

The Congress Party—and not only that—was split both horizontally and vertically, and led to a chain reaction in some of the state legislatures, thereby disturbing the delicate power balance still further. Mere cold figures and statistical data could hardly tell the whole story or capture the real magnitude of what had happened. However, even in those terms, with an average of more than one legislator changing his label each day and for some time, again on an average, one government collapsing each month, it was only natural that the phenomenon of defections continued to claim some attention. Contrary to popular impressions of the times, the number of defections during 1971-73 period was much larger than that during 1967-1971. The flow had continued unabated; only the direction had kept on changing with the winds of time. In fact, defections had by the 70s ceased to make news because they had become so routine and so very much part of the system and political culture that the people got insensitized to their occurrence. They no more had news value.

During 1967-73 some 45 State governments were toppled in quick succession with as many as some 2,718 cases of defection by legislators in the direction of the highest bidder. Over 60 per cent of all legislators all over the country were involved in the game. Many changed their affiliations more than once and some of them as many as four or five times. One MLA was found to have defected five times but succeeded in being a minister for only five days. The 'operation alliance' and 'operation topple' went side by side. The climax was reached soon after the 1971 elections to the Lok Sabha, when three governments collapsed through defections within one week—the last week of March 1971.

Constitutional Amendments

As the first attempt at an anti-defection law, the Union Cabinet approved the draft of a legislation on 24 July 1970. Its provisions were based on the majority report of the Committee of Defections and were to the effect that (a) the Constitution be amended to restrict the strength of the Council of Ministers; (b) the Prime Minister of India or the Chief Minister of a State, if he or she is not already a Member of the Lower House, be elected to it within six months; and (c) a new article be incorporated in the Constitution disqualifying a defector from holding a ministerial post or other office of profit for a period of one year.

Before the dissolution of the Lok Sabha in December 1970, the Prime Minister convened a conference of the representatives of the Government and of the Opposition parties and groups to hammer out some agreement on the draft 'legislative provisions' seeking to outlaw defections. The conference, however, dispersed in a mood of mutual distrust, with the government suspecting that some Opposition elements were out to wreck the whole process, and the Opposition critics blaming the ruling party for not being serious about stopping defections. The 1971 elections to the Lok Sabha returned the Congress under Smt Indira Gandhi's leadership with a two-thirds majority, enough to carry through any constitutional amendments without the support of Opposition parties. However, it was after considerable further procrastinations for over two years and a long period of expectancy that an anti-defection Bill was finally introduced in the Lok Sabha on 16 May 1973. It was a relatively short document consisting of 10 clauses. It sought to amend eight articles of the Constitution namely articles 75, 101-103, 164 and 190-192.

According to the Statement of Objects and Reasons appended to the Bill, when the Report of the Committee on Defections was considered "it was felt that the recommendations that a defector should be rendered ineligible for certain offices of profit for a stipulated period would not provide an adequate solution and that it would be more appropriate to amend the Constitution with a view to disqualifying a defector from his continued membership of the Legislature". Actually, none of the recommendations of the Chavan Committee having a bearing on the problem of defections had been incorporated in the Bill. On the other hand, proposals which were bitterly opposed by some members of the Committee or which were not at all considered by the Committee found a place.

The only crucial provisions so far as the problem of defections was concerned were those pertaining to disqualification from membership and the new role and importance proposed to be assigned to political parties. Clauses 4 and 8 of the Bill sought to disqualify a person from continuing to be a member of Parliament or State Legislature if he voluntarily gave up the membership or voted or abstained from voting against the direction of the party by which he was set up as a candidate for election or which he joined after such election.

It was specifically provided that the proposed disqualification would not apply to those cases where a legislator resigned from or voted against his party by reason of split in the party. Political party was defined to mean any party classified as a recognized political party under election laws or any other party recognized by the Speaker or Chairman of the House as a political party and consisting of not less than 1/15th of the total membership of such House. Clauses 5 and 9 provided that the President or the Governor, as the case may be, would not entertain any question regarding the disqualification of a legislator unless it was referred by the political party concerned.

Thus, under the Bill political parties for the first time were to acquire constitutional recognition and status and party bosses an unprecedented hold over the minds and souls of the elected representatives of the people. As it was, almost all the political parties in India—big or small—had already acquired the characteristics of establishments with all the vested interests in *status quo* and institutional resistance to progress and change. The Bill might have had the unhealthy effect of freezing this state of affairs and even strengthening the party establishments. The Bill was strongly opposed through the media and otherwise on the following grounds:

- Indian voters, by and large, had no real involvement in party activities and little commitment to any party ideology or programme. Only a negligible percentage of voters happened to be members of any party at all. Even among those who might be nominally enrolled members only the fewest had any idea of what the party stood for. In a system where the people really voted more for a person—the leader or the candidate—and not for a party programme or policy, where parties lacked ideological clarity and organizational stability and where the people were getting more and more frustrated and disillusioned with the politics of slogans and grossly corrupt and decadent party establishments, it was highly questionable if the party-bonds should be given any constitutional recognition and rigidity. The Bill would have liked the legislators to be deemed bound to the party on whose label they won the election. It seemed to proceed on the preposterous and phoney assumption that the people elected lamp-posts of parties and not persons. It was true neither in law nor in practice. Inasmuch as under the scheme of our Constitution, the legislators represented their territorial constituencies and not political parties and neither the representatives nor the electorate seemed to take seriously any party principles or political ideology, etc., it could not be really contended that there was an unbreakable bond between the representative and the political party under whose banner he contested the election. The basic relationship really was between the legislator and the people whom he represented and not between him and his party. While he might belong to a political party, the party was no sacred cow, it could not be above the people. It was only a means and not an end.

- An analysis of the available empirical data showed that the single important factor responsible for defections causing instability in marginal-majority State governments had been the existence of a large number of independent legislators who occupied an eminent position—both qualitatively and quantitatively—as top actors in the game of seeking position and power through defection dynamics. The Committee on Defections was aware that 'not an inconsiderable part of the political instability can be directly or indirectly traced' to the role of independents and their attempts to bargain and balance between parties or combinations thereof.

However, the Bill left the independents completely out of the purview of the disqualification clauses. An independent was left free to vote as he liked to retain greater freedom of action and choice or to join any political party—even a party against whose candidate he may have won the election on an anti-party platform—with any motivation whatever, without incurring any disqualification.

Incidentally, in some cases, candidates were termed 'independents' merely because the parties to which they belonged were not recognized for purposes of allotment of separate symbols. Also, in cases where the candidate was really a no-party candidate, there was on his part a definite commitment of continuing 'independence' and of not changing his 'independent' label. After winning the election on an independent platform and against party candidates, if a person joined a political party, he was as much a defector as a party-man who resigned from the party to join another party or to become an 'independent' after being elected on its ticket.

To the extent that the independents were not covered, the provisions of the Bill were highly discriminatory and in effect, put a premium on legislators staying 'independent' or as members of smaller 'unrecognized' parties so as to be in a better position to bargain for personal benefits by manoeuvring the fall and formation of governments from outside the parties without losing their seats in the legislature.

Implied in the provisions of the Bill there was a distinction between defection by individuals and by groups inasmuch as group defections were often termed as party splits. The basic presumption behind the proposed distinction between individual and group defections seemed to be the belief that the latter were based on honest ideological differences or on disagreements on principles or policy and were not in any way motivated by considerations of personal gain in terms of money, office or power of patronage, etc.

A close examination of various splits in the political parties in India showed that the motivation behind party splits and bulk defections were often not very different from those that moved the individual defectors. The presumption of nobler intentions and of honourable differences thus being invalid, the distinction became merely so much balderdash. After all, whether it was one member who crossed the floor or it was a group of members, the nature and content of the act was the same. We could not dub an individual floor-crosser as a defector and disqualify him from membership while allowing a group to go scot-free under the cloak of a party split.

Actually, it was usually the group defections engineered by faction leaders which attempted to and often succeeded in toppling government with the defectors sharing the spoils amongst them. The party split was only an incidental by-product of defection politics. Out of the 1969 acts of defection, as many as 535 could be termed as group defections. In most of these cases, the groups involved were so sizable that one of the necessary consequences was the split of the party concerned.

Apart from the Congress split, prominent group defections were those leading to formation of the BKD in UP, Vishal Haryana Party in Haryana, Telengana United Front in Andhra Pradesh, Kerala Congress and the Indian Socialist Party in Kerala, Jan Kranti Dal, Soshit Dal and Loktantrik Congress in Bihar, Bangla Congress, People's Democratic Front and National Democratic Front in West Bengal, Janata Congress and Punjab Janata Party in Punjab, Jan Congress in Orissa and MP, Janata Party in Rajasthan and many others. In some cases of break-away splinter group defections, ideology or honest programmatic differences were the least significant motivations; in fact they were paraded merely as a cloak for the more real and relevant causes and motivations which were basically self-interest and power-oriented. Several defectors adorned the *gaddi* of the Chief Minister of their state following the splits or group defections led by them. With a few exceptions, the large number of defectors who seized other ministerships belonged to small or large groups of defectors. Except in situations of marginal majorities, it was relatively more difficult for a lone defector to bargain with an organized party.

Even where group defections as at the Centre were not followed by a change of government, it could not be said that the actors in the drama were moved by any considerations of higher principles and the like. They merely failed to achieve their ambitions and ends because of their political miscalculations and because of better tension management and more astute and courageous leadership by Smt Indira Gandhi. Thus, there was no justification for excluding group defections under the guise of splits from the operation of the disqualification clauses.

- It cannot be seriously denied that in a majority of cases, legislators defected and re-defected because of temptations of office, money or status or because of the denial of the same. The most important motivational force behind defections had by and large been prospects of political power and the lure of ministerial office. When over 200 defectors had been rewarded with ministerial *gaddis* and some 15 with Chief Ministerships, it was a pity that despite the categorical recommendation of the Chavan Committee no provision for debarring defectors from ministerial or other offices of profit found a place in the Bill.

  Disqualifying defectors from continuing as legislators without any provision for disqualifying them from ministerial or other offices of profit meant that under the existing provisions of the Bill, it was quite constitutional and legal for a defector to be appointed a minister for a period of up to six months or to bargain for some other more lasting office of profit. Thus, even at the risk of losing their seats, defectors could find the game of defection and of toppling governments profitable.

- The disqualification provisions appeared to be against the basic freedom of association and opinion guaranteed by the Fundamental Rights Chapter of the Constitution. The freedom of association and opinion did include the freedom of changing associations and opinions. Also, articles 105 and 194 guaranteed the freedom of speech and expression in the Houses of Legislatures at the Centre and in the States. Any legislation—even if it be a constitutional amendment—which restricted the freedom of choice or bound the vote of a legislator was clearly tantamount to tampering with the fundamentals of the Constitution and making a mockery of democracy.

- Disqualifying legislators on grounds of their defection from the party or a vote against the party was likely to lead to endless litigation involving Members of Parliament and State Legislatures and their conduct inside and outside their respective Houses. The procedures and proceedings of the Houses could become subject-matters of frequent questions and discussions in courts of law thereby bringing legislatures and the Judiciary into greater conflict and creating a situation where some legislators themselves might look to the courts for protection of their rights vis-à-vis legislatures.
- Lastly, any attempt to freeze the existing party position coming at a point of time when the ruling Congress commanded sweeping majorities at the Centre and in most of the States, was understandably likely to be misconstrued and viewed with suspicion by the Opposition parties. Also, under any objective assessment, taken as a whole, it seemed extremely doubtful whether the proposed constitutional amendment could prevent defections or serve any other useful purpose. The amendment bill in fact, was a remedy worse than the malady. It cold merely create the illusion of action without anything being really done to prevent unprincipled defections.

  Viewed from a broader perspective, defections themselves happened to be the outward trappings or superficial manifestations of a much deeper malaise eating into the vitals of our political culture and threatening the very system which we had so assiduously nurtured. Hypocrisy had become such an integral part of the character of the chief actors on the political stage that even repeated hammer-blows had little impact. What ailed the body politic was known; the remedies were also not unknown. What was lacking was the will or the desire to really do something.

Finally, the Constitution (32nd Amendment) Bill 1973 was referred to a Joint Committee of the two Houses. However, before the Committee could complete its deliberations, the Lok Sabha was dissolved and the Bill lapsed. Another Bill on the subject was introduced in the next Lok Sabha on 28 August 1978, but it was opposed at the stage of introduction itself both by some ruling party members and the Opposition as certain features of the Bill did not satisfy them. After some discussion, the motion for introduction of the Bill was withdrawn by leave of the House.

Anti-Defection Law and After

The two, 1973 and 1978, efforts to amend the Constitution to ban defections thus proved abortive. But, after the Congress Party was returned with large majority in December 1984, Prime Minister Rajiv Gandhi took the earliest opportunity to outlaw defections. The Constitution (52nd Amendment) Act popularly known as the Anti-defection Law was passed by both the Houses in January 1985. It received the President's assent on 15 February and came into force on 1 March 1985. It amended articles 101, 102 and 190 and 191 of the Constitution regarding vacation of seats and disqualification from membership of Parliament and the State Legislatures and added a new schedule (10th Schedule) to the Constitution setting out certain provisions as to disqualification on grounds of defection. The main provisions of the Schedule were as follows:

Para 2

(1) An elected member of Parliament or a State Legislature, who was elected as candidate set up by a political party and nominated member of Parliament or a State Legislature who was a member of a political party at the time he took his seat would be disqualified on the ground of defection if he voluntarily relinquished his membership of such political party or voted or abstained from voting in the House contrary to any direction of such party; (2) an independent member of Parliament or a State Legislature would be disqualified if he joined any

political party after his election; (3) a nominated member of Parliament of a State Legislature who was not a member of a political party at the time of his nomination and who had not become a member of any political party before the expiry of six months from the date on which he took his seat would be disqualified if he joined any political party after the expiry of the said period of six months.

Paras 3-4

No disqualification would be incurred where a member claimed that he belonged to a group representing a faction arising from a split in a party or merger of a party in another provided that in the event of a split the group consisted of not less than one-third of the members of the legislature party and in case of a merger of not less than two-thirds of the members of the legislature party concerned.

Para 5

No disqualification was incurred by a person elected to the office of the Speaker or the Deputy Speaker of the House of the People or of the Legislative Assembly of a State or to the office of the Deputy Chairman of the Council of States or the Chairman or the Deputy Chairman of the Legislative Council of a State, if he severed his connection with his political party.

Para 6

(1) The question as to whether a member of a House of Parliament or State Legislature had become subject to disqualification would be determined by the Chairman or the Speaker of the respective House; where the question was with reference to the Chairman or the Speaker himself it would be decided by a member of the concerned House elected by it in that behalf; notwithstanding anything in the Constitution, no court would have any jurisdiction in respect of any matter connected with the disqualification of a member of a House; and (2) all proceedings in relation to any question as to disqualification of a member of a House

under the Schedule would be deemed to be proceedings in Parliament within the meaning of article 122 or, proceedings in the Legislature of a State within the meaning of article 212.

Para 7

Notwithstanding anything in the Constitution, no court had any jurisdiction in respect of any matter connected with the disqualification of a member of a House.

Para 8

The Chairman or the Speaker of a House was empowered to make rules for giving effect to the provisions of the Schedule. The rules were required to be laid before the House and were subject to modifications/ disapproval by the House.

Even before the Anti-defection Law was passed by Parliament, as indicated earlier, serious doubts were expressed in regard to its constitutionality and advisability. Also, it was apprehended that legislative measures alone would not be an effective remedy against the malady of defections. Thus, treatises on the politics of defection published in 1969 and 1974 pointed out a number of politico-constitutional and legal grounds on which an anti-defection law could be questioned.[1] After the Anti-defection Law came into operation, it was criticized on several grounds, viz., that it was violative of the basic structure of the Constitution, that it was beyond the competence of Parliament and that it gave preference to expediency over principles.

The Supreme Court somehow upheld the validity of the 10th Schedule but found that there were legal infirmities in the passage of the Anti-defection Law inasmuch as the Constitution Amendment

---

1 Subhash C Kashyap, *Politics of Defection*, National, New Delhi, 1969 and *Politics of Power,* National, New Delhi, 1974.

Bill had not been ratified by the requisite number of State Assemblies before being presented for the President's assent. Also, the Speaker's functions under the 10th Schedule called for a judicial determination of issues under the law. The process of determining the question of disqualification could not be considered part of the proceedings of the House and as such not amenable to judicial review. The Supreme Court struck down Para 7 of the Schedule barring the jurisdiction of Courts and declared that while operating under the Anti-defection Law, the Speaker was in the position of a tribunal and therefore, his decisions like those of all tribunals were subject to judicial review.[2]

Intriguingly, the number of defections at the Union and State levels during the 10 years (1985-1995) far exceeded the total number of defections during the three decades preceding the enactment of the anti-defection law. Several Governments were formed and brought down through the operation of the politics of defection during the 10 years of the operation of the law.[3]

At the level of the States, some of the things that happened were bizarre, to say the least. Notwithstanding the Anti-defection Law, some of the Governments, *inter alia*, in Nagaland, Mizoram, Tamil Nadu, Pondicherry, Manipur, Goa, Sikkim and Meghalaya were brought down through defections. There were problems under the Anti-defection Law in several other States as well, as in Madhya Pradesh, Gujarat, Bihar, Andhra Pradesh, Kerala, UP, Punjab, Himachal Pradesh, Haryana and Arunachal Pradesh. No particular party could be blamed, as they all behaved according to a very similar pattern. The irresponsible manner in which the Speakers and the Governors exercised their powers brought disgrace to their high offices and sometimes led to the brink of open confrontation with the judiciary.

---

2 Kihoto Hollohan vs Zachillhu and others, 1992 Supp(2) SCC 65.

3 Subhash C Kashyap, *Anti-Defection Law and Parliamentary Privileges*, Tripathi, Bombay, 1995 (2nd edition, Universal, New Delhi, 2003)

27

The Emergency Aberration

The founding fathers of our Constitution felt that extraordinary situations could arise under which it might not be possible for the normal scheme of the Constitution to function and it might become necessary to suspend the operation of certain parts or provisions to protect the independence and the security of the nation and to safeguard the Constitution and the democratic system. Dr Ambedkar claimed that the Indian federation, unlike any other federation, in times of emergency, could convert itself into an entirely unitary State. The position was upheld by the Supreme Court in *Gulam Sarwar vs Union of India* (AIR 1967 SC 1335).

Briefly, the Emergency provisions of the Constitution envisage two kinds of emergencies: (i) a National Emergency under article 352 due to threat of war, external aggression or armed rebellion, and (ii) Financial Emergency under article 360.

The provisions of Article 352 were made more stringent in 1978-79 by the Constitution (44th Amendment) Act, 1978 which came into effect from 20 June 1979. This was done after the sad experience of the Emergency declared on 25 June 1975 on grounds of 'internal disturbance'. To prevent the misuse of emergency provisions, the words 'armed rebellion' were substituted for 'internal disturbance', a written communication of the decision by the Union Cabinet was made an essential pre-condition for the issue of a Proclamation by the President, and the entire procedure for emergency provisions was streamlined to ensure dependence on approval of Parliament, particularly of the Lok Sabha.

There have been three proclamations of National Emergency in India. The first emergency was proclaimed in October 1962 at the time of the Chinese aggression. The second emergency was declared on 3rd December 1971 in the wake of the Pakistani aggression. The war with Pakistan culminated in the unconditional surrender of the West Pakistan forces in Bangladesh. The Prime Minister informed the Lok Sabha that the instrument of surrender was signed in Dacca at 16.31 hours (IST) on 16 December 1971 by Lt Gen AAK Niazi on behalf of Pakistan Eastern command. Lt Gen Jagjit Singh Aurora, GOC-in-C of the Indian and Bangladesh forces in the Eastern Theatre accepted the surrender and Dacca was then the free capital of a free country. There was prolonged applause and acclaim in the Lok Sabha. It was a moment of the greatest glory for Indira Gandhi's personal leadership.

Both these Emergencies—the first and the second—on grounds of external aggression were widely accepted as fully justified. It was, however the third Emergency proclaimed in June 1975 that was considered as the greatest affront to parliamentary institutions and the worst aberration in India's parliamentary history affecting the prestige and functioning of Parliament.

Loknayak Jayaprakash Narayan, the popular Sarvodaya leader—a staunch socialist turned Gandhian—and the most prominent hero of the 1942 'Quit India' movement, had launched in March-April 1974 an agitation against corruption and in support of electoral, educational and other reforms. Although his movement was professedly non-violent, he was reported to have suggested early in 1975 that at some future date he might have to call upon the armed forces to revolt.

A number of prominent Congress Party members of Parliament including Mohan Dharia, Chandra Shekhar and Krishan Kant, openly expressed their sympathy for JP's movement and advocated that Indira Gandhi should enter into a dialogue with him. However, she rejected this suggestion and felt that a conspiracy was being hatched to dislodge her from power and find another leader for the party.

Elections for the State Assembly were held in Gujarat on 8 and 11 June 1975 after a period of 16 months of President's rule introduced in February 1974 and extended twice. No party or group of parties succeeded in winning an absolute majority; the Congress obtained 40 per cent of the votes and 75 of the 182 seats. Further, the elections to the Rajya Sabha from Gujarat resulted in two seats being won by the Janata Front and one by the Congress. All this was considered a severe blow to the Congress and to Mrs Gandhi's supremacy.

Almost simultaneously with the Congress setback in the Gujarat elections came the ruling of the Allahabad High Court on 12 June 1975 declaring null and void Mrs Gandhi's election to the Lok Sabha and disqualifying her from contesting election to either House of Parliament for a period of six years. The judgement quite naturally strengthened the momentum of opposition to her leadership even though the judge had granted her a 20-day stay of his order to allow her to appeal to the Supreme Court. According to both Indian and foreign sources, after the ruling, Mrs Gandhi considered resigning the premiership while awaiting the Supreme Court's verdict on appeal. She was dissuaded from doing so by her senior colleagues.

Supreme Court judge, Justice VR Krishna Iyer, heard on 23 June 1975, Mrs Gandhi's application for an absolute stay order, which would allow her to retain both her seat in Parliament and the premiership until the Supreme Court had heard her appeal. His order, issued on the following day, granted her a conditional stay, allowing her to retain the premiership and to address Parliament in that capacity, but not to vote in Parliament or to draw her salary as a member.

A meeting of leaders of opposition parties, other than the CPI which stood with Mrs Gandhi, was held on 25 June 1975. Jayaprakash

Narayan was present when it was decided to launch a week's civil disobedience campaign on 29 June 1975 in support of their demand for Mrs Gandhi's resignation. On the same evening, JP publicly announced the decision of launching the civil disobedience campaign. Accusing Mrs Gandhi of leading the country towards dictatorship, he appealed to the people to be prepared to refuse to pay taxes, to court arrest and to go to prison. In his appeal to the army and the police he was reported to have said: "Government servants should not obey any unjust orders. The military's responsibility is to protect Indian democracy; their duty is to protect the Constitution. The police are trained to act blindly; they should also think. Have they no self-respect, or are they there just for the sake of bread..."

Shortly after dawn on 26 June 1975, a proclamation under clause (1) of Article 352 of the Constitution was issued by President Ahmed declaring that "a grave emergency exists whereby the security of India is threatened by internal disturbance". Although the state of Emergency proclaimed on 3 December 1971 at the outbreak of war with Pakistan was still in force, it was considered necessary to proclaim a second simultaneous state of Emergency based on the alleged threat to internal security. This was the first time in 25 years (since the commencement of the Constitution) that a state of Emergency was declared on the ground of a threat to national security from internal disturbance. Mass arrests followed. 'Extremist' organizations were banned. Extraordinary powers were assumed by the government under several laws and constitutional amendments. There was severe criticism of the misuse of powers. Opposition leaders linked the declaration of a fresh emergency on 25 June 1975 with the Allahabad High Court's decision. Six Congress Members of Parliament who had not attended the meetings of the parliamentary party which reaffirmed their faith in Mrs Gandhi's leadership—Mohan Dharia, Chandra Shekhar, Ram Dhan, Krishan Kant, T Lakshmi Kanthamma and SN Mishra were suspended from party membership on 26 June 1975. Dharia, Kant and Mrs Kanthamma were expelled from the party on 8 August.

Press Censorship: Press Censorship was introduced on 26 June 1975 for the first time since India became independent, newspapers being forbidden to publish inter alia reports which affected India's relations with foreign countries, denigrated the institution of Prime Minister; might cause disaffection among members of the armed forces or public servants, or might bring the Government into hatred or contempt. Several leading Delhi newspapers did not appear on 26-27 June 1975. This was officially attributed to a power failure in the street where they were published, but it was unofficially reported that the power lines leading to their offices and also to that of *The Motherland* (Jan Sangh daily), which was published in another street, had been cut during the night of 25-26 June. *The Statesman* and *The Hindustan Times,* which had appeared on 26 June, suffered from a similar 'power failure' at their Delhi offices on the following day. The papers resumed publication on 28 June, with the exception of *The Motherland*, which was closed down because it refused to abide by the censorship regulations.

Vidya Charan Shukla was appointed Minister of State for Information and Broadcasting (in independent charge of his portfolio) on 28 June 1975 vice Inder Kumar Gujral, who took over the former's previous post of Minister of State for Planning. Warning editors against attempts to elude the censorship, Shukla told them on 2 July that the Government's measures were 'irreversible' and that 'the press, like everyone else, will just have to live with them'. He warned all foreign correspondents in New Delhi that they would be liable to expulsion if they failed to submit their dispatches or broadcast scripts for censorship. Even the publication of parliamentary proceedings by newspapers was subjected to prior censorship.

Despite some bitter criticism by some opposition members, the two Houses of Parliament approved the proclamation of Emergency by large majorities. But, in the general elections that followed, the ruling Congress (I) under the leadership of Indira Gandhi lost and a Janata Party Government was formed. It was the Constitution (44th Amendment) Act, 1978 which confined the suspension of article

19 only to situations of war or external aggression, and enunciated that freedoms under article 19 could not be taken away. Also, the same amendment laid down that under no circumstances could the enforcement of rights under articles 20 and 21 be denied even during an Emergency.

Several cases involving Emergency provisions were decided by the Supreme Court before the 1978 amendment. These dealt with matters arising during periods of the first and second Emergencies proclaimed in 1962 and 1971. The Court upheld the Presidential order suspending the right of a citizen to move the court to enforce the provisions of articles 21 and 22 (*Mohan Chowdhury vs Chief Commissioner*, AIR 1964 SC 173). In *Makhan Singh vs State of Punjab* (AIR 1964 SC 381) the Court tried to balance the Fundamental Rights of the Citizens with the Emergency provisions and the needs of the security of the State. While conceding that if national security is in peril, individual rights must give way to the state, the Court said:

> "How long the Proclamation of Emergency should continue and what restrictions should be imposed on the Fundamental Rights of citizens during the pendency of the emergency, are matters which must inevitably be left to the executive because the executive knows the requirements of the situation and the effect of compulsive factors which operate during periods of grave crises."

But, the court also held that it had the power to judge and examine the validity of emergency legislation under which persons were detained with *mala fide* intentions or under excessive delegation of powers to the Executive. In another case, the Court upheld the validity of the statute which invested the Executive with drastic powers and observed that the power to detain without trial was basically an Executive act not subject to judicial review (*Sadhu Singh vs Delhi Administration*, AIR 1966 SC 91). In *State of Maharashtra vs Prabhakar Pandurang Sanzgiri* (AIR 1966 SC 424), the Court upheld the liberty of a detenu to send his book outside the jail for publication since there was no nexus between the Government order preventing it and the purpose of the enforcement of Emergency rules. The stand was reiterated in *K Ananda Nambiar vs Chief Secretary* (AIR 1966 SC 657) where Justice Gajendragadkar asserted that even during the operation of emergency, in considering the effect of a Presidential order suspending the enforcement of fundamental rights, the order should be strictly construed in favour of the citizens's fundamental rights. In *Ram Manohar Lohia vs State of Bihar* (AIR 1966 SC 740), it was held that the order of detention must *prima facie* be proper, that 'maintenance of law and order' could not be equated with 'maintenance of public order' and that action under the Defence of India Rules would be valid only if taken in the 'interests of public order' and not merely 'in aid of law and order'. While protecting the paramount interest of the security of the State during Emergency, citizen's rights to freedom could not be taken away without the existence of justifying necessity specified in Defence of India Rules. On this ground, the Court declared a detention 'clearly and plainly *mala fide*' (*G Sadanandan vs State of Kerala*, AIR 1966 SC 1925). In *PL Lakhanpal vs Union of India* (AIR 1967 SC 1507), the Supreme Court overruled the decision in the *Sandhu Singh* case and held that principles of natural justice should apply to the decision to review an order of detention. The Court went further in *State of Madhya Pradesh vs Bharat Singh* (AIR 1967 SC 1170) when it said:

> "All executive action which operates to the prejudice of any person must have the authority of law to support it, and the terms of Article 358 do not detract from that rule... article 358 does not purport to invest the State with arbitrary authority to take action to the prejudice of citizens and others: it merely provides that so long as the Proclamation of Emergency subsists, laws may be enacted and executive action may be taken in pursuance of lawful authority, which if the provisions of Article 19 were operative would have been invalid."

In *Mohd Yayub vs State of J&K* (AIR 1968 SC 765), the Supreme Court clearly observed that there was no scope for judicial review to find out any nexus between exercise of power under article 359 and security of India in view of the suspension of the enforcement of Fundamental Rights in the interests of the security of the State by the President. In *Bhut Nath vs State of West Bengal* (AIR 1974 SC 806) also, the Court declined to hold the continuance of emergency void. Justice Iyer said that the argument that there was no real emergency fell outside the orbit of judicial control. The position was reiterated in *Collector of Hyderabad vs Ibrahim and Co.* (AIR 1975 SC 1275). The Court said:

> "The executive order immune from attack is only that order which the State was competent, but for the provisions contained in article 19, to make. Executive action… which is otherwise invalid is not immune from attack, merely because a Proclamation of Emergency is in operation when it is taken."

There appeared to be a considerable shift in the approach of the Supreme Court to cases of violation of Fundamental Rights vis-à-vis emergency provisions arising during the Proclamation of internal Emergency (1975-1977). Thus, in the *Habeas Corpus* case, the Court refused to interfere in matters of detention of persons as it believed that the intention was to keep preventive detention controlled exclusively by the executive. Detenus could not move any court for the writ of *habeas corpus* if a *prima facie* valid detention order existed (*Additional District Magistrate vs Shivkant Shukla*, AIR 1976 SC 1207).

In *Union of India vs Bhanudas* (AIR 1977 SC 1027) again, the Court held that all rights of personal liberty under articles 19, 21 and 22 could be suspended during national Emergency due to Presidential Orders under article 359. Most of these Court verdicts lost validity after the 44th amendment inter alia amended article 352, 358 and 359.

In the *Minerva Mills* case, it was held that the judiciary could act if it was established that the Union Government acted *mala fide* or on irrelevant or no facts. The remedy otherwise could be only political. A matter like the satisfaction of the President was beyond the Court. Only if it was shown that there was, in fact, no satisfaction at all, or the satisfaction was absurd, perverse or *mala fide*, the exercise of power would be unconstitutional. Courts could certainly act under their power of limited judicial review in such a case (*Minerva Mills vs Union of India*, AIR 1980 SC 1789).

The years of Mrs Gandhi's Prime Ministership will probably be remembered most for the aberration of the imposition of internal Emergency and some bitter pills of authoritarian legislation and administrative excesses in implementation. The period however was significantly eventful in many other ways and left certain indelible imprints on Indian policy. War with Pakistan was won most decisively. Bangladesh was liberated. Gracious and triumphant in victory, India signed the Simla Agreement with Pakistan. Sikkim became an integral part of the Union of India. The far-reaching Indo-Soviet Treaty of Friendship was signed. After Independence in 1947 perhaps the moment of highest glory in Indian history was when on 16 December 1971 amidst deafening cheers and unprecedented scenes of enthusiasm in Parlimant, Mrs Gandhi announced the surrender of nearly hundred thousand strong armed forces of Pakistan before an Indian General in Dacca and the emergence of Bangladesh as a fully sovereign nation. Mrs Gandhi's personal leadership rose to the greatest heights and also fell to the lowest levels. If the resounding victory over Pakistan in the 1971 War was the high mark of her leadership, the second year of the Emergency was the low level which left her politically in near isolation. Praised and lauded as Goddess Durga and Shakti and as India's pride in the first year of the fifth Lok Sabha, she was also to earn disdain as the villain in the forced sterilizations during the last year.

28

Succession in Prime Minister's Office

Remembering Rajiv Gandhi*

When on the night of 21 May 1991, I heard the unbelievable from a friend's telephone, the instinctive reaction was to rush to 10 Janpath. On reaching there, I remembered how one morning only about a month earlier, Rajivji had received me there despite his terribly busy schedule and with literally thousands waiting for him outside. He was as usual, very affectionate and friendly. His sweet words, "*Kashyapji, kaise hain*" still ring in my ears. I had gone primarily to present to him two of my latest books with which he was somewhat connected. He had himself contributed a valuable 'Foreword' to the first book, *The Political System and Institution Building under Jawaharlal Nehru* and the second book was written at the instance of Mrs Indira Gandhi, who had personally gone through its detailed synopsis and made extensive comments. The title of the book *History of Parliamentary Democracy—From the Earliest Times to the End of the Nehru Era* was inspired by Rajivji himself. I returned from the meeting satisfied and happy.

---

* First published in *The Financial Express,* 2 June 1991 soon after late Rajiv Gandhi's tragic demise.

I was very pleasantly surprised therefore, when in the afternoon I received a telephone call from Rajivji's Secretary as a follow-up to the meeting and asking me to rush a note to him by the same evening. I was told that Rajivji was considering me for contesting a seat for Lok Sabha from a Delhi Constituency. As if meeting with exemplary courtesy and without prior appointment was not enough, the follow-up telephone touched me to the depths of my heart.

On that tragic 21 May night, standing in front of 10 Janpath, my mind also went back to another gruesome day in our history when shots were fired at Mrs Indira Gandhi. Having been in the special plane that brought Rajivji from Calcutta to Delhi, I was a witness to his being an embodiment of tremendous poise, superhuman equanimity and unique dignity throughout those moments of extreme anxiety followed by deep anguish, shock and sorrow. When the sad news of Mrs Gandhi being no more was finally conveyed from the cockpit, the gloom that descended was too stunning for words. The senior leaders present, however, soon realized that the country had to continue and that they had a serious responsibility to discharge at that critical moment. The dignitaries and top national figures aboard the plane included the Speaker, Dr Bal Ram Jakhar, Mr Uma Shankar Dixit, Mr Pranab Mukherji, Mr Abdul Ghani Khan Choudhry and Mrs Sheela Dixit. When at the instance of Dr Jakhar, I had to explain some points to Rajivji, he heard me with great patience and courtesy. The question was whether under the Constitution, Rajivji could be sworn in as the Prime Minister right away or only after the 13 days' mourning was over and formalities of election were completed with the senior most Minister acting as PM in the interim. In all fairness to him, Rajiv Gandhi himself seemed to agree that it was necessary to wait for 13 days, not realizing that if he did not take over at once, he might not have been allowed to become Prime Minister by the 'senior' after 13 days of mourning. A senior minister very categorically and strongly asserted the view that immediately the senior-most minister had to take over. In fact, he almost shouted in disagreement when it was pointed out that so far as the Constitution was concerned, the

President could appoint anyone right away as the Prime Minister if in his judgement the appointee was the one most likely to win the confidence of the House of the People. There was no constitutional requirement of prior election as the leader of majority party etc. This was countered by saying that the conventions were very clear, twice earlier in case of the death of the Prime Minister (Nehru and Shastri) the senior-most Cabinet Minister GL Nanda had taken over. At the end, with remarkable modesty, Rajivji said very softly—almost in my ear—that he did not much understand all those constitutional points. Putting his hand on my shoulder, he added that Dixitji was a senior man and understood all these things better and if he (Dixitji) was convinced then he (Rajivji) would also agree. Much else that happened on the flight is better left unsaid. I was happy to be able to convince Dixitji with the help of the text of the Constitution which Mrs Sheela Dixit was able to produce from her purse. The rest is history but I can still feel Rajivji's hand on my shoulder.

Charming

My earliest remembrance of Rajivji is of seeing him in Washington DC sometime in 1966 when he and Sanjay accompanied Mrs Gandhi to the United States probably from London. In his early twenties, he was handsome and charming and gave the impression of being a jolly happy-go-lucky young man. Next I once saw—only saw—him at 1, Akbar Road in jeans and shirt, most unassumingly walking in and out and making some enquiries from the senior staff around. I believe it was soon after Mrs Gandhi had resumed the Prime Ministership of the country.

I remember how during a visit to Trinity College at Cambridge, we were thrilled to see the signatures of two of our Prime Ministers—Jawaharlal Nehru and Rajiv Gandhi in the Admission Register of the College. Both of them had been students there and we were proud to have met at lunch the professor who had been Rajivji's tutor.

When after a stint as an international civil servant in Geneva, I joined as Secretary-General of Lok Sabha, Rajivji was a Member of Lok Sabha. He sat almost in the middle of the House facing the Speaker. It was, therefore, impossible to miss him from the table. His interventions in debates were few and far between but he had already made two very powerful speeches on the need for social change and development strategy.

My mind goes back to the day when the customary group photograph for the Seventh Lok Sabha members was being taken. There was a little scramble among senior leaders for chairs as usual. When Rajivji passed near me, almost instinctively and out of natural courtesy, I offered to him my seat in the front row. But a stickler to rules of propriety, he politely declined and as a first-term member, he gracefully decided to stand in the fifth row instead. Such of course, is the stuff of which real eminence is made.

Mature

As Prime Minister during his very first year, Rajivji gave remarkable evidence of having matured fast. His performance in the House was superb and worthy of a seasoned parliamentarian. It was a delight to hear him make his points with sweet reasonableness. He spoke well, sought the cooperation of all and was willing to listen to the voice and views of others. An example of bonhomie: Prime Minister Rajiv Gandhi once told the Lok Sabha, "We also have promised that we will carry the opposition with us. And I am happy to say, Sir, that we carried almost all the opposition with us. There are one or two exceptions." Prof Madhu Dandavate was quick to retort, "We have promised that we will carry the Government with us."

It was unfortunate that roughly after a year something seemed to have gone wrong. Suddenly, the climate in the House changed. Some very unkind things were said about him. His own style also changed. But despite the misinformation campaign and stories about his inaccessibility and temper, it must be said that even in moments of heat, anger and acrimony in the debates, Rajiv's famous smile, poise and balance never left him. If anything, his wit became sharper and he began to excel in repartees. An example: Prime Minister Rajiv Gandhi said, "You can see the strength of our party in front of you". Mr HM Patel remarked, "Looking ahead". Rajiv then said, "I am looking ahead. You will see in 1990... We will be occupying even that row." Prof Madhu Dandavate pointing upwards interjected. "It is because after some years, we will go to that 'Upper House'". Quick came the Prime Minister's retort: "Sir, we are not in a hurry to send him to that 'Upper House'. But, we are glad that he acknowledges that the Congress will be replacing the Opposition Leaders (even) on those benches, when they leave."

Again, a question arose whether solar energy could provide strength and sustenance to the Government or the Opposition? Prof Dandavate asked Prime Minister Rajiv Gandhi in the Lok Sabha if it was a fact that in 1981 an aeroplane fuelled entirely by solar energy crossed the English Channel successfully and if so, on the basis of the experience gained, if the government would explore the possibility of successfully using the solar energy for flying aeroplanes. When Mr Gandhi confirmed that a plane did cross the English Channel, Prof Dandavate quipped: "Solar energy is so powerful that the entire Government can be run on it". However, Mr Gandhi shot back: "We can help the opposition with solar energy. They can go and sit outside."

Amiable

Also, in personal behaviour, he always remained most unassuming, amiable and sweet. He had an open mind and he could be convinced by reason. I remember once he was to speak in Lok Sabha in regard to a certain matter. He was already in the House and the Speaker was in his chair. It was found that if he spoke, rules required that various group leaders be allowed to speak. A bitter and unpleasant controversy was likely to emerge. When the position was explained to Rajivji on a chit that I sent to him, he had hurried consultations with a couple of his colleagues and conveyed his agreement not to speak, by a nod of his head. Perhaps an ugly situation was saved. The only person, I learnt later, who was perhaps sorry was the one who had worked on the draft for him until very late hours on the previous night.

Once when Rajiv during a fierce debate used a certain expression meaning 'untrue', the Speaker ordered it to be expunged as unparliamentary. While some Congress members protested at Prime Minister's words being expunged, Rajiv Gandhi himself most gracefully accepted the expunction. Also, there were occasions when the Government or the Prime Minister would like certain things to be done but which could not be permitted under the rules. While smaller ministers would be insistent and sometimes even angry at their wish not being respected, Rajiv Gandhi always accepted the position that if something was impermissible under the rules, it just could not be done.

I remember once at one of the luncheon meetings, during informal conversation, I mentioned to the Prime Minister a matter that had got inordinately delayed by a few months because the file was said to be in his office. He was most surprised and sorry and said that it could not be so as he was himself most anxious that that matter was expedited in public interest. He immediately asked the Minister in PMO who was present, to pursue the case which she did. Within a few days, there was a meeting with the Prime Minister, Speaker, concerned ministers and others present and the things were sorted out. Incidentally, I also recall the experience of seeing extreme forms of yesmanship in action with everyone trying to accept every word that the PM uttered as gospel truth and nobody really helping him in taking a decision. He, on his part, however, wanted to hear genuine reactions, new ideas and views that were different. I must say that he listened to disagreement with respect.

During the period that I was Secretary General Lok Sabha, one of the duties discharged by me was the returning officer for the presidential election. The Congress candidate was R Venkataraman, the electoral process was full of controversies and apprehensions. After the conclusion of the election, at a casual meeting I mentioned about the election and suggested the need for some reform in the process of the election, Rajivji asked for a full note. (See the chapter 'Electing the President')

Humble and Compassionate

Above everything, Rajivji was very human. At one of the dinners to which he had invited my wife and I, he noticed that a senior cabinet minister and I were wishing each other with a friendly embrace. He walked to us. The minister was somewhat embarrassed and immediately explained that we were old university pals and were meeting after a long gap. Rajivji laughed most heartily and remarked towards the minister. "Now, I know why you exercise such a clout in Parliament." At another dinner, when I told Rajivji that my wife was a great admirer and wanted to see him from near, he laughed, immediately introduced her to Mrs Sonia Gandhi and said: "*Kashyapji to hum sabko house mein guide karte hain.*" He was indeed so sweet, kind and human.

I am reminded of another party at which my son was introduced to Rajivji by the host. This young man of the new generation, quite uninhibited and oblivious of the fact that he was before the Prime Minister of the country started explaining to him at length some ideas about planning strategies and processes in India not taking into account in their projections the role and impact of the fast changing technological inputs. From a distance, I could see that Rajivji was giving him a patient hearing and at the end of it all he simply told my son in a very friendly tone, "That is precisely what I have myself been telling these people but they do not seem to appreciate". He invited the young man to see him some time. This would have surely won the heart of any youth for ever.

I recall the day in Lok Sabha when soon after the House was adjourned, as I stood up to leave, no less a person than the Prime Minister himself walked over to the Secretary-General's seat at the head of the table of the House. While I looked at him with some surprise and anxiety as if to ask if something had gone wrong or whether there were some instructions from the Leader of the House, he gave me another of those lovely smiles and said that he was just wanting to see out of curiosity as to what all was there on the Secretary-General's table to enable him to function as he did and more particularly the mechanism for communicating with the chair during the sittings of the House. Such was the sweet child-like simplicity we shall always miss.

Opposition Leader

When he ceased to be Prime Minister and was Leader of the Opposition or later still only leader of the Congress Parliamentary Party, there were occasions when on some constitutional issues I was asked to give my objective analysis and views, I was told these were required by Rajivji. I do not know how many of them were actually asked for by Rajivji himself, or if any of them reached him at all. But, I did learn that in the matter of the position of the Leader of the Opposition, several experts had insisted that he could continue as such even after pledging full support to the Chandra Shekhar Government. When I advised otherwise, he did not frown at me but appreciated my candid and well-argued view that he could not continue as the Leader of the Opposition because by definition, Leader of the Opposition must be from the opposition and his party was not in opposition but stood in support of the Government. Not only did he accept the position but also offered to vacate 10 Janpath which was allotted to him as the Leader of the Opposition.

What is now left of this most handsome man on the Indian political scene are only memories. Some of the humble souls like mine can treasure and cherish them only within our bosoms. May his soul rest in peace and may his rich legacy help us to build a united nation, an integrated society and a better tomorrow.

29

Minority Government on Congress Crutches

Gowda as Prime Minister

Sometimes what appear to be serious Constitutional crises have their source in matters of purely personal ambitions and private concerns of politicians. A 13-Party United Front minority government headed by HD Deve Gowda of the Janata Dal was formed on 1 June 1996 with the outside support of the Congress Party. The experiment, however was short-lived.

There appeared some sudden signs of descending darkness at noon in the Gowda camp on 30 March 1997. Congress President, Sitaram Kesari, had finally thrown a bombshell by announcing the withdrawal of Congress support from the minority United Front Government. There were widespread rumours of the imminent fall of the Gowda Government. Kesri staked his own claim to be called upon to form a new Congress-led Government. Under the circumstances, the ideal thing for Gowda would have been to himself offer to seek the confidence of the House by having a sitting of the House the very next day. Since the Lok Sabha was sitting and only on recess, a sitting could be called by the Speaker at hours' notice. In the absence of such an initiative by Gowda, the President had to act. Obviously, he was well advised when he decided to leave the question of the loss of majority support to be determined on the floor of the Lok Sabha. In doing so, Dr Shankar Dayal Sharma acted with the utmost alacrity and sagacity. He asked Gowda to seek a fresh vote of confidence and prove majority support by 11 April.

Several constitutional issues were being raised in the official fora, political parties and media. Perhaps, there was some overplay of a sense of crisis situation. The United Front, after the initial shock reactions, appeared to be in a somewhat conciliatory mood and requested the Congress to reconsider the decision to withdraw support. Initiatives for peace talks and negotiations for mutual accommodation were taken up at various levels by individuals and groups in both the camps.

Peace-makers and mediators tried to identity the issues that queered the pitch between Gowda and Kesri. It was an indicator of the depths to which we had fallen that the intelligentsia, the ordinary citizens and even the politicians themselves, in private conversation, freely talked about the real issues involved being entirely different from those given out to the public. There was no relationship or similarity between the public and private faces of actors in the political arena.

Politics and public life were getting murkier every day. The matters of the greatest personal concern to politicians both in the Congress and the UF were the allegations of various kinds of criminal and other offences like bribery, forgery, conspiracy, murder, tax evasion, FERA violations etc. Sometimes these were used to blackmail political opponents and make them fall in line.

Police enquiries and/or CBI investigations were going on in a number of cases and some of these were expected to come to a head soon. It was not unnatural, in fact it was quite human for those involved to want that the pressure on them be eased somehow. To ensure this, they needed to have a friendly government and an administration that was not hostile to their interests. Also, there were those who harboured personal ambitions of reaching some high offices in the polity or of continuing and prospering in them if they were already there. Interests of all such eminent men, irrespective of their party labels, had to be protected and accommodated.

Therefore, any solution that was finally worked out to get out of the impasse had to address itself to these more mundane matters. Issues of constitutional provisions and principles, party ideologies, secularism, national interest, etc., were largely for public consumption only. These were used to camouflage and mask the more concrete personal interests or problems, calling for bargaining, mutual give and take, adjustment and the like. The issues to be settled had nothing to do with ideological, programmatic or even political differences. The bargaining was to revolve round two major items, viz., (i) the sharing of offices of President, Vice-President and Ministers between the Congress and UF partners and (ii) the official approach to the then on-going police enquiries, CBI investigations and court proceedings in criminal cases against politicians, ministers and legislators of rival parties both at the Union and State levels. The number of the worthies involved was already very large. In case of one major party, as many as over 100 members were threatened with action.

In any healthy democratic polity, those in power should not use the machinery of the State—particularly the law enforcement and investigative agencies—for purposes of settling scores with the rivals in politics, parties or persons, or for bringing them round to submission through official blackmail. On the other hand, it is equally wrong for any party or person to try to threaten the Government with 'operation-topple', only in order to seek an indefinite moratorium on the processes of law or to escape prosecution and punishment for the crimes committed.

In the very nature of things, the points of agreement between the United Front and Congress leadership were likely to lack transparency. They had to be arrived at behind the scenes and a strategy had to be worked out to enable every party to present before the people and its own party workers a sellable public face.

So far as constitutional position was concerned, it was quite clear that the President had to appoint the Prime Minister and the other

Ministers on the advice of the Prime Minister. After the Council of Ministers was so constituted, it was collectively responsible only to Lok Sabha. Therefore, the question of its having or losing the confidence of the house was entirely a matter between the Government and the Lok Sabha.

There were under the Rules of Procedure of the Lok Sabha several procedural devices for expressing lack of confidence in the Government of the day. There was a specific provision for a no-confidence motion which could be brought up by any member almost at any time. There was no provision either in the Constitution or in the Rules of Procedure for any 'confidence motion' as such. A practice had, however, developed of the President asking the Prime Minister to seek a vote of confidence when he was not the leader of an assured majority in the House at the time of appointment or when he ceased to be so as a result of subsequent developments.

When a motion expressing confidence in the Government was received, it was covered by and treated under only the general rules for the admission and consideration of ordinary motions. While the practice was unfortunate and an affront to the dignity of the occupant of the office of Prime Minister, it was certainly an improvement on the President involving himself in receiving and verifying lists of supporters of competing claimants for the Prime Ministerial chair, allowing signature campaigns or parades of legislators for head counts and the like.

The sitting members of the Lok Sabha, irrespective of their party affiliations, did not want to undergo the risks and travails of a mid-term poll. Also, the United Front Government could hardly survive without the Congress support and the Congress could not hope to have a say or share in power without the support of partners. These compulsions could bring about some rapprochement in mutual interest. If this happened before 11 April, the spectre of a showdown on that day could be averted.

A question that was being asked was what would happen if no compromise was arrived at. Once Gowda was convinced of losing the confidence vote, he could himself then submit to the President resignation of his Government and advise the President to dissolve the House as Shri Charan Singh had done. The advice under the circumstances could not however be binding on the President who would have to use his own discretion to decide whether to explore the possibilities of an alternative Government before going again to the electorate in a general election. In fact, the situation would be substantially the same if Gowda lost on a vote and then resigned.

The President could take the view that the BJP as the single largest party was first accorded an opportunity to try to form its government. Its Government lasted only 13 days. The other parties also thereafter had an opportunity. The 13 parties in the United Front had formed a coalition Government with the Congress promising support from outside. Thus, all the parties had been tried and the only legitimate course left was to dissolve the House and order fresh elections. In the alternative, the President could decide to start the process of Government formation all over again and first invite the BJP as the single largest party to form a government followed by the Congress, the second largest party. Still, it was also entirely likely that after the Gowda Government was defeated or resigned, new political alignments emerged and determined the shape of things to come. The President would have to use his discretion and take a decision in his wisdom on whether to dissolve the House and order fresh elections or to explore possibilities of forming an alternative government.

Be that as it may, the other constitutional issues being raised were: (i) what would happen to the Presidential election if the House was dissolved; and (ii) could the Budget be passed without being affected by the current controversy between the Congress and the United Front and would there be a constitutional crisis if it was not passed?

Articles 52-62 of the Constitution concern the office of the President. The President is to be elected by an electoral college consisting of the elected members of the Lok Sabha, Rajya Sabha and State Assemblies. The term of the office is five years. Election for the new President must be held before the term of the incumbent expires.

It has been held in an Advisory opinion that the election cannot be postponed or invalidated on the ground of the electoral college not being complete or fully constituted.

Therefore, strictly legally, it may be possible to hold Presidential election even after the dissolution of Lok Sabha. However, holding Presidential election without the 543 Lok Sabha members would be most untenable and a violation of propriety in the election of the head of the State. It would, therefore, be necessary either to dissolve Lok Sabha only after holding the Presidential election or to complete general elections to Lok Sabha expeditiously so that the Presidential election could follow and get completed by July when the President's term expired. In any case, no serious constitutional crisis was likely to arise because the Constitution also clearly lays down that even after the expiration of his term, the incumbent President would continue to hold office until his successor took over.

As for the Budget, a Vote on Account for two months, that is, up to the end of May had already been taken. If a change of Government took place or general elections were to be held, it would be perfectly admissible to seek another Vote on Account for a further period of say two months, June and July. Thereafter, the new Government could get the Budget including the Demands for Grants, the Appropriation and Finance Bills, etc., passed with any modifications and improvements that it may deem necessary in keeping with its policies.

The Budget had to be passed by the House and not by the Government, strictly technically, therefore, it could still be discussed and voted with the agreement of parties while the Gowda Government continued as a caretaker. However, since financial control of Parliament is ensured largely through budgetary scrutiny and voting on demands for grants of various Ministries and Departments, although not exactly illegal or unconstitutional, it would be unethical and a travesty of parliamentary norms if the Budget was passed in a hurry by short-circuiting the budgetary processes of parliamentary scrutiny of budget estimates, in-depth examination of demands for grants by the Standing

Committees and debates on the floor of the House. The biggest joke doing rounds was that different political parties were agreeable to passing the Budget 'in national interest' as was done in March 1991 after Chandrashekhar's resignation. With almost lightning speed and without discussion, the General and Railway Budgets, Appropriation and Finance Bills were passed.

It must not vest only with the parties whether the Budget should be subjected to debate and scrutiny or whether it could be straightaway passed. The device of Vote on Account was available to tide over such problems. Also, there seems to be no difficulty in leaving the final passage of the Budget to the next Government that takes over without or after fresh elections. The outgoing Government cannot bind the succeeding Government by a budget that may not be in keeping with its policies and priorities.

It was thus clear that media fears notwithstanding, the political scenario did not really present anything like a constitutional crisis. Whatever little problems were to come up could get solved within the system. The Constitution provided the remedies. The real crisis was political and moral and centred round the personal interests of the main players in the political drama.

30

From Gowda to Gujral

Constitutional Crisis in Retrospect

The political circus that was going on in India's capital for nearly three weeks in March 1997, at last concluded on a somewhat happy note with the 'new' Government headed by IK Gujral receiving the confidence of Lok Sabha. The new Prime Minister was a cultured man and a sophisticated diplomat. He was committed to the nation and its people.

But, preceding the assumption of office by Gujral, Indian politics had descended to its lowest depths. What happened would go down in history as a great slur and a stigma on our democracy. That the 13-Party minority coalition government of several fronts—Federal Front, Left Front, etc.,—and factions headed by Gowda could not last long, was known. But, the end came untimely and too suddenly. If the Gowda Government did not hesitate to use all weapons in official armoury to weaken and demoralise the other side, Kesri was equally unscrupulous in his 'operation topple'. When his threats did not work, he pulled the rug of outside support. No principles, ideologies or welfare programmes for the people were involved on either side. It was a naked struggle for power and self survival on all sides. It was claimed by some that those in power were selective in instituting police enquiries, CBI investigations and court cases against their rivals and were in fact indulging in witch-hunting and official blackmail. This was sought to be met by counter blackmail of support withdrawal.

What happened thereafter was even more bizarre. The Gowda government lost on a confidence vote on the floor of the House by a massive vote on 11 April. As per usual practice, the President asked Gowda to continue until alternative arrangements were made. Normally, one would have expected the President to act immediately to start the process of alternative government formation. But, in a masterly demonstration of Presidential passivism, no steps were taken by the President to even start the process of government formation for a week. He kept waiting and watching, meanwhile leaving it, to parties, petty manipulators and power brokers to get their act together and somehow cobble another coalition of disparate elements to rule the country.

It seems the President had decided in his wisdom to have the financial business—Vote on Account or Budget—passed under the stewardship of the defeated Gowda Government itself and think of the new government, etc., only afterwards. The Houses of Parliament were required to meet on 21-23 April to complete the financial business. This, it was pointed out, was an untenable position unless it was proposed to dissolve Lok Sabha.

The President was later reported to have asked three prominent leaders to find out a solution of the impasse by 21 April, as if it was their duty to form a government and not the clear constitutional responsibility of the President himself. It is definitely the job of the President to appoint the Prime Minister. He can appoint anybody who he thinks can command the confidence of the House, but appoint he must and that too without delay. He cannot simply wait and watch like UP Governor Bhandari for the feuding Prime-ministerial aspirants to settle among themselves. For the first time, the President seemed to be putting himself on the wrong side of strict propriety by giving a clear impression that he would like a Congress-UF patch up in order to be able to install another Front Government. But party or front leaders could not be allowed to behave like a private limited company and take the nation for granted. Democracy is said to be government by the people and we call our system representative parliamentary democracy or participatory democracy. But, in the whole process of government formation, the people seemed to have had no role and no voice. Also, most surprisingly, they appeared unconcerned spectators only.

Finally, the President got into action after United Front succeeded in electing a leader and arriving at a fresh understanding with the Congress. Soon, the earlier directive of transacting financial business was substituted by seeking confidence for the new government.

Once again, the President missed an opportunity to send a message to the House under article 86(2) asking it to elect its leader just as it elects the Speaker. The person so elected could be appointed the Prime Minister. This procedure would have been in keeping with the spirit of the Supreme Court judgement in the Bommai case, the Sarkaria Commission Report and the Allahabad High Court judgement in the UP case. The decision would have been entirely on the floor of the House and the President would have stayed above all politics and controversy. Also, the whole thing would have been entirely constitutional and one leading to a more stable government. In any case, it was a better option than asking three or 13 leaders to work out a solution.

A second UF Government was in office in less than a year. Gowda was out and Gujral was in. Except for the TMC ministers and one Yadav casualty, the Gowda team itself had become the Gujral team.

It is inconceivable how merely by changing the leader, the defeated United Front Government could be reinstated. But this was done throwing all legitimacy to winds.

The two positive results of the installation of the 'new' government were that the 11th Lok Sabha continued and that the elections for the office of the President could be held and completed on time with the 11th Lok Sabha members participating therein.

The option of fresh polls was discarded in the name of the people. But everybody knew that the sole consideration was the vested interest of members themselves who were afraid of going to the people and of losing all the benefits and perks of office including the one crore per year (later raised to two crore per year) development fund (MPLAD Scheme) at their disposal.

The question that was being asked once again was, how long could the United Front government last? Could a decent man survive in the snake pit of today's politics without compromising on decency and principles?

Congress President Kesri while withdrawing support had given nine grounds for the Congress decision on 'principles'. Not a word was said or heard in regard to any change in the matter of those principles or grounds of disagreement with the United Front.

The Coordination Committee was said to be the new panacea to resolve all possible conflicts and ensure stability of the government. But, the question being asked was what would happen if there was no agreement in the Coordination Committee after some party or group with adequate numbers decided to pull down the government. The public face of differences in the Committee would perhaps again be different from the real issues of personal or party interests.

The minimum that the people could demand was that the understandings made between the leaders must be transparent and openly declared. They were entitled to know what had changed in the policies and programmes of the Front, which once again made Congress offer unconditional support. Was the country held to ransom for three weeks or more only due to personal incompatibilities of two leaders or were there some behind-the-scene dealings on CBI investigations, withdrawal or soft-pedalling of court cases etc. Were issues of crime and corruption in politics going to be buried? If so, were they being used only for witch-hunting and as official blackmail in power games for achieving personal and partisan ends?

31

Sordid Defection Drama

When after categorically losing majority support Janata Dal Prime Minister VP Singh did not gracefully resign on 23 October 1990 and instead obtained a 15-day reprieve from the President, it was widely feared that what would follow would be politics with no-holds-barred and with the sole 'value' and the single 'issue' being of somehow sticking to power. While the people continued to hear the idiom of patriotism, social revolution, sacrifice and love for the poor and the backward, the political scenario was getting murkier, depressing and even disgusting. The sordid drama was on for all to see.

On 5 November 1990, a clear split took place in the Janata Dal when two separate meetings of the two factions under their respective leaders were held. The officially controlled electronic media also clearly announced the fact of the split. The VP Singh faction claimed that out of 140 Janata Dal members, 83 attended its meeting and expressed full confidence in VP Singh's leadership. The Chandra Shekhar and Devi Lal (CD) faction, on the other hand asserted that 68 members were present at its meeting and elected Chandra Shekhar as their leader. Whether those parting company with VP were 57 or 68 it was obvious that they were more than the one third required for a split and with the split in the Janata Dal, VP Singh lost even the last ditch battle. The strength of Congress (I), BJP and their allies in Lok Sabha being what it was with the added votes of the CD faction of the Janata Dal, what was left of the VP Ministry with all the support of the Left parties, was a tally of less than 150 members in a House of 525. Singh should have seen the writing on the wall and resigned on 5 November. The 'never-say-die' PM however continued in the saddle.

While more than one-third members of the Janata Dal in Lok Sabha claimed a split and formation of Janata Dal (S) VP Singh quickly expelled 25 of those members including Chandra Shekhar. The Speaker, acting even more promptly, declared them 'unattached'. VP Singh claimed that the expulsions preceded the claim of party split and since the residual number of the members of the break-away group was thereby reduced to less than one-third, there was no valid split and the break-away members were liable to be disqualified under the Anti-defection Law. Even though Chandra Shekhar formed the Janata Dal (S) Government and won the confidence of the House on a substantive motion, all the members of the ruling Janata Dal (S) were either those who had been expelled by VP Singh and declared 'unattached' by Speaker Ray or those against whom show-cause notices for disqualification under the Anti-Defection Law had been issued by the Speaker in the exercise of his powers under the aforesaid law. The Speaker's action covered all the members of the Council of Ministers headed by Chandra Shekhar.

It was argued on Chandra Shekhar's side that para 3 of the 10th Schedule of the Constitution recognized the legitimate right of members to bring about a democratic realignment of forces in the House by way of a split in an existing party. From the time of split, each faction had to be deemed to be a separate 'political party' for purposes of disqualification on ground of defection and 'original political party' of each member of either faction for purposes of the split. Thus, on the date of the crucial vote in the House on 7 November, 30 members were members of the party named Janata Dal (S) headed by Chandra

Shekhar and were subject to its whip. A 3-line whip was actually issued by the Chief Whip of the Janata Dal (S), Mr Harmohan Dhawan asking all its members to be present in the House and to vote against the VP Singh Government on the confidence motion. All the 30 obeyed this whip. The official Janata Dal could have no jurisdiction over these 30 who were then, under the law and in fact, members of another party. Any whip issued to them by the official Janata Dal, therefore, was infructuous and *ab initio* without jurisdiction.

Under para 3 of the 10th Schedule of the Constitution, it was ordained that a member 'shall not be disqualified' on the ground of voluntarily giving up 'membership of his original political party' or for voting 'contrary to any direction issued by such party' if he 'makes a claim' that he belonged to 'the group representing a faction which has arisen as a result of the split in his original political party and such group consists of not less than one-third of the members of such legislature party'. Thus, what was significant was that the Speaker was not required to go beyond the member's 'claim' regarding the fact of the split. His only job was to see that the break-away group was not less than one-third of the membership of the original party.

There would have been no scope for any petition if the most unconstitutional, *mala fide* and fraudulent step of expelling 25 members had not been taken and followed by their instantaneous recognition as 'unattached' members by the Speaker. The Constitution or the Anti-defection Rules significantly did not make any mention of 'expulsions' or 'unattached' members. While expulsions are a party matter, no notice thereof could be taken when they followed a split. In any case the members concerned should have been given, as is normal, full opportunity to explain their position before declaring them 'unattached'. In fact, after the Anti-defection Law, there can be nothing like an 'unattached' member. Wantonly expelling members and making them unattached were dubious devices to attempt to thwart or make inoperative provisions of the Constitution which legitimized party splits and as such these attempts, were nothing short of a fraud on the Constitution.

This dragged on until finally Rabi Ray decided on 11 January 1991 to give benefit of doubt to the ruling party and recognized the split as a one-time process which began and closed on 5 November. Janata Dal (S) was recognized as a political party with 54 members. The seven members who joined after the date of split were disqualified.

Pathetic attempts were made to deny the fact of the split. VP faction complained that the split had not been effected constitutionally as if the party constitution provided any legitimate means or methodology therefor. Once they had voluntarily parted company and elected their own leader, they were no more members of the official Janata Dal headed by VP Singh and no more amenable to his disciplinary jurisdiction. Expulsions by VP Singh of members in the CD faction were as meaningless as the expulsion of Singh himself by CD faction. If the expulsions had preceded the separate meetings and the actual split, it was another matter.

The position under the Anti-defection Law in the 10th Schedule of the Constitution, as it then existed, could be briefly put inter alia as follows:

- If a member voluntarily resigned from or voted in the House against the directives of the party on whose symbol he or she was elected then he or she would be liable to be disqualified from membership.
- No disqualification would be incurred in cases where split in a party or merger of a party in another is claimed. In the event of a split, at least one-third of its members must decide to quit or break away and in case of merger the decision should have the support of not less than two-third of the party members. Para 3 of the 10th Schedule was very clear that from the time of the split, the break-away faction was to be deemed to be a separate political party for purposes of the Anti-defection Law. If a member made a claim that he and any other members of his legislature party constituted the group representing a faction which had arisen as a result of a split in his original party which

consisted of not less than one-third of the members of such party, members would not incur disqualification.

- The question of disqualification was to be determined by the Speaker but he was to take notice of an alleged defection only when a petition in writing was received from a member. Rule 7(7) provided that the procedure to be followed by the Speaker was to be the same as adopted in privilege cases by the Committee of Privileges. A reasonable opportunity must be allowed to the member complained against to represent his case and to be heard in person. Every single case of alleged defection had been referred by the Speaker to the Committee of Privileges for enquiry and the process had often taken very long. There was thus no immediate effect of defection and there had been cases where the House had completed its life and got dissolved without any determination on the alleged defection or liability to disqualification.
- The jurisdiction of courts was barred in respect of matters connected with the disqualification of members. However, this particular provision had been struck down as *ultra vires* by the High Courts of Punjab and Haryana and finally by the Supreme Court.
- The Anti-defection Law (10th Schedule to the Constitution) and the rules framed thereunder did not provide for expulsion of a member from his party for his activities outside the House nor did they provide for anything like an unattached member. A practice had however developed to declare as 'unattached' a member who was expelled from the party. He continued to be a member of the House and fully entitled to all the rights of a member. The Anti-defection Law was not attracted.

Thus, while the Anti-defection law sought to curb the evil of defection, it left scope for democratic realignment of forces in the House by way of merger of two or more parties or split in an existing party. The President while addressing the Conference of Governors in October 1988 had expressed his anxiety for 'the democratic structure of the State' if 'wrong or ill conceived decisions' were given under the Anti-defection law. The President's warning needed to be heeded at all levels.

So far as the Anti-defection Law was concerned, the position in the instant case was crystal clear. There was a split in the Janata Dal. There were two separate Janata Dal parties in Lok Sabha in effect and they had to be recognized as such. No notice could be taken of the expulsions which followed the split. The mischievous device of expelling 25 members had obviously been resorted to with a view to nullify the split on the ground that the remaining numbers in CD faction did not constitute one-third of the Janata Dal membership. That would also oblige them—so thought the VP faction—to either vote for VP on the crucial motion on 7 November or run the risk of being disqualified under the Anti-defection Law. If the provisions of law and the rules and past experience of defection cases were any guide, nothing like this could happen. If an attempt to thwart and make inoperative the provisions of the Constitution which permitted as legitimate split in parties, was allowed to succeed, it would have been nothing short of a fraud on the Constitution.

Also, it must be remembered that the Government would have fallen already with the votes of the members sought to be disqualified and under the Anti-defection Law also there was no provision even to bar them from constituting the Government and being ministers. The real issue was political and the battle lines were sharply drawn. Threats of expulsion or disqualification could prove phoney and change nothing of what was coming on 7 November. There was every reason to expect and believe that the highest traditions of objectivity, impartiality and a non-partisan approach would prevail and the Constitution, the Rules and the established practices would be followed in letter and spirit.

VP Singh submitted the resignation of his Council of Ministers after losing on the floor of the House on a confidence motion. On 10 November 1990, the leader of the break-away group, Chandra Shekhar formed the new government. This also was short-lived. With the Congress discontinuing its support to his ministry, Chandra Sekhar resigned. Thus, two governments—those of VP Singh and Chandra Shekhar—fell in quick succession during the ninth Lok Sabha.

During the 10th Lok Sabha period till the end of 1995, there had been as many as a dozen group defections or party break-ups in legislature parties—not all of them deserving the protection under the 'split' or 'merger' clauses. The Telugu Desam Party, the Jharkhand Mukti Morcha, the Shiv Sena, the Samajwadi Party, the Indian Union Muslim League, the Assam Ganatantra Parishad, the Janata Dal and Janata Dal (A) were all reduced in strength because of successive defections. The greatest beneficiary in the entire process was the Rao Congress and the worst loser the Janata.

By protecting the defectors in the name of splits or mergers, the Anti-Defection Law could be said to have been a source of stability for the Congress Government which graduated from a minority to a majority government. Every time that the Rao Government faced a no-confidence motion, there were additions to its strength through defections.

In March 1992, it was the group of six from TDP which defected and finally merged with the Congress (I). The July 1992 no-confidence motion led to the defection of the 20-member Ajit Singh group from the Janata Dal and the July 1993 no-confidence motion nabbed the famous 'seven saviours' from this break-away Janata Dal (A).

As the year 1993 was coming to a close, on 30 December 1993, 10 of the 13 Janata Dal (A) MPs led by Ajit Singh himself defected to the Congress raising the strength of the Congress party to 267 (including the Speaker) in an effective House of 528 with 16 vacancies. Thus the Congress acquired a slender majority. With more than two-third members joining in the move, it was described as a merger for purposes of the Anti-defection Law. Even though after a long wait, Ajit Singh was duly rewarded with ministership.

On 21 June 1994, the Janata Dal (B) underwent a major split with 14 of its 39 members in Lok Sabha raising the banner of revolt against the leadership—particularly the Ram Vilas Paswan-Sharad Yadav-Lalu Prasad Yadav troika. This was the fifth break-up in the Janata Dal family. The rebels who formed a separate group—first called Janata Dal (G) and later named Samta Dal—included prominent names like those of George Fernandes, Nitish Kumar, Rabi Ray, Chandrajit Yadav, Syed Shahbuddin, Hari Kishore Singh, Yunus Salim, Abdul Ghafoor and others. On 28 June, the break-away group elected George Fernandes as the leader even as Bommai said that all the 14 rebel MPs stood expelled from the Janata Dal (B). Chandrajit Yadav and Syed Shahabuddin were elected as the Leader and Deputy Leader of the new Parliamentary party. Samta Dal itself broke into two with leaders pulling in different directions.

From a perusal of decisions by Speakers in disqualification pleas, it seemed that the phenomenon of split had become very largely something that only concerned and took place within a Legislature Party. The only worry of intending defectors was to see that they somehow constituted the one-third number of their Legislature Party membership. The moment this magical figure was reached, the defectors requested the Speaker to recognize them as a party and give them separate seats and in most cases the Presiding Officers obliged. Legally, this was most untenable and contrary to the provisions of the Constitution. The 10th Schedule contained no concept of a split in the legislature party as such. Also, there was no provision for splits in the State or other units in case of an all India party. To seek the protection of the 'split' clause against disqualification for defection, it had got to be shown that

- there was a split in the original political party, that is, the party outside the legislature which put up candidates to fight elections to the Houses of Legislatures;
- one-third or more members of the Legislature Party claiming the protection actually belonged to a group representing one of the factions of the political party arising as a result of its split.

If the cases of group defection that had taken place during 1992-95 in the Houses of Union Parliament and State Legislatures were judiciously examined on this basis, it could be seen that in overwhelming majority of cases there was no split and the defecting members deserved to be straightaway disqualified under the 10th Schedule of the Constitution. Of course, the Constitution (91st Amendment) Act, 2003 has since omitted the provision of party split as a protection against disqualification on grounds of defection. Also, it disqualified for appointment on remunerative political posts all those disqualified for membership on the grounds of defection.

32

The Manipur Imbroglio

As the year 1994 was coming to a close and the new year 1995 was beginning, certain constitutional, legal and parliamentary procedural issues were expected to arise out of the developments in the state of Manipur. For example, it was asked what action should be taken in certain situations that could arise on 9 January 1995 when the State Assembly had been summoned to meet for ascertaining the confidence of the House in the Council of Ministers headed by Shri Rishang Keishing. Some of the situations were purely hypothetical or mere anticipation of likely scenarios emerging.

The facts in brief were as follows:

- On 9 December 1994, while Manipur was under President's rule and the Manipur Legislative Assembly was under suspended animation in terms of the Presidential proclamation, Speaker Borobabu Singh issued show cause notices to 31 MLAs why they should not be disqualified under the Anti-defection Law on grounds of defection.
- On 13 December 1994, when the Manipur Legislative Assembly had an effective strength of 56 members (in a House of 60, four

seats were vacant), Shri Rishang Keishing claimed the support of 36 members. The convincing majority support was confirmed by the physical presence of members before the governor as also in writing. Accordingly, President's Rule was revoked and Shri Rishang Keishing was sworn in as the Chief Minister on the same day.

- On 16 December 1994, the MLAs who were under notice for alleged defection, contested the grounds and filed their replies with the Speaker. The hearing fixed for 21 December 1994 was not held although the MLAs presented themselves.
- On 21 December 1994, on a petition by 22 of the 31 MLAs under notice, the Gauhati High Court admitted the writ, listed it for the next day and directed the Speaker meanwhile not to pass any order pursuant to the notices of 9 December 1994. A copy of the order, the Speaker was said to have passed, disqualifying 23 MLAs including the 22 petitioners the same day, in the afternoon and after the court's order was fully in the knowledge of the Advocate of the Secretary of the Assembly.
- On 22 December 1994, the Gauhati High Court passed a further order to the effect that the operation of the notices dated 9 December 1994 shall be stayed and the petitioners shall be entitled to participate and vote in all the proceedings of the House pending disposal of the petition. The operative portion was ordered to be furnished to the counsel of the Speaker and the petitioners. The counsel for the Secretary Manipur Assembly did not inform the court even at this stage on 22 December 1994 of the orders regarding disqualification said to have been passed by the Speaker on 21 December 1994.
- A Press Note announcing the Speaker's decision allegedly of 21 December 1994 was also actually issued only on 22 December 1994, that is, after the Speaker was fully aware of the High Court orders not only of 21 December 1994 but also of 22 December 1994. It was on the evening of 22 December 1994 that for the

first time it was announced (through AIR Imphal) that 23 MLAs had been disqualified by the Speaker on 21 December 1994.

- When the matter came up again before the Gauhati High Court on 23 December 1994, the court expressed a strong 'suspicion regarding the factual position of (the Speaker) passing the order on 21 December 1994'. In any case, the court held that even before this alleged date and time of the Speaker passing the order, the High Court's order of stay in the matter had been passed on 21 December 1994 and duly served and was already known to the Advocate of the Assembly Secretary. Quoting Supreme Court rulings in similar cases, the High Court held

(a) that the Speaker was bound by the stay order and was not entitled to ignore it.
(b) that the Speaker's action in passing orders of disqualification was illegal and all proceedings taken after the knowledge of the stay order were a nullity.
(c) that the orders of disqualification passed by the Speaker were a nullity and *non est* in the eyes of law.
(d) that the petitioners shall be entitled to take part the Assembly proceedings and vote as MLAs.
(e) that the orders of disqualification of petitioners shall stand stayed and suspended.

- The Manipur Legislative Assembly was summoned by the Governor (Lt Gen VK Nayar) to meet at 11 am on 23 December 1994. Being the commencement of the first session of the year, the Governor was to address the Assembly which was to consider a motion of confidence in the Rishang Keishing Ministry. However, at about 10 am on 23 December 1994, the Secretary to the Governor informed the Assembly Secretary that the Governor had resigned and his resignation had been accepted and that he would, therefore, not be able to address the Assembly at 11 am. The new Governor was appointed at 12.15 pm on 23 December 1994.

- Under the circumstances, the Council of Ministers and MLAs supporting the Government did not attend the Assembly on 23 December 1994. However, a few (22) Opposition members with Speaker Borobabu Singh in the Chair held a meeting at which a vote of no-confidence in the Ministry was passed, 'Governor's address' was laid, a motion for the disqualification of 23 MLAs on grounds of defection and another motion for expelling them from the membership of the House for allegedly misbehaving in Assembly premises were adopted. Since only the Opposition members were present, all the decisions were reportedly taken 'unanimously' within a record time of one hour. The Assembly was adjourned *sine die* on 23 December 1994.
- The new Governor (ON Srivastava) prorogued the House on the advice of the Cabinet on 23 December 1994 evening.
- On 24 December 1994, Secretary to the Governor conveyed to the Secretary to the Chief Minister, an order of the same date summoning the Assembly to meet at 1100 hours on 9 January 1995 'in the Assembly Hall'.

The questions that arose and were very relevant and important were:

- Whether the 23 MLAs who were disqualified by the Speaker but whose disqualification was stayed and suspended by the Gauhati High Court, continue to be members of the Assembly entitled to participate and vote in the Assembly proceedings?
- Whether the meeting held on 23 December 1994 could be considered a sitting of the Assembly and whether its proceedings during 11 am to 12 noon were valid?
- Whether the so called 'expulsion' of the 23 MLAs by the aforesaid meeting on 23 December 1994 had any validity in law?

The only tenable and constitutional position in regard to the above points was as follows:

- In *Kihota Hollohan vs Zachillhu & others*, the Supreme Court had *inter alia* established beyond any shadow of doubt.

  (a) that para 7 of the Anti-defection Law (10th Schedule of the Constitution) which sought to bar the jurisdiction of courts in matters connected with the disqualification of members on grounds of defection was void as it had not been validly passed under article 368(2) of the Constitution;
  (b) that the Speaker's functions under the 10th Schedule called for a judicial determination of issues under the law;
  (c) that the process of determination of questions of disqualification could not be considered part of the proceedings of the House and as such not amenable to judicial review;
  (d) that while operating under the Anti-defection Law, the Speaker was in the position of a tribunal and therefore, his decisions like those of all tribunals were subject to judicial review by High Courts and the Supreme Court under articles 136, 226 and 227 of the Constitution insofar as infirmities based on violations of constitutional mandates, *mala fides*, non-compliance with rules of natural justice and perversity were concerned.

In view of the above position of the law, it was quite clear that so far as the Anti-defection Law was concerned, the Speaker's order of disqualification stood stayed and suspended and the disqualification was to be treated as *non est* and a nullity in the eyes of law. The 23 members continued to be members of the Assembly fully entitled to participate in its proceedings and to vote.

- The Governor was not only the Head of the State but a constituent part of the State Legislature. Article 168 of the Constitution provided that the Legislature of the State consisted of the Governor and the House (or Houses) of the Legislature.

  Under article 174 of the Constitution, the House of the Legislature was to be summoned 'by the Governor' at such time and place as he deemed fit. The Governor could time to time, prorogue or dissolve the House.

Articles 175 provided for the 'Right of the Governor to address and send messages to the House or Houses'. It said that the Governor 'may' address the House or send messages. Under article 176, however, at the commencement of the first session after each general election and 'at the commencement of the first session of each year', the Governor 'shall' address the Legislative Assembly and inform the Legislature of the causes of its summons.

From the above analysis, it would be seen that since in the Manipur case the sitting of the Assembly on 23 December 1994 was to be 'the commencement of the first session' of the year, an address by the Governor was constitutionally mandatory. The use of the word 'shall' in article 176 as contradistinguished from 'may' in article 175, left no ambiguity at all in this matter. Further:

(a) from 10 am to 12.15 pm on 23 December 1994 one of the two constituent parts of the Assembly, the Governor of Manipur did not, in effect, exist,
(b) the Secretary to Governor had before 11 a.m. informed the Legislature Secretary of the Governor's inability to address and also told him about the new time to be fixed for the address,
(c) the constitutional requirement of the Governor's address was not fulfilled,
(d) the laying and distribution of Governor's address was obviously unauthorized; there could just be no Governor's address when there was no Governor and the inability to address had been conveyed duly; and
(e) the unanimous decisions by only the 22 opposition members—also a minority of members—without any discussion or observance of rules of procedure regarding motions for expulsion of 23 members established a *prime facie* case of *mala fide*.

In these circumstances, the proceedings of 23 December 1994 held during 11 am to 12 noon could not be considered to be valid under the Constitution. At best, in view of the very special situation, the Assembly could be considered to have stood adjourned sine die without transacting any business.

It had to be appreciated that the Assembly is summoned by the Governor (not by the Speaker). The Governor informs the House of the causes of its summons, that is, of the Government business to be transacted. It would be a strange proposition to say that the proceedings can continue without any official Government business and without the presence of the Government or anyone to represent it.

A situation arose in Lok Sabha when Lok Sabha was summoned to meet on 20 August 1979 but the then Prime Minister wrote to the Speaker the same day that he and his Council of Ministers had resigned, the House met but was adjourned *sine die* without transacting any business. A sitting of the House in the absence of or in a situation of boycott by the Opposition was conceivable and there were many precedents but a sitting without the Government representation was incongruous and inconceivable.

The plea that the proceedings would stand protected or immune from judicial interference under article 212(1) as explained in *Keshav Singh*'s case (Spl Ref No 1 (1965)(1) SCR 413) on the ground of there being mere procedural irregularity was most untenable as the Manipur case was not one of procedural irregularity but a substantial matter of violation of mandatory constitutional requirements and of basic *mala fide*. It was not as if some rule of procedure was not followed during the session or a sitting of the Assembly, actually there was no valid session or sitting at all.

- Since there was no valid sitting of the House, there could be no proceedings and no decisions. The so-called 'expulsion' of the 23 MLAs was therefore as much a nullity and *non est* as the Speaker's decision to disqualify them. They continued to be members of the House. However, it would have been most advisable to approach the High Court in the matter and obtain its orders/directions in the matter. While Court's orders existed in the matter of disqualification, no orders seemed to have been sought on the validity of the 23 December 1994 proceedings of the Assembly and the 'expulsion' of the 23 members.

There was no legal force in the Opposition's contention that the Rishang Keishing Ministry stood defeated in the Assembly on a no-confidence motion on 23 December 1994.

A valid sitting of the House was entirely conceivable in the face of boycott by opposition members on 9 January 1995. In the absence of the Speaker, Deputy Speaker and members of the panel of Chairman, the House could on the spot elect any member to preside over the proceedings of the day.

It was not for the Speaker or Deputy Speaker to summon or not to summon the House on 9 January 1995. Summoning of the House was the prerogative of the Governor and he had already summoned the House. The Speaker's duty was to preside over the sittings of the House and to regulate its business in accordance with the Constitution, the laws and the rules of procedure. He had to function as a servant of the House, not its master. The will of the House and its members was supreme. There was the well-known story of the Speaker of the British House of Commons who said that he had neither eyes nor ears and that be could see and hear only what the House, of which he was the servant, willed. Also, one of the Speakers was said to have been held forcibly in his seat by two of the stout members when the House was anxious to transact some business despite the Speaker's unwillingness.

The Legislature building and the Assembly chamber belonged to the members and were for them. They were not the Speaker's property and could not be locked against the *bona fide* members of the House or against the majority of the elected membership.

If the Speaker disregarded the orders of the High Court and did not allow the 23 MLAs to participate and vote on grounds of disqualification, he would be committing a blatant contempt of court and would be guilty of violating the laws of the land and the Constitution. The legal remedy available would again be under the writ jurisdiction of the Hon'ble High Court.

So far as the continuation of the ministry was concerned, there should be no legal difficulty because the council of ministers was responsible to the Assembly and the ministers held office during the pleasure of the Governor. Thus, so long as the Governor was convinced that the Righang Keishing Ministry enjoyed the support of the majority and was being prevented forcibly and illegally from vindicating it on the floor of the House, there was no reason why he should dismiss it. Its continuance was legal and legitimate.

When the Governor arrived to address the House, it was unthinkable that any right-thinking Speaker could show such disrespect and affront to the Head of the state as to order that 'the main Gate of the Assembly campus and the doors of the chamber' be 'closed under lock and key' against him or for that matter against the members of the House to whom it belonged. The Governor and the members would be there within their rights and to fulfil their constitutional obligations. If the members were obstructed in the discharge of their duties, it would be breach of parliamentary privilege and contempt of the House. Since it would also be a violation of Court's orders, it would be construed as contempt of court and the contemner could be ordered to be arrested and brought before the court.

If the Speaker, Deputy Speaker and members of the panel of Chairman decided to remain absent when the Governor came to address, he could be conducted to the House by the Leader of the House. When the House met after the Governor's address, a member could be elected to preside over the day's proceedings.

Apart from conducting other official business, the House could consider suitable action against those showing disrespect to the Governor and the House. They could be charged with breach of parliamentary privileges, contempt of the House and unbecoming conduct. Also, notices for removal, if already given more than 14 days earlier, against the Speaker and Deputy Speaker could be taken up for disposal by the House.

An alternative scenario could be that the Speaker remained present and disallowed entry only to the 23 members and that too not on the ground of disqualification but on the basis of 'expulsion by the House'. The legally safe course for these members would have been to approach the Hon'ble High Court under appropriate writ jurisdiction to seek annulment of the proceedings of the Assembly on 23 December 1994 for disqualification of members on grounds of defection. Court's order had to be obtained before the motion of confidence was taken up by the Assembly. Once the court declared the disqualification a nullity or stayed it, the 23 members could certainly assert their right and enter the assembly on the force of the court order.

In case, the legality, legitimacy or *bona fides* of the membership of all the 36 members supporting the Ministry headed by Shri Keishing was clearly established but they were forcibly prevented from expressing it on the floor of the House or if the House had to be adjourned due to disturbances without voting on the confidence motion, the Governor could, as a last resort, take recourse to being himself satisfied of the majority backing of the ministry.

On 7 January 1995 the Gauhati High Court ordered restoration of *status quo*, quashed the disqualification orders against the 23 members and invalidated the entire proceedings of 23 December 1994.

33

Farce and Fraud in Andhra

Role of the Governor and the Speaker

The farcical drama played in Andhra Pradesh during the last days of Rama Rao regime was played in many parts. First, the Prime Minister and the ruling party at the centre were feigning utter innocence, non-interference and neutrality in the entire scenario built up to explode during the week after some of the chief actors had played polo at the Race Course in Delhi for quite some time. Also, the Andhra Governor was the indomitable Krishna Kant. As the head of the State, he was called upon the play the most crucial role in the crisis. His five-year term had expired and for fairly long he was kept waiting for orders of extension or otherwise. As another Governor commented, his stay in Raj Bhawan was practically on daily wage basis. Was it necessary or fair to keep the highest State functionary in such a state of uncertainty and readiness to leave at the shortest possible notice? Did it not make Krishna Kant susceptible to suspicion of being manipulated or pressurized to serve partisan interests in the over all political power game even though he undoubtedly belonged to the dwindling tribe of the few honest and honourable men in politics. He had been a great success as a Governor. He was popular and was respected. He had ideas and courage of his convictions and the will to speak out unpleasant truths. Perhaps that made a decision in his case difficult. Once out, he could a menace to the powers that be. But, perhaps all that should have been reason enough for him to refuse to serve on daily wage basis, to honourably walk-out of the cage and breathe freely with his like-minded compatriots. In any case, for quite some time, he had shown exemplary courage in resisting all pressures to arbitrarily and unconstitutionally dismiss Rama Rao and at once install Naidu as the Chief Minister.

Second, when the Chief Minister Rama Rao called on the Governor at 7:45 am on 25 August 1995 to recommend dissolution of the Assembly 'owing to certain unhappy circumstances', the Governor had absolutely no reason to doubt that the former was the supreme leader of the ruling TDP and that he enjoyed absolute majority support in the House. TDP under his leadership had won a massive mandate of the people. He was called upon to form the Government which had beyond any shadow of doubt proved on the floor of the House its overwhelming majority. If the precepts of British parliamentary polity were to be strictly followed, the House must have been dissolved when the Chief Minister recommended dissolution. Under article 167(c) of our Constitution, the Governor could have only ascertained from the Chief Minister if the decision to recommend dissolution of the House had been taken by the Council of Ministers.

Three, the Governor's initial reactions to seem to agree to the recommended dissolution of the House and to accept the advice of the Chief Minister to dismiss certain ministers were on perfect grounds. After the Chief Minister had left, some dissident ministers met the Governor between 9:30-10 am. TDP MLAs opposed to Rama Rao's continuance had assembled in the Darbar Hall of Raj Bhawan. Even though the Governor appeared before them briefly, he was very right in not agreeing to have a head count.

There was hardly any need or justification for the Governor asking the Speaker to verify the signatures of TDP MLAs on the memorandum submitted to him. Instead of letting the Secretariat accomplish the technical task of signature verification and reporting to the Governor, the Speaker went a step forward and held a shameful roll-call to physically verify in the Committee Hall of the Legislature Building, the strength of the break-away group of the TDP. It must go down in our parliamentary history as the only case where the Speaker assumed such a role of virtually presiding at a party faction meeting. Whatever the game of numbers, it was entirely an internal party feud of the TDP, all the actors were TDP members and the question was one of struggle for leadership within the party. It was not even an issue of the Chief Minister or the Government enjoying majority support of the members of the Assembly.

Party battles have to be fought and leadership and other issues sorted out within the party. If Rama Rao as the leader was convinced of having lost majority support, he should have himself resigned honourably and allowed another leader to be elected by the Telugu Desam Legislature party. If he did not do so and the Party wanted to change their leader, the only legitimate course open was to a convene a meeting of the party in accordance with the provisions of the Legislature Party Constitution.

No such meeting was legally convened by the functionaries authorized to do so nor was there any evidence of a special meeting having been requisitioned. No split in the party was claimed either. The meeting said to have been held on 24th night, if any, could not be regarded as regular or valid. In any case, neither the Governor nor the Speaker could legitimately concern themselves with internal matters of a party.

Fourth, the Governor acted wisely and rightly in not responding to the Chief Minister's request to appoint a Speaker *protem* simply because the Chief Minister had no confidence in the impartiality of the Speaker or the Deputy Speaker. The Governor could not appoint any Speaker *protem* when the Speaker and Deputy Speaker were both very much in position. Also, the question of their continuance or removal could be decided only by the Assembly in ac cordance with the prescribed procedure.

Fifth, the Governor showed sagacity in finally deciding to go by the Supreme Court decision in the Bommai case and the Sarkaria Commission recommendations to leave matters of majority support, confidence in the government, etc., to be decided by the Assembly on the floor of the House. But, it was hardly proper or necessary for him to summon an emergence session of the House and ask the government to seek a fresh vote of confidence within the shortest possible time-frame ever laid down by a Governor in a similar situation. In fact, the Governor could have told the dissidents to fight their battle within the party or to wait for the next Assembly session to move a vote of no-confidence in the Council of Ministers if they so liked. Till it lost on the floor of the House, it was entitled to continue as the legitimate Government of the state and it was no function of the Governor to monitor or verify continuance of majority support constantly on a day to day basis.

Sixth, the Speaker is only the Presiding Officer of the House. He has to take the chair and regulate the proceedings of the House in accordance with the rules. He cannot recognize or de-recognize party affiliations of members. These are now determined only by people at the time of election. The Speaker comes to have a role under the Anti-defection Law in the 10th Schedule only if and when he receives a petition seeking disqualification of a member on the ground of disobeying a directive of his party. Speaker's decision on the petition is subject to appeal and judicial review by the High Court and the Supreme Court. The Speaker was therefore ill advised to accord recognition to Naidu as the leader of the TD Legislature party. It was hardly legal or constitutional. But, the Governor was right in not accepting the CM's contention of asking the Speaker to ignore any whips issued by Naidu. Issue of whips is purely a party affair and the Governor or Speaker have no role to play. On the matter of recognition of the leader and the Speaker exceeding his jurisdiction and playing a partisan role, the remedy for the CM's supporters was to approach the courts which they did. But, perhaps they were very inadequately briefed in matters *lex parliamenti*. There was still much that Rama Rao could question and seek the protection and verdict of the courts.

Whatever the constitutional and legal issues involved, all these were sidelined by the Chief Minister Rama Rao being taken seriously ill and hospitalized. From the hospital bed, he submitted his letter of resignation to the Governor.

The imbroglio simmering for a week at least temporarily appeared to have resolved with the sick Chief Minister submitting the resignation of his equally sick and emaciated Government to Governor Krishna Kant, the party properly electing a new leader on 31 August 1995 and the Governor inviting him to take oath of office on 1 September. The comic-tragic drama finally came to a close with the demise of Rama Rao. It was a sort of happy ending for the anti-NTR forces.

There may have been merits in the criticism of the projection of his wife by Rama Rao and the former's abrasive manners and unwarranted interference in matters of State but it is also a fact that the powerful liquor lobby and some industrial houses proved to be as much his undoing as his wife or his progeny or the succession struggle.

But, what should concern us is the importance of some of the very fundamental constitutional questions in regard to the respective roles of our high functionaries going far beyond the Andhra developments.

While a great deal was talked about at various fora about the spectre of uncertainty of Governments and need for greater stability, it was not appreciated that the sorry state of affairs was reached only because, most unfortunately, we had molested the Constitutional provisions in processes of operation and interpretation. Governors and Speakers and others had arrogated to themselves powers that never belonged to them and could never have been intended to be entrusted to them by the makers of the Constitution.

The Constitutional position is that under article 164(1), the Chief Minister is appointed by the Governor. Other ministers are appointed by him on the advice of the Chief Minister. They hold office during the pleasure of the Governor which means that they can be removed by the Governor on the advice of the Chief Minister. A point which, however does not seem to have been adequately stressed or analysed either by the various commissions including the Sarkaria Commission or even by the Supreme Court so far is that the founding fathers made a very significant and deliberate distinction between the 'Ministers' and 'Council of Ministers'. While the Governor can dismiss any minister on the advice of the Chief Minister, our Constitution nowhere authorizes the Governor to dismiss the 'Council of Ministers'. Under Clauses (2) closely following Clause (1) of article 164, it is categorically stated that the Council of Ministers shall be collectively responsible to the Legislative Assembly. This means that, the Government would be answerable for all its acts of commission and omission to the House and if at any time the Council of Ministers prove themselves unable to be answerable or responsible and lose the confidence of the House, they must resign.

In Britain, even a Prime Minister defeated on the floor of the House has the option to recommend dissolution of the House and seek a fresh verdict from the people and since 1783 there has not been a single clear case of dismissal of a Cabinet by the Sovereign. In India, a governor may not accept the advice of a chief minister whose party does not constitute the majority of the House or in whom the House has specifically expressed no confidence by a vote. But, the governor is entitled to expect that once the government is defeated on the floor of the House on a no-confidence motion or on an issue amounting to such expression, the chief minister would forthwith submit his resignation. If he is so unreasonable and obdurate as to refuse to do so, the governor has a remedy under article 356 to recommend to the President failure of the constitutional machinery. The President (Union Government) can then issue the necessary directions and warnings to the State Government and if nothing works then as a last resort consider the need for the take over of the functions of the government of the State. It is under the Presidential proclamation under article 356 that the State Council of Ministers can then stand dismissed.

The governors have not been clothed with any powers to every now and then or at any time simply tell a chief minister that a doubt has arisen about his retaining majority support of Assembly members and therefore an emergency session of the House is being summoned whereat he must afresh prove his majority.

It could not have been intended that the Governors and Speakers should all the time play politics or that the legislators should, day and night, all the year round, indulge in only manipulating ministerships or the like for themselves or offering their support to the highest cash buyers thereby all the time keeping the chief ministers and their governments on time or interest left for serving the people or attending to their problems. Should the chief ministers remain dependent on the shifting loyalties of legislators and on the need to keep their flock together and win new adherents through tension management techniques of distributing spoils, favours and gains from crime and corruption?

Once the electorate has returned a clear verdict in favour of a party, a leader and a programme and the Government is duly constituted and has demonstrated its majority strength on the floor of the House, it should be normally expected to last its full five-year term. The Governor, the Speaker and the legislators must all mind their legitimate constitutional business. The Government must be left undisturbed to govern in accordance with the popular mandate unless and until a vote of no-confidence is passed by the Assembly on the floor of the House. And, this cannot be a daily affair. It can arise only when the Assembly is in session and even then under the rules, a no-confidence motion can be discussed only once a session.

To ensure accountability and see that the Government does not cease to be responsive to popular opinion and responsible to the House, the Constitution already provides in article 174 the safeguard that a period of more than six months must not intervene between two sessions of the House.

There is no provision for a vote of confidence as such either in the Constitution or in the Lok Sabha Rules of Procedure. There are, of course, specific rules for no-confidence motions as a separate category. When the so-called confidence motions are brought up, they are treated only under the most general category of ordinary substantive motions.

It is a pity that an entirely farcical extra-constitutional and illegitimate practice has been started by the governor-politicians on their own or at the behest of their masters in Delhi to ask the chief ministers at the slightest pretext to seek votes of confidence within a few days—may be five days or 30 days—as may be arbitrarily fixed by them.

This has promoted a climate of perpetual instability of governments, insatiable illegitimate demands by the legislators with threats of overthrowing governments through horse-trading, role of money and mafia power in making and unmaking governments and ultimately holding the people at large to ransom and making them suffer in utter helplessness at the hands of whosoever proves the successful bidder and wins power to rule over their lives.

It is time, and before it gets too late, to accept an honest interpretation of the scheme of our Constitution under which first of all, MLAs are expected to be in the State capital generally only on receipt of summons for a session of the Assembly. Once the session is over, they are expected not to pollute, crowd and corrupt the social life of the Capital or disrupt the functioning of the government and administration by all the time politicking and playing power brokers or liaison officers for private interests. Their legitimate place during non-sessions is in their constituencies or in the field at large to listen to the people's problems and grievances and to serve them through constructive work and positive contributions.

Second, there is no justification for any occasion whereunder the governor can or should be allowed to dismiss the Council of Ministers on his own. It is not the business of the Governor or the Speaker to keep constantly monitoring or even to verify on request on a day to day basis the support enjoyed by the government, the party or the leader in power. The forum for settling rivalries within the party is the party itself and question of the Government enjoying majority support can be tested only on the floor of the House by a motion of no-confidence, on a major policy issue or on a vote on demands for grants during sessions of the Assembly.

Lastly, every member of the House, unless he is elected as an independent, belongs to the party on the symbol of which he is elected. The Speaker has hardly any role in the matter. Political parties under the Constitution are mentioned only under the 10th Schedule. There is no automatic disqualification of any member going against his party directive. Cognizance of disobedience is to be taken by the Speaker only when he receives a petition in that regard. Even after the Speaker's decision is arrived at, may be after long drawn enquiry, evidence and arguments, the question of disqualification or otherwise is subject to judicial review at the level of High Courts and the Supreme Court.

34

Mayawati Government

Perverse Role of the Speaker

Serious apprehensions of violence, utter disorder and pandemonium in the UP Vidhan Sabha on 19 June 1995 fortunately did not come true. It was feared that the Samta Party of Mulayam Singh Yadav with the support of its muscle power and its loyal partymen and with Dhaniram Verma as the Speaker would do everything possible to make it impossible for the House to function and provide the needed sanction and legitimacy to the Government of Ms Mayawati. That way, it was believed, the President would be left with no option but to impose President's rule.

What happened on 19 and 20 June 1995 was in a sense a sort of anticlimax. Even the usual fireworks were missing, no unseemly noises were raised, no furniture was broken, not even blows were exchanged. The entire operation was unbelievably peaceful and orderly and accomplished with clockwise precision. Happenings behind the scenes, what arrangements were made and what compromises struck which made all this possible, would one day make an interesting story. But, it all ended very tamely with a little drama by Speaker Dhaniram Verma for public consumption only.

The Speaker arrived, made a brief statement about the unconstitutionality of the Government, adjourned the House *sine die* and quietly left. Members of the Mulayam Singh party also equally quietly walked out while majority of members remained glued to their seats ignoring the adjournment announcement, electing another person to take the chair and proceeding to conduct normal orderly business of the House. Neither side met with any resistance in doing what it decided to do. The whole thing appeared quite pre-arranged and well-rehearsed.

A Motion for removal of Dhaniram Verma from the office of Speaker was passed unanimously and the Government of Ms Mayawati secured the much needed unqualified confidence vote of the House. Nevertheless, the conflictual situation and the confrontationist scenario between the Governor and the Speaker in regard to their respective role perceptions and areas of jurisdiction gave rise to certain constitutional issues which needed dispassionate analysis. Media reports indicated considerable confusion in the public mind and the experts expressed contrary views.

The simple facts were that with the break-up of the SP-BSP coalition and the extension of unconditional support to BSP by the single largest party in the House, that is, the BJP, the Governor invited the BSP leader Ms Mayawati to form the Government and asked her to seek a vote on confidence by 20 June 1995.

Speaker Dhaniram Varma acting more as a partyman than as the Speaker of the Vidhan Sabha, recognized in great haste a break-away group from the BSP in utter disregard of the constitutional provisions in the 10th Schedule. The Business Advisory Committee as constituted by him violated set parliamentary practice of having the committee reflect the composition of the House and represent all the parties in proportion to their respective strength in the House. He went so far as to openly declare himself to be a partyman first and only then the Speaker of the whole House. No other Speaker in history was known to have made such a perverse claim. Flouting all moral standards, conventions and parliamentary propriety, he tried to prevent the House from considering a Motion for his own removal from the office of Speaker. Also, he discarded the order of Government business. Finally, he questioned the Governor's action of appointing the Chief Minister and refused to place before the House, the Message sent by the Governor.

It was certainly not one of the legitimate functions of the Speaker to pronounce on the legality of the Government or to declare the Governor's choice of Chief Minister as 'unconstitutional'. Also, it was not difficult to make out a case of *mala fide* and vested interest against Speaker Dhaniram Verma because by adjourning the House and by not allowing it to consider the Governor's Message, he was in effect, scuttling the pending Motion for his removal.

The function of the Speaker is to preside at the sittings of the House and to ensure that it functions smoothly and in an orderly manner in accordance with the Constitution, rules and conventions. He is there to regulate the proceedings in accordance with the wishes of the House. The House is the master of its procedure. The Speaker is a servant of the House. He is neither above the rules nor above the House. He cannot shut the House against itself and make it disfunctional nor can he substitute his own judgement for that of the House. It is obvious that majority of the UP Vidhan Sabha was anxious to transact lawful business and wanted the sitting to continue. The capricious adjournment by the Speaker against the wishes of the House could very legitimately be disregarded by the House. Whatever prestige and powers he has are drawn from the House and exercisable only on behalf of the House. Even the power to adjourn the House is derived from the House and is not a constitutional power.

It was constitutionally untenable and politically most unfeasible to suggest that after the perverse and unwarranted adjournment of the House against the wishes of the House, one should have had recourse to judicial interference to have the adjournment set aside. It was forgotten that even in the Punjab case in 1968, after all the recourse to law courts and the Governor's ordinance forbidding adjournment of the House, it was ultimately the House itself that had to disregard the adjournment by the Speaker and hold its sitting with the Deputy Speaker in the chair. That alone settled the issue and the courts also accepted the legality of the proceedings. The Manipur case made the position even clearer that the House was the master of itself and it was for the House to decide whether and when it was sitting as the House. Courts always tried to stay away in such matters concerning the Legislatures, and rightly so.

In the absence of the Speaker and the Deputy Speaker, under article 180 (2) 'such other person as may be determined by the Assembly, shall act as the Speaker'. The House was thus within its right to put Barkhu Ram Verma in the chair and carry on the proceedings. This was bound to be a temporary, *ad hoc* arrangement and in itself could have no impact on the continuance of the duly elected Speaker who could be removed only by the House passing the Motion for his removal after the prescribed 14 days' notice. Barkhu Ram Verma did not become the Speaker and Dhaniram Verma did not stand removed on 19 June. The removal came only on 20 June when a Motion for removal was passed by the House in accordance with the Rules.

While the Governor had no right to interfere with the procedure or the proceedings of the Assembly or to issue any directives or directions to the House or to the Speaker, he certainly had a very specific right to send Messages to the House under article 175(2) of the Constitution.

When such a Message is sent by the Governor, it is laid down in the Constitution that the House 'shall with all convenient dispatch consider any matter required by the Message to be taken into consideration'. The provision has three clear implications. One, the use of 'shall' makes it obligatory for the House to consider the Message. Two, it has to be done at the earliest. Three, the use of the word 'any matter' makes it clear that the message may concern 'any matter' including the order of business in the House etc. Of course, the House is free not to accept the suggestions made in the Message.

What Governor Motilal Vora sent was not a direction or directive but a Message to the House for consideration. It was incumbent on the House to consider it with all convenient despatch and it was the constitutional duty of the Speaker to ensure that this was done and facilitated. He had no business to come between the Governor and the House. Perhaps the Speaker forgot that besides being the Head of the State, the Governor was also a constituent part of the Legislature in as much as article 168 *inter alia* provides that the Governor and the two Houses (in case of UP) constitute the State Legislature. Not respecting the Governor's Message and not allowing the House to consider it vitiated the entire proceedings conducted while Dhaniram Verma was in the Chair. The House itself was fully competent to annul them including the Speaker's announcement of 'adjournment'.

The sitting of the House held with Barkhu Ram Verma in the Chair and with majority of the members present must therefore be deemed definitely to be a valid sitting of the House, transacting lawful business and arriving at binding decisions. It cannot be questioned in a court of law on the ground of any procedural irregularity, etc., as article 212 categorically rules out court interference in the proceedings of a legislature. It says that "the validity of the proceedings in the legislature of a State shall not be called in question on the ground of any alleged irregularities of procedure."

Thus, it was entirely constitutional and valid for the UP Vidhan Sabha holding its sittings with Barkhu Ram Verma in the chair, willingly accepting the suggestions in the Governor's message, passing the motion for the removal of the Speaker and the Vote of Confidence in the Council of Ministers.

It was a matter of the deepest anguish that partisan actions of Speakers like Dhaniram Verma keep bringing the high office of the Speaker into disrepute and disgrace.

35

The 'Unconstitutional' President's Rule

Allahabad High Court Judgement

On 19 December 1996, the Lucknow Bench of the Allahabad High Court delivered its historic judgement disposing of the six writ petitions filed in the shape of public interest litigation challenging the constitutional validity of the Presidential Proclamation of 17 October 1996 reimposing President's Rule in UP under article 356 of the Constitution.

It seemed unfortunate that the Allahabad High Court judgement did not evoke the kind of interest among jurists, media and others that it should have. Hardly any incisive analysis appeared. This might have been so perhaps because the judgement did not get reported promptly and its full text was not easily available. It ran into 210 pages and called for an in-depth study.

The High Court 'quashed' the 'reimposition' of the President's Rule as 'unconstitutional'. To avoid any constitutional deadlock, it directed that the judgement would come into effect only prospectively from 26 December. The Supreme Court admitting a Special Leave Petition against the judgement, stayed its operation. However, the judgement would probably go down as one of the most significant and far-reaching in our constitutional history.

While each of the three judges on the Bench recorded their reasons separately, the court unanimously held that the Presidential Proclamation of 17 October 1996, 'subsequently approved by Parliament' was 'unconstitutional, issued in colourable exercise of power' and 'based on wholly irrelevant and extraneous grounds which therefore could not 'be allowed to stand'. The indictment could hardly be more severe or more serious inasmuch as it was for the first time ever that an act of the President performed on the advice of the Council of Ministers and approved by the two Houses of Parliament was held to have been a colourable exercise of power based on irrelevant and extraneous grounds, declared unconstitutional and quashed. One of the judges referred to 'non application of mind' while the other doubted if the Governor was 'really serious' about installing a responsible ministry and categorically said that the Governor was 'wrong in not realizing that President's Rule is the last resort' or that 'perhaps he did not understand the legal position correctly'.

Much before the judgement came, it was argued by the present writer that the 'fresh Presidential proclamation of October 17 in effect extended or continued the already one-year old Presidential rule in Uttar Pradesh' (*Sunday Observer*, 27 October–2 November 1996). The proclamation was unconstitutional—a fraud on the Constitution in view of article 356 (5). By calling it a 'fresh' proclamation for 'reimposition' of President's Rule, the fact of the continuation of the President's Rule beyond one year could not change. What could not be done directly could not be done indirectly either. The Gowda Government had done what even Parliament could not do except during Emergency. It was suggested that the most democratic and constitutional way out of the impasse was for the Governor (i) to summon the Vidhan Sabha to meet under article 174(1) and (ii) to send a message under article 175(2) requiring the House to elect its leader. The leader so elected could then be appointed by the Governor as the Chief Minister.

On both these counts, the position was upheld not substantially but literally in full by the Full Bench of the High Court. Justice

BM Lal very aptly observed, "without any interregnum gap, between revocation of previous Proclamation and issuance of fresh Proclamation, the position becomes that although in form it was a fresh Proclamation yet in substance and in fact, the President's Rule is continuously in force in Uttar Pradesh with effect from 18.10.1995. Therefore, it cannot be said, that a new circumstance or ground emerged whereby clause (5) could have been bye-passed, giving it legal colour of new proclamation under clause (1) of article 356, and thus the impugned Proclamation dated 17.10.1986 is a subterfuge suffering from malice in law and has the effect of achieving indirectly what cannot be achieved directly."

The same view about the unconstitutionality of the Proclamation was expressed in different words by the other two judges, namely Justice B Kumar and Justice M Katju. They held that President's Rule in the given situation could not be continued beyond one year and that what was done was nothing but continuation.

All the three judges in their separate judgements repeatedly upheld the suggestion that the only way out under the situation in UP was for the Governor to leave it to the House to indicate the name of the leader who had the support of the House and could be appointed Chief Minister. References were made to the Prime Minister in Japan being designated by the Diet and to the recent ideas emerging from think tanks in the UK in regard to the desirability of the Queen consulting the Commons in situations of unclear majority. Rodney Brazier even suggested summoning of the House of Commons for choosing a person who could be invited by the Queen to form the Government. Justice Kumar spoke of 'the idea of taking assistance from the legislators' being afloat in India as well . He agreed that 'new situations called for new solutions'. In Justice Kumar's view, "If a few persons, namely, the leaders or elected members of political parties can be consulted outside the House, it is not reasonably understandable, which constitutional provisions or conventions would be violated if all elected members of different political parties assemble, together to answer the problem... This solution would be better than to keep the matter in suspense or uncertainty for an indefinite period... It would rather be in keeping with the democratic spirit pervading all our constitutional provisions. It will very well fit in with the whole scheme of the Constitution."

Justice Katju put the argument most strongly and very clearly when he observed that "the Legislative Assembly not only can meet but has to meet in a situation like the present one where the Governor is unable to decide in whom the Assembly has confidence". When the Governor is unable to find anyone who in his opinion is likely to enjoy the confidence of the House, "the only rational and democratic alternative (short of dissolution of the House) is that the Governor should ask the House itself as to in whom it has confidence. For this purpose, the Governor must summon the House under article 174 and send a message to it under article 175 (2) informing the Legislative Assembly that he has not been able to find anyone who in his opinion is likely to enjoy the confidence of the House, and hence the House itself should inform him as to in whom it has confidence so that the Governor could appoint such a person as the Chief Minister".

Referring to Solicitor-General's arguments, Justice Katju remarked, "I find it strange to say that the Assembly cannot even choose (whether by way of election, consensus or otherwise) a person who will enjoy its confidence. Nothing could be more repugnant to democracy... the confidence must be of the Assembly and not of the Governor... Who can be in a better position than the House itself to inform the Governor about the person in whom the House has confidence". His Lordship concluded by holding that the UP "Assembly may now be summoned under article 174 and the members sworn in as early as possible with a message under article 175 (2) requesting it to meet and deliberate and inform the Governor within a reasonable time as to the person in whom it has confidence, so that he could be appointed as the Chief Minister".

Second, since the Constitution provides that there 'shall' be a Council of Ministers, under articles 163 and 164, it was the Governor's constitutional obligation to constitute a popular Government after the completion of the electoral process, the Government so appointed would have been responsible to the Assembly and not to the Governor. If the Governor found it difficult to decide on whom to call to form the Government, he could take recourse to article 175 (2), send a message to the House to elect its leader who could then be appointed by him as the Chief Minister.

Justice Lal said that the term 'Government' used in article 356 (1) "refers to elected Government and, not the President's Rule. Clause (1) of article 163 uses the word 'shall'. The word 'shall' indicates mandatory sense. Therefore, it is not the discretion of the Governor to appoint a Chief Minister or not to appoint. Constitutionally, he is bound to appoint a Chief Minister. Here his discretion is limited to choosing the Chief Minster if no party has a clear majority .But it is not open for the Governor to say that he will not appoint a Chief Minister… Political justice can only be extended at this juncture to the electorate through their representatives by adhering to the provisions of articles 174 and 175 of the Constitution". His Lordship bemoaned how the great patriotic people of Uttar Pradesh had been 'unconstitutionally deprived of their right of forming a democratic Government'. He saw no reason why the Governor could not invoke articles 174 and 175 and ask the members of the Legislative Assembly to indicate the name of the leader in whom they had confidence so that the same person could be appointed Chief Minister.

The more closely one read the learned judgement delivered and the reasons recorded separately by the three distinguished Judges, one was left wondering along with Justice Katju, why after all the rational and democratic alternative available to the Governor was not used and why the MLAs elected by the people were not allowed to meet even for the limited purpose of informing the Governor as to the person in whom they had confidence.

36

Discussing Governor's Conduct*

A Historic Ruling

All rulings from the chair are, by definition, fair and final which cannot be questioned and deserve the highest respect. Politics and party perceptions apart, Speaker Sangma's ruling of 6 March 1997 admitting notice of a motion for the recall or the UP Governor Bhandari would go down in parliamentary history as one of the most straightforward, significant, objective and honest rulings from the chair.

In his comprehensive ruling, Speaker Sangma had wisely drawn attention to the constitutional requirement of the Council of Minister being collectively responsible to Lok Sabha. He had referred to the 'discordant notes and confusing signals from the government on the law and order situation in UP'. It was to be expected that the UF Government would heed the stern warning of the Speaker. If they could not act as a team, they needed to be moved out without delay.

So far as the ruling and the admission of the notice were concerned, the Speaker had gone strictly by the Rules and the provisions of the

---

* From *Indian Express*, 13 March 1997 under the title 'Sangma's UP Ruling—A Crisis of Consensus'.

Constitution. It was the constitutional duty of the Union *inter alia* to protect the State against 'internal disturbance' and to ensure that its government 'is carried on in accordance with the provisions of the Constitution' (article 355). This responsibility became more marked when the State happened to be under the President's Rule.

There was nothing new in Lok Sabha discussing the acts and conduct of a Governor could not be discussed in Lok Sabha where these were supposed to have been performed on the advice of the Council of Ministers of the State because in those cases the proper forum was the State Legislature concerned. But, where the Governor's act was in his discretion or on direction or advice from the Union Government, these could certainly get discussed in Lok Sabha. This position was also upheld by a ruling of the Speaker in 1974. But, if it was proposed to discuss the conduct of a Governor and censure, disapprove or condemn it, that could be done only on a substantive motion under Rule 184. Subject to this, during the continuation of the President's Rule, all the acts and conduct of the Governor were quite legitimately liable to be discussed in Parliament.

There was hardly any justification for the BJP euphoria over the ruling of Speaker Sangma. The ruling was on merits. It may need clarification that notices of motions, etc., were not given by political parties but by individual members. The notices stood in the names of Jaswant Singh, Atal Bihari Vajpayee, Murli Manohar Joshi and Pramod Mahajan. Besides demanding the recall of Bhandari, the motion sought to condemn his conduct in publicly disagreeing with the Union Home Minister Indrajit Gupta on his remark regarding UP heading towards 'anarchy, chaos and destruction'.

It may be educative to look at some precedents. In 1967, the Lok Sabha discussed a motion under Rule 184 recommending that the then governor of West Bengal be dismissed. In 1968, a motion disapproving the manner and procedure adopted by the Bihar Governor in installing BP Mandal as Chief Minister was discussed. The Speaker had then ruled that 'the conduct of the Governor as an individual could not be debated but the official action of the Governor could be debated'.

The closest precedent one remembered is that of 1970 when also the motion specifically asked for the recall of the Governor. The notice was under Rule 184. It was admitted for being discussed and voted upon. The State concerned then also was UP. The then Governor was Gopala Reddy who passed away the other day. Among those giving notice of the motion. Atal Bihari Vajpayee's name appeared as much in 1970 as it does in the present motion in 1997 motion was actually moved by Prakashvir Shastri while in the present case it is to be moved by Jaswant Singh.

It was on 19 November 1970 that the motion disapproving 'the conduct of the Governor of Uttar Pradesh' in handling the constitutional crisis there and recommending that the 'Governor be recalled' was discussed. The Governor had declined to dismiss the Congress (R) Ministers despite the explicit recommendations of Chief Minister Charan Singh. Even though Charan Singh had offered to prove his continuing majority on the floor of the House, the Governor, armed with the advice of the Attorney-General, asked Charan Singh to resign as with the break up of the coalition and withdrawal of Congress (R), he had no right to continue as the Chief Minister of the coalition and his advice was no longer binding on the Governor.

There was lengthy correspondence between the Governor and the Attorney-General and Rashtrapati Bhawan and Raj Bhawan in the matter of seeking the Attorney-General's advice and between the Chief Minister and the Governor in regard to the removal of ministers and asking Charan Singh to resign. Some 18 prominent members also wrote to the President. All this correspondence makes interesting reading. When Charan Singh did not resign, the Governor reported failure of constitutional machinery and President's Rule was imposed on 2 October 1970. The motion for Governor's recall was discussed for six hours on 19 November 1970 but was negatived.

The situation in March 1997 was more critical and unique inasmuch as the real conflict was within the UF Government with the Prime Minister, the Home Minister and the Parliamentary Affairs Minister speaking in different voices. If the motion was defeated, the position of the Home Minister—a man with a reputation for impeccable integrity, honesty and ability—would be in the mud and it would be sad if he was left with no honourable alternative to walking out in disgust. On the other hand, if the motion was adopted, Gowda would have to ask Bhandari to resign or advise the President to withdraw his pleasure, that is, dismiss the governor. In either case, the UF Government faced a tricky predicament. Also, there were serious differences among members within the UF and the congress in regard to the motion.

The most advisable way out for Governor Bhandari would have been to submit his resignation and since that did not happen, the UF and the Congress could have both saved their faces by not issuing whips and allowing their members to vote freely on the motion. That way, whatever the decision of the House, embarrassment to UF Government and the Congress Party would have been avoided. But, what was preferred was some tight-rope dancing and behind-the-scene agreements and arrangements to defeat the motion and later change the Governor.

37

The Uttar Pradesh Drama

Supreme Court Verdict*

At all the national and international fora, we are never tired of taking pride in ours being the largest democracy in the world which has survived for over half a century despite many a crises. We conveniently forget that constitutionalism implies a limited Government, that the quality of Rule of Law is predictability and that it excludes rule by personal will or individual discretion. Our Constitution ordains a Government that is representative of the people and responsive and responsible to the people.

Opinions about political parties are bound to vary and every citizen is free to hold and propagate his views for or against a political party. But, there is something fundamentally wrong with our psyche and political morality if we go about expressing our resolve to be ready to go to any lengths and gang up to do 'anything to prevent a recognized national party from forming a Government even if the people return it with the best mandate vis-à-vis all the other parties or if a nominated head of a State uses his so-called discretionary powers to

---

* From *Deccan Herald*, 1 March 1998.

summarily dismiss in an election eve coup, a legitimately-constituted and functioning Government of the largest party with 174 members of its own and appoints a government of a break-away group of merely 22 members. This was precisely what the UP Governor did in UP.

Thanks to the Governor, the crisis forced on the BJP Government in UP left it rather strengthened. Had he followed the constitutional norms and left it to the floor of the State Legislative Assembly to decide the question of confidence or lack of it in the Ministry, perhaps the tally might not have been so impressive. Also, the whole drama in UP that culminated in the virtual election of the Chief Minister by the Assembly under the direction of the Supreme Court could considerably affect the trend of voting for Lok Sabha in the final phase and it might not have been easy to deny to the BJP and its allies some 245 or more seats and every likelihood of forming a Government at the Union level.

However, more important than the fate of the political parties and victories or defeats in the political power games were several constitutional questions to which the developments in UP had given rise. These needed to be looked at and analysed in depth from an objective and non-party angle.

First was the question of the Governor's role. If we look carefully at the provisions of the Constitution in articles 163 and 164, it would be obvious that the council of Ministers is not responsible to the Governor. It is collectively responsible only to the Assembly. It is therefore not part of the functions or the authority of the Governor to dismiss the Council of Ministers which has not lost the confidence of the members on the floor of the House.

Both the Legislature and the Judiciary had shown beyond any shadow of doubt that the action of the UP Governor in summarily and in unseemly haste dismissing the Kalyan Singh Government on poll eve was wrong, unwarranted and perhaps not based on *bona fide* considerations. That he did not heed the advice even of the President of the Republic made his position more inexplicable and unpardonable.

The High Court did the right thing in ordering the reinstatement of Kalyan Singh and continuation of *status quo ante*. The Supreme Court also did not interfere with this order of the High Court and refused to stay it. However, it directed convening a special session of the Legislative Assembly with the single point agenda of holding a composite floor test of the respective strengths of the two claimants of the Chief Minster's chair. In effect, it amounted to an election of the Chief Minister by the House. Majority went in favour of the incumbent Chief Minister Kalyan Singh. After the results were reported to the Supreme Court on 27 February 1998 Jagdambika Pal's petition to the Court was also dismissed. The final curtain on the drama fell with Chief Minster Kalyan Singh dropping Jagdambika Pal from his Cabinet on the same day.

The other important constitutional question was that of the President-Governor and the President-Caretaker Cabinet relationship. The Governor, according to the Constitution (articles 155-156) is appointed by the President and holds office during the pleasure of the President. Normally the President acts on the advice of the Council of Ministers. But this is only because the Council of Ministers has behind it the support of the House of the People to which it is responsible. But in a situation where the Council of Ministers has lost the support of the House, has resigned and has been asked by the President only to continue to take care of the day to day administration, and where in fact, there is no Lok Sabha in existence, the Council of Ministers loses all credentials to give to the President binding advice. Actually, a Caretaker Government is responsible and accountable to the President himself. The President is being extra nice in seeking the advice of a Caretaker Prime Minister.

There could be no difficulty in the President transferring or dismissing the Governor. In the absence of the Lok Sabha and a Government responsible to Lok Sabha, if necessary, the President could address the nation directly and explain the position. He had to be wide awake 'to preserve, protect and defend the Constitution'.

But, perhaps efforts should have been made to mark time and let elections pass.

The third and the most important constitutional question was that of the lesson we could draw from the developments in UP and to what extent these could influence the shape of things at the level of the Union Parliament.

The three major problems plaguing Indian polity are those of hung Houses, instability of governments, frequent elections and unprincipled defections for forming or toppling governments. To meet these problems, the present writer had been suggesting that in case no party or pre-poll alliance of parties secured a clear majority in the House, the President could simply send a message to the Lok Sabha asking it to elect its leader so that he was appointed the Prime Minister and once so appointed he should be removable only on a constructive motion of no-confidence passed on the floor of the House and containing the name of the successor. This could be done by a simple amendment in the Rules of Procedure.

After the Supreme Court verdict in *Jagdambika Pal vs Union of India* (Air 1998 SC 998), the device of election of the Chief Minister by the House could be said to have had the sanction of the Supreme Court itself. This ensured that the President remained completely above political controversy, decision on Government formation was taken on the floor of the House, the malady of horse-trading was contained, the heavy cost and strain of frequent elections was avoided and government was ensured reasonable stability.

38

Bihar Assembly Dissolution

Supreme Court Judgement Revisited

Following the announcement of results to the Bihar Legislative Assembly held in 2005 but before the Assembly could meet, President's Rule under article 356 was imposed on the recommendation of the Governor (Buta Singh) vide notification dated 7 March 2005 on the ground that no political party was in a position to form a government. The Assembly, however was kept under suspended animation. The Governor sent to the President two reports on 27 April 2005 and 21 May 2005 stating that according to various reports, MLAs were being lured by money, posts, etc., that political instability may give rise to further horse-trading by various parties and that, therefore, it would be desirable to dissolve the Assembly. The second report of the Governor also specifically made the point that a 'particular party (under Nitish Kumar) may be close to getting majority' and 'claim may be staked to form the government'. This report was received by the Union Government on 22 May 2005 and on the same day, Union Cabinet met at about 11 pm and decided to accept the report and sent a fax to the President (Dr APJ Abdul Kalam), who was in Moscow, recommending dissolution of the Bihar Assembly. The President faxed back his approval. The notification dissolving the Assembly was issued on 23 May 2005.

Delivering a historic judgement in *Rameshwar Prasad vs Union of India* (AIR 2005 SC 4301), the Supreme Court held the dissolution of the Bihar Assembly to be unconstitutional but did not direct return to *status quo ante*. A few points emerging from the judgement could be high-lighted:

First, much was made by some politicians and political parties of the judgement of the Constitution Bench not being unanimous but a 3:2 majority judgement. The effort was thereby to dilute the severity of the indictment by taking recourse behind the arguments of the two judges who disagreed with the majority and found the Governor's role above-board and the dissolution of the Assembly in order. This did not make much sense when it was remembered that many of the most historic and path-breaking judgements of the Supreme Court had been majority judgements only, for example, in the *Kesvananda Bharti* and the *Bommai* cases. It is always the majority judgement that is the binding verdict of the court and becomes the declared law of the land.

Second, so far as the text of the judgement was concerned, it was difficult to disagree with what it said but there was much to be said about what it failed to say. Even though the question of the validity of the proclamation of President's Rule (7 March 2005) was not raised, in fact, that was the original sin. The purpose of holding elections was to elect people's representatives and to constitute a democratic government. That is why article 164 provides that the Chief Minister 'shall' be appointed and other ministers appointed on his advice. Thus, an obligation was cast upon the Governor to appoint the Chief Minister. He could theoretically appoint anyone but he had to appoint someone. Normally, of course, he would appoint only one who was likely to command the confidence of the House because the Council of Ministers had to be collectively responsible to the Assembly. A Council of Ministers that did not enjoy the support of the House or lost it, must quit.

The Governor could not take the plea that no government could be formed unless he exhausted all the possible options available to him including the one of asking the House itself to elect its Leader. In Bihar, Governor Buta Singh did nothing of the sort and rushed to recommend imposition of President's Rule under article 356 which, under the Constitution, was a device of last resort to be used when everything else failed—when the discharge of Union responsibilities under article 355 did not yield results, when directions issued to State government under articles 256-257 were not complied with and when under article 365, it could really be held that the government of the State could not be carried on in accordance with the Constitution. Imposition of President's Rule immediately after the election without allowing the newly elected House to meet was nothing short of a contempt of the electoral exercise and the verdict of the people. The representatives whom the people elected could not be so unceremoniously sent home on the arbitrary advice of a Governor.

Third, when President's Rule was imposed and instead of being dissolved, the Assembly was kept under suspended animation, obviously the hope was that through some realignments or garnering of fresh support, some leader could be in a position to claim majority and stake claim to form a government. Thus, the possibility of realignments and change in loyalties of members was anticipated and accepted as legitimate.

Fourth, what has held to be unconstitutional by the Supreme Court was the Presidential notification of 23 May 2005 dissolving the Bihar Assembly with the President exercising powers under article 174(2) read with article 356. In the whole drama, there were at least four prominent actors involved.

- The Governor—a very prominent and active politician and former Union Home Minister of the ruling party—was obviously not sent to Bihar to allow or facilitate the installation of an opposition government. Presumably, the Governor was doing what, according to his best lights, would be appreciated by the

High Command, that is, even if he had not been specifically asked to make the report that he did. Unfortunately, the arguments of likely horse-trading advanced by him were most untenable because for dealing with defections (or sale-purchase of legislators) we had the 10th Schedule of the Constitution and even thereunder the law came into play only after the defection had taken place and not at the prospect or threat of defection. Also, there could be change of loyalties or a group defection which was entirely legal and protected under the merger clause. In any case, there was no provision that could justify dissolution of the House on grounds of threatened defections. In fact, in several instances both at the Union and State levels, governments were formed, facilitated or enabled to survive by defectors only. What was necessary for the life and legitimacy of a government was its ability to command the confidence of the House. For defection, the individual member involved might have to pay by earning disqualification but the government remained in order so long as it did not lose the confidence of the House. Governor Buta Singh perhaps gave himself out when he spoke of the likelihood of Nitish Kumar staking claim to form government as the real justification for his recommending dissolution. It was not only the Governor speaking of the fear of horse-trading but Prime Minister Dr Manmohan Singh himself referred to the worst kind of horse-trading going on in Bihar. The Governor was only one of the players and perhaps the most insignificant. He only made a recommendation, gave his own assessment of the situation. He took no decisions and no action. He had, in fact, no power to do either. Bihar being under President's Rule, the powers of the Governor to dissolve the Assembly under article 174(2) stood transferred to the President.

- The second and the most important player in the Bihar drama was the Union Cabinet headed by Prime Minister Manmohan Singh. The Cabinet armed with all the relevant information from all available sources, after careful consideration, took the decision to recommend to the President issuance of the notification dissolving the Assembly. It could not be disputed that it was the responsibility of the Cabinet to satisfy itself on points of law and fact before deciding on dissolution. It could be nobody's case that the Governor's report or recommendation was binding on the Cabinet. In any case, the unseemly haste in which decision was taken and sought to be rubber-stamped by an obliging President equally promptly could not be justified.

- The third, and constitutionally and legally, the most responsible player was the President who allowed himself in his noble simplicity perhaps, to be misled and hurried into signing a blatantly 'unconstitutional' notification. He could have asked the powers that be to wait, he could take' his own time, could make necessary consultations and should have taken a decision only after careful consideration. Also, he could send the matter back to the Cabinet for reconsideration. And, even thereafter, no President could be bound by any 'unconstitutional advice' or advice to do something palpably 'unconstitutional'.

  When in December 1970, dissolution of Lok Sabha was recommended by Prime Minister Mrs Indira Gandhi, President Giri asked her if the Cabinet had considered it. Even after a recommendation letter came to him from the Cabinet, President Giri kept it for consideration and when notification was issued, it read, "The President, on the recommendation of the Council of Ministers and after careful consideration..." One President withheld his assent to a Bill passed by both the Houses and another refused assent to a Bill unanimously passed by both the Houses. The President's role was definitely not that of a rubber-stamp. He could and must assert his constitutional authority whenever necessary. Inasmuch as what was declared as 'unconstitutional' by the Court was the Presidential notification, one could not absolve the President's office of his constitutional responsibility. One had to be more careful in future.

- Fourth and the last but not the least responsible player was the Supreme Court itself. While declaring the dissolution 'unconstitutional', it was difficult to understand, how could the Court allow the beneficiaries of that unconstitutional act to get away with the loot. The primary duty of the Court was to adjudicate disputes and to provide relief and remedy to victims of injustice and unconstitutional acts. In this case, in view of the ground realities, 'pragmatic' considerations etc., elections based on unconstitutional dissolution were allowed to be held and the petitioner or public interest got no relief from the apex court. That election results brought a stable government was another matter. The moment the Court announced that it was allowing the electoral process to continue, the judgement and its arguments became a matter only for academic debate. It was worth considering whether the Courts were not laying too much emphasis on laying down high principles for future generations making immediate adjudication of a dispute and relief to petitioners and public interest a casualty.
- The judgement concentrated on the Governor's role and reiterated earlier recommendations about the type of persons who should not be appointed as Governors. It appeared to be too soft on the role of other players particularly the Union Cabinet when it merely said:

> "The Governor may be the main player, but Council of Ministers should have verified facts stated in the report of the Governor before hurriedly accepting it as a gospel truth as to what Governor stated. Clearly, the Governor had misled the Council of Ministers."

And we might add, the Council of Ministers misled the President. It was a moot question whether more responsibility attached to advisers who misled or to high functionaries who got misled.

Lastly, it was impossible to agree with those who, for political party reasons, jumped on the judgement to demand resignation of the Union Government. The Government had every right to continue so long as it did not lose the confidence of the Lok Sabha. However, the Court would have done well to flag the responsibility of the Union Cabinet squarely and laid down some guidelines for future correctives.

39

Constitutionality of Central Teams to States

In June 1998, a fierce controversy erupted on the issue of the constitutionality of the Government of India's action in sending teams of officers for an on the spot study and assessment of the ground situation in Tamil Nadu, Bihar and West Bengal. The opposition dubbed the BJP-led coalition government's action unconstitutional. The team that visited West Bengal was reported to have been badly snubbed by the State's then Home Minister, Budhadev Bhattacharya as 'unwanted guests'. Notwithstanding the fulminations of the West Bengal Minister and the use of undignified and rebellious language challenging the authority and ability of the 'weak' Central Government to dare issue a proclamation, leadership at the Union level showed exemplary maturity in not over-reaching to the political rhetoric and instead retaining its restraint in the matter of taking recourse to article 356. However, the matter needed to be examined dispassionately with reference to the position as it emerged from the constitutional provisions.

Article 356 empowers the President *inter alia* to take over the functions of the State Government if he is satisfied on a report from the Governor 'or otherwise' that a situation has arisen in which the

Government of the State cannot be carried on in accordance with the Constitution.

It was categorically stated by Dr Ambedkar in the Constituent Assembly that the article was being kept in the Constitution as a matter of abundant caution to be used as a last resort when all other methods failed and that it was not likely to be used ever and could remain a dead letter.

Unfortunately, during the last 58 years (1950-2008) this article has been abused and misused repeatedly on blatantly partisan considerations; on nearly 120 occasions, elected State Governments have been dismissed. This has been done by almost every party while in power and always vehemently condemned by every party when in opposition. Most often Governor's report has been considered enough for satisfying the President. Also, there have been allegations of Governor's office being misused for securing from docile occupants of the high office reports dictated by the Union Government and required as justification for pre-planned and politically motivated imposition of President's Rule.

Even though rarely followed in implementation, the principle is well-established by court judgements as in the *Bommai* case and in reports of Commissions like the Sarkaria Commission (1986) and the Constitution Commission (2002) that article 356 should be used only as a matter of last resort when everything else failed.

In the instant case, in May-June 1998, there were pressing demands that were being made for imposition of President's Rule and dismissal of governments in some States. The then Union Government headed by Atal Bihari Vajpayee, however was committed not to misuse article 356 for partisan ends. Also, it was aware that the matter was subject to judicial review and its action could be held by the Court to be *ultra vires* the Constitution.

If the Union Government did not depend entirely on the Governor's report and was anxious to be otherwise satisfied and therefore decided to have the position studied on the spot in a nonpartisan manner by a team of officers, its approach deserved to be welcomed as unexceptionable and commendable. It was the only Central Government that had taken a firm and principled stand and even risked its survival on not dismissing the State Governments for partisan considerations.

If the Vajpayee Government had followed the precedents set by the Congress, Janata and United Front Governments, it could straightaway dismiss the State Governments in West Bengal, Tamil Nadu and Bihar. It was not necessary to send any fact finding teams of officers. It was therefore most astounding that the Government was being frowned upon for trying to use all available alternatives and to exhaust all possible options before merely seeking or accepting Governor's report and imposing President's Rule.

The legitimacy of the authority of the Union Government to send a team of officers to any State is inherent in the provision of article 356 whereunder the President has to satisfy himself on the Governor's report or otherwise, that is, by any other means.

There is also the most fundamental principal that the Government of India is the Government of whole of India—including every State and Union Territory. The relationship is that of the whole with its parts. Even in matters like law and order which are assigned to the States, the ultimate responsibility is that of the Union Government. If the State Government fails to maintain law and order and/or is not being run or cannot run according to the Constitution despite action by the Union Government under article 355, then only, as a last resort, President may issue a proclamation under article 356.

Without taking recourse to article 356 and dismissing elected State Government and imposing President's Rule, there is much that can be done under article 355 which casts a constitutional responsibility on the Union Government to protect the States from external aggression and 'internal disturbance' and ensure that the State Governments function in accordance with the provisions of the Constitution. This means that the Union Government has to be constantly monitoring and overseeing the situation in regard to *inter alia* 'internal disturbance' which includes 'law and order' and constitutional functions of the Government. Naturally, the power to take any action to fulfill this responsibility must be read in article 355 itself. Sending a fact finding team of officers is the most innocuous step that can be conceived in that direction.

Article 246 and the Seventh Schedule to the Constitution provide for distribution of legislative powers between the Union and the States. The executive powers of the Union are coextensive with its legislative powers. However, article 246 is not a complete code and certain powers are conferred on the Union and the State legislatures and governments by or under several other articles of the Constitution. For example, special responsibilities are cast upon the Union in matters like protection of minority rights (articles 350A and 350B), safeguarding the interests of the Scheduled Castes and Schedule Tribes (articles 338 and 339) and application of fundamental rights to the armed forces (article 33). Under article 256 and 257, the Government of India can issue such directions to a State as may appear to be necessary in the exercise of its executive powers and discharge of its responsibilities.

Article 365 provides that if any of the directions given by Government of India under any article of the Constitution are not complied with, 'it shall be lawful for the President to hold that a situation has arisen in which the Government of the State cannot be carried on in accordance with the provisions of the Constitution' and the President may as a last resort, dismiss the recalcitrant State Government by a proclamation under article 356.

Thus, under various constitutional provisions not only was there every legitimacy and justification in sending to any State teams of Government of India officers but such a step should have been appreciated by all those federalists who stood for States' rights and had been opposed to misuse of powers under article 356.

40

Surrender to Blackmail

Appointment of a Chief Minister*

Tamil Nadu Governor, Fatima Bibi appointed, Ms Jayalalitha as the Chief Minister of the State even though she stood convicted of corruption charges and disqualified for membership of the Legislature. The 2001 controversy surrounding the appointment as Chief Minister of a person convicted of corruption and disqualified for membership raised serious calling for a nation-wide debate.

What the Tamil Nadu Governor—a former Supreme Court judge—did drastically altered the norms of political discourse and conduct. Gone were the days when mere suspicion of wrongdoing, adverse finding by a Committee or Commission of inquiry or framing of charges would invite resignation of a holder of public office. Corruption was said to have ceased to be an issue in public life.

It was argued unabashedly and without any moral or legal compunctions that under article 164(1) of the Constitution, the Governor had an unfettered right to appoint anyone as the Chief

---

* From *The Statesman*, 8 June 2001.

Minister as if while there were qualifications and disqualifications for being 'members', there were none for being 'ministers'. Article 164(4) was being interpreted to mean that even disqualifications for membership did not apply to occupying ministerial office for six months.

There could be legitimate difference of opinion on whether the court judgement convicting Ms Jayalalitha on corruption charges and awarding a three-year sentence was correct or whether the 1997 interpretation given by the Election Commission to Section 8(3) of the Representation of People Act 1951 and the rejection of her nomination paper by the Returning Officer on that ground were good in law. Ms Jayalalitha had filed an appeal in the TANSI corruption case. She could also file an election petition challenging the rejection of her nomination paper. She would on a point of law, question the *vires* of the Election Commission directive in regard to the interpretation of Section 8(3) of Representation of People Act. But, these were all matters which were in the exclusive judicial domain and one had to have the patience and good sense to await the court's verdict. Meanwhile, the law as it stood had to be respected.

There was no doubt that the Tamil Nadu Governor had a very difficult task to perform. Even though Ms Jayalalitha herself could not be said to have received any mandate of the people, the parties under her leadership had swept the polls and a clear majority of legislators had elected her as the Leader. She and her followers appeared entirely unwilling to accept anyone else. If she was not sworn in immediately, the Governor might have been accused of flouting the people's mandate and of indulging in anti-democratic conduct. Also, with the likely demonstrations, rioting and immolations in support of the self-proclaimed mother of Tamil Nadu, serious law and order situation might have been created and the State thrown in turmoil. The Governor, under the circumstances, acted swiftly and presumably accepted Ms Jayalalitha's assurances of having the disqualification removed and getting elected to the legislature within six months. She was obviously for a more pragmatic approach and a safer path of least resistance, leaving it to the law courts to wrestle with interpreting the letter and the spirit of the Constitution and the niceties of Rule of Law.

But, adoption of such soft options and surrender to threats of mob violence and blackmail may have dangerous ramifications for the future of Indian polity, constitutionalism and Rule of Law. While the popular will deserves all the respect, democracy is inconceivable without Rule of Law. Everyone, howsoever high, is bound by the Constitution which the people have given to themselves. The Governor also takes an oath under article 159 to 'preserve, protect and defend the Constitution and the law'.

While under article 361 the Governor enjoys personal immunity from being proceeded against in a court of law, it certainly does not follow that the highest courts are precluded from pronouncing on the unconstitutionality of certain acts. In fact, acts of Governors, including the appointment of Chief Ministers, have been subjected to judicial review.

It would have been ideal if the Governor could have advised and in a suave manner convinced 'Amma' not to stake her claim to Chief Ministership until removal of disqualification. If that failed, the Governor had to follow the Constitution and the law. Between politics and the Constitution, the latter had to have precedence.

Article 173 of the Constitution lays down the minimum qualifications for membership of houses of State Legislature in terms of age and citizenship and says that additional qualifications may be prescribed by Parliament by law. Article 191(1) lays down the disqualifications. The persons who are specifically disqualified for membership are: holders of office of profit under the Government, persons of unsound mind so declared by court, persons who are undischarged insolvents, those who are not citizens of India and those who are disqualified by or under a law made by Parliament. Section 8(3) of the Representation of the People Act 1951 specifically provides that a person convicted of an offence and sentenced to imprisonment for not less than two years shall be disqualified from the date of such conviction and for six years after release.

Thus, non-citizens, those below the age of 25 in case of Legislative Assembly and 30 in case of Legislative Council, insane or insolvent persons, those holding office of profit and those convicted of certain offences are disqualified for membership of the legislature.

The foundational principle of parliamentary polity is that the Executive comes out of the Legislature, remains part of it and always responsible to the popular House. The members of the Council of Ministers, therefore have got to be from among the members of the Legislature. The principle is actually reinforced by clause (4) of article 164.

The basic principle requiring Ministers to be Members of the Legislature clearly suggests that only those eligible or qualified to be Members can be appointed as Ministers or Chief Minister. Anyone who stands disqualified for being a Member, stands doubly disqualified for being appointed as a Minister or Chief Minister so long as the disqualification lasts.

Any other interpretation would be an argument in futility and may lead to absurd results (*reduction ad absurdum*). This, if a person not qualified or disqualified for membership could be appointed and could continue as a Chief Minister for six months, then not only those convicted of some of the most heinous offences but even those who were not citizens of India, were below 25 years of age, were occupants of offices of profit under the Government, or were insane or insolvent would become eligible for Chief Ministership. After all, if a person convicted lower court could hope to be completely exonerated on appeal in six months' time, it was also conceivable for a non-citizen to become a citizen, holder of an office of profit giving it up, an unsound mind returning to sanity, an insolvent becoming solvent or a below 25 getting to be 25 in the next six months. That certainly could never be the intent of the founding fathers nor could that ever be an acceptable interpretation.

True, the conviction by the lower court might not be upheld by the higher courts and Ms Jayalalitha might be ultimately held not guilty. On the grounds of balance of convenience, it could argued that depriving her of the Chief Ministership would have caused irreparable loss to her and to the people. But then, it was equally conceivable at that point of time that conviction was upheld by the highest court and in that case the appointment of a guilty person as Chief Minister could be said to have meanwhile caused irreparable damage to the people and the polity and therefore balance of convenience should have dictated greater caution. After all, contesting an election for membership of the legislature or being a minister is not a fundamental right.

The above position was later upheld by the Supreme Court when it said that a person who is disqualified for being a member of the Legislature cannot be appointed a minister or Chief Minister for six months taking refuge under article 164(4). The standards expected of a minister who is not a member should be the same as, if not greater than, those required of a member (*BR Kapur vs State of Tamil Nadu*, AIR 2001 SC3435).

41

Relevance and Role of Governor's Office

Goa and Jharkhand Cases

I

Constitution works on a delicate system of checks and balances. Once the norms are given a go-by anywhere, a vicious cycle is set in motion and one wrong used to justify another wrong with wrongs alone getting multiplied. The office of the governor has been mired in controversies almost from the commencement of the Constitution. From time to time, Governors of different States have been accused of partisan behaviour and of acting as agents of the party or parties in power at the Union level. It would be desirable to try to analyse the constitutional position in regard to the need, position and powers of the Governor's office.

The office of the Governor under the Constitution is one of great responsibility and dignity. The Governor was envisaged on the one hand as the executive head of the state and on the other as the representative of the Union in the State. He was expected to be a vital link between the Union and the State, to act as the eyes and ears of the Union and to generally ensure that the government of the State was carried on in accordance with the Constitution and particularly to see that the interests of the Union are safeguarded. Unlike the President, the Governors have to exercise some important functions under their discretionary powers also. In view of this and in the context of many fissiparous tendencies now and then, raising their ugly heads, the office of the Governor becomes even more relevant now than it was ever before.

The Governor is appointed by the President (that is, the Union Government) and holds office during his pleasure, Subject to such pleasure, the term of the office is five years. Governor takes an oath 'to preserve, protect and defend the Constitution and the law' and to devote himself 'to the service and well-being of the people' of the State. Unfortunately, the parties that come to power at the Union level treat it as a part of the patronage or spoils system. Governorship becomes a reward for past loyalty and a tacit assurance of protecting party interests in the future. Thus, the office degenerates into that of an agent of the party/parties in power in New Delhi. The Sarkaria Commission and the National Commission on the Constitution had both suggested salutary norms to govern the selection of Governors only from among eminent persons not too intimately connected with active party politics. Such advice, however, did not seem to make sense to powers that be. Unfortunately, parties in power have come to treat the Governor's office as part of the patronage or spoils system. All parties have been equally guilty in the matter.

In exercise of their functions, the Governors must act impartially, constitutionally and not as party politicians anxious to serve party interests or please party bosses. As it is, the Governor's office was often misused both by the Union Government and by the Governors themselves. The crucial areas giving birth to controversies and allegations of partisan conduct had been (i) appointment of the Chief Minister in case of a hung house, and (ii) reporting failure of constitutional machinery and recommending President's rule.

Where the elections return a 'hung' House with no single party or pre-poll alliance being in a position to command majority support on its own, the role of the Governor in choosing the Chief

Minister becomes most delicate and difficult. Unless the fullest care and caution are exercised, Governor may get involved in unseemly political controversies. The unfortunate stand of some of the Governors in the matter has in fact been largely responsible for the continuing phenomenon of horse-trading and instability of Governments. The governors will be well advised not to play the dirty game of promoting horse trading and indulging in counting the heads of MLAs.

The Sarkaria Commission, the Supreme Court (in the Bommai case) and the Constitution Commission have all held that the question of majority support should be settled only on the floor of the House. The Governor cannot act as a policeman keeping a head-count of supporters of different parties and leaders or verifying the lists of supporters, their signatures and the like. Sarkaria Commission recommended and the Constitution Commission endorsed the recommendations that in case there is no single party having absolute majority in the House, the Governor should adhere to the following order of preference in calling the leaders to form the Government: (i) leader of pre-poll alliance, (ii) leader of the largest single party, (iii) leader of post-poll alliance, (iv) leader of the group of parties some of which promise support to the Government from outside, and lastly (v) leader who in Governor's own judgement was most likely to command a majority in the Assembly.

As for the Governor's powers under article 164(1), it is necessary to look at and analyse the text of the article. It says that (a) the Chief Minister is appointed by the Governor, (b) and other ministers are appointed by the Governor on the advice of the Chief Minister. The Council of Ministers so constituted is collectively responsible to the Legislative Assembly. This means that only the person likely to be most acceptable to the House ought to be appointed as the Chief Minister. The ministers hold office during the pleasure of the Governor. It is clear that a distinction for purposes of this article has been made between the Chief Minister and the other ministers and only the latter depend for their continuance on the pleasure of the Governor which in effect means the pleasure of the Chief Minister. Since the Ministers are appointed on the advice of the Chief Minister, they remain subject to removal by the Governor at any time on the advice of the Chief Minister. Article 156 of the Constitution also says that the Governor holds office 'during the pleasure of the President'. Nobody can suggest that that means that the President himself can dismiss any Governor without the advice of the Prime Minister. The fact is that the Governor is appointed on the advice of the Prime Minister and can be removed only on his advice.

Article 164(2) says that the Council of Ministers is collectively responsible to the Legislative Assembly, that is, quite clearly not to the Governor. The Constitution does not anywhere say that the Governor has the power to remove or dismiss the Council of Ministers. Only individual ministers can be removed by him on the advice of the Chief Minister. The Council of Ministers must hold office so long as it does not lose the confidence of the House. The question can be decided only on the floor of the House on a motion of no-confidence. Also, in parliamentary polity, for continuance in government, it is not necessary to have majority 'for'. What is required is that majority should not be 'against'.

The Governor cannot act as a constant policeman over the House. It is not his business to keep a tally of the numbers supporting the Government from day to day. He is not supposed to keep making a head count of MLA s with or against the Government. The matter is entirely between the Government (the Council of Ministers) and the House. The unfortunate stand of some of the Governors had in fact been largely responsible for the continuous phenomenon of horse-trading and instability of Governments.

Misuse of the high office of the Governor, however, can constitute no argument against the continued relevance of the office. If constitutional offices begin to be scrapped because some of their occupants indulge in unbecoming conduct, very soon hardly anything would be left. Democracy itself may face a question mark.

II

Goa Governor's Coup d'etat

Goa was notorious for defections, instability, intense infighting for ministerial posts and frequent change of Chief Ministers and Governments. The saddest part of the whole affair was that providing good governance to the people had become the last priority of the politicians and parties. It was all a naked struggle for power, sharing ministerships, and getting-rich-quick at the expense of 'we, the people'.

Thanks to Governor, SC Jamir, the office of Governor once again was in the news in February 2005. The facts of the case were simple. Four members of the BJP-led coalition Government in Goa resigned from membership of the House. The Government was said to have lost its majority. Immediately, the Congress leaders built pressure on the Governor to dismiss the Government without any need of a floor test. The Governor asked the Government headed by Parrikar to prove its majority on the floor of the House.

On 2 February 2005, the Assembly Speaker declared the confidence motion carried. But before putting the motion to vote amidst noisy scenes and turmoil, he ordered one member out. Within minutes of the Parrikar Government winning the confidence of the House, the Governor staged a coup. The Government headed by Parrikar was summarily dismissed. Congress Party leader, Pratap Singh Rane was swiftly installed as the new Chief Minister. The justification given for Governor's action was (i) that the Speaker's action in having one member removed was unconstitutional and (2) that under article 164(2) of the Constitution the Governor had full authority to dismiss the Government.

Under the scheme of our Constitution, each State Legislature is supreme and sovereign within the sphere assigned to it. Each house is the master of its procedure. The validity of any proceedings of the House cannot be questioned by any outside authority. Even courts cannot question it 'on the ground of any alleged irregularity of procedure' (article 212 of the Constitution).

Smooth and orderly conduct of the business of the House is the responsibility of the Speaker. Within the House and in all matters connected with the business and procedure of the House, his word is final. If the Speaker's conduct is found to be unworthy of the office, he can be removed by the House itself by a resolution. Only in the exercise of his powers under the Anti-defection Law (10th Schedule) his decisions are subject to judicial review.

The Governor cannot constitute himself into a court of appeal over the acts of the Speaker or decisions of the House. The Speaker represents the House and the Governor is not his boss. The Constitution does not give to the Governor any authority to declare an act of the Speaker unconstitutional or to reverse the decision of the House on grounds of procedural irregularity etc. Governor's powers are limited to (a) sending a message to the House, (b) addressing the House, (c) withholding assent to a Bill and (d) in case of failure of constitutional machinery to recommend President's Rule.

It was obvious that while the Speaker's conduct might not have been entirely above blame and he probably acted in a partisan manner, the Governor had no authority to declare his act unconstitutional or to arbitrarily reverse the decision of the House. Two wrongs do not add up to one right. The act of the Governor was blatantly undemocratic, patently unconstitutional and positively partisan. Also, it was unprecedented inasmuch as never before any State Government in India was so dismissed by a Governor immediately after winning the confidence of the House. All this must have been known to policy makers in New Delhi. The decision to use the Governor's office for the dirty job must have been entirely political and motivated by the desire to keep the Central Government and Congress High Command away from the odium particularly at a time when elections were on in three States.

III

Jharkhand Imbroglio

When in March 2005, Governor Sibtey Razi of Jharkhand appointed Shibu Soren as Chief Minister, it was obvious that none of the salutary constitutional principles in the matter were kept in view and all norms were flouted. Instead of following the order of preference indicated by the Sarkaria Commission (1986) and the Constitution Commission (2002) and inviting the leader of the largest pre-poll alliance who incidentally also happened to be the leader of the largest single party, the Governor decided to appoint a person who in his own judgement was able to provide a stable government. Even if the Governor wanted to go by the head-count, 41 members constituting majority were paraded before him at the Raj Bhawan. It was highly improper for the Governor to decide to meet some of the supporting members separately and individually. It was beneath the dignity of a Governor to act as an investigating or interrogating police officer. The conduct of the Governor generated almost universal condemnation for jeopardizing respect for democratic institutions and constitutional offices. It had, in fact, caused tremendous damage to the image of the Congress Party and its leadership. However, it seemed extremely unlikely that he was acting on his own without tremendous outside pressures. After all, Sibtey Razi as a person was a very decent man.

Once the constitutional culture and democratic norms were given a go-by, a vicious cycle was set in motion and one wrong was used to justify another wrong with wrongs getting multiplied. Houses of Parliament not being allowed to function was a case in point.

After 40 Jharkhand MLAs physically presented themselves before the President, it was to be expected that the Governor would be asked to explain the grounds that led to his decision to appoint Shibu Soren. If the President was not satisfied, he could give a bit of his mind to the

Governor. The President could also call the Prime Minister and ask him to look into the matter. A polite hint should have been enough for the Prime Minister to do the needful. The minimum that could be done without much loss of face for anyone was to immediately hold a sitting of the House to ascertain its confidence in a leader.

A way for the Governor to stay out of controversy could have been to send a Message under article 175(2) asking the House itself to elect its leader who could be appointed the Chief Minister. That way, the decision of majority support would have been taken on the floor of the House, chances of horse-trading would have been minimized and it would not have been necessary to ask such a Chief Minister to seek a vote of confidence again. When the basic question to be determined was of who commanded the majority support in the House, the most obvious and logical course was to ask the House itself. After all, in the 1998 UP case, the High Court had ordered the reinstatement of the former Chief Minister and the Supreme Court had ordered a special session of the Assembly to have a composite floor test between two contending claimants to Chief Ministership. (*Jagdambika Pal vs Union of India*, AIR 1998 SC 998]

Article 212 forbids the Judiciary questioning the proceedings of the House on any ground of irregularity of procedure. In Jharkhand, the proceedings were not being allowed to be held. The issue of questioning the proceedings could arise only after the proceedings were held. Also, if the Constitution is flouted and the matter is brought before the court, the court must act to protect constitutional principles.

In the entire drama, the constraints and compulsions of the Governor could be understood even if not appreciated but it was difficult to understand the stand of the distinguished Speaker of Lok Sabha insisting on a reference being made to the Supreme Court for an advisory opinion under article 143. Supported by media attention, an effort was made to whip up a legislature versus judiciary confrontation. The real strength of the Speaker is that he speaks on behalf of the whole

House, above all party considerations. In this case, however, major parties in Opposition were against the move. Later, the ruling alliance and the Government also washed their hands off the controversy and disclaimed any support to the proposal of seeking advisory opinion of the Supreme Court.

Also, opinion under article 143 cannot be sought in a matter where the Supreme Court has already given a judgement. In the Jharkhand case, howsoever generally worded, the exercise appeared to be seeking Supreme Court's advice against its own orders issued in precisely the same matter. Finally, the holding of the truncated Conference of Presiding Officers at heavy cost to public exchequer was an ill conceived and infructuous undertaking. Speakers can speak for the Legislature only when their Houses, irrespective of party labels, are united behind them. The Conference was yet another vindication of de-institutionalization of our institutions and of our conduct in making them dysfunctional.

[illegible] above [illegible] jurisdiction. [illegible] However, upon [illegible] the ruling alliance had the [illegible] that [illegible] and threatened any support to the proposal of securing advisory opinion of the Supreme Court.

An advisory opinion cannot be sought in a matter where the Supreme Court has already given a judgement. In the [illegible] case, however, [illegible] appeared to be asking the Supreme Court to [illegible] its own orders issued in [illegible] the same matter. Finally, the holding of the Conference of Presiding Officers [illegible] was an [illegible] and unconstitutional [illegible]. Speakers can speak for the Legislature only when their Houses [illegible]. The Conference [illegible] gives another indication of [illegible] institutions and of [illegible] conduct in making them dysfunctional.

42

Much Ado about Nothing

Parliament vs Courts

Too much fuss was kicked up over the courts in *Raja Rampal vs Speaker Lok Sabha* (2007) concerning the expulsion of MPs for what had come to be called the 'Cash for questions' scandal. Media stories spoke about the Legislature and the Judiciary being pitted against each other and of the impending confrontation or face-off between the two. Fortunately, nothing of the sort was borne out by the facts. It was difficult to find out if some elements had a vested interest in creating the image of a conflictual and confrontationist situation where none existed. As the Lok Sabha Speaker said, there was no 'confrontationist move', both the Legislature and the Judiciary deserved respect, none was supreme, each organ had to operate within its jurisdictional limits. So long as the *Lakshman Rekha* set by the Constitution was not crossed, there could be no question of confrontation.

Issue of notices by the courts was merely for (i) informing the parties impleaded, (ii) giving them an opportunity to have their say in the matter and (iii) seeking their assistance in interpreting the constitutional provisions. It was not a decision or a judgement on the facts of the case or on points of law. Mere issue of notice could not be construed as an intrusion in the parliamentary domain.

Similarly, if either House of Parliament or functionaries thereof did not respond to the notices and decided not to be represented before the court, it meant no disrespect to the court. So far, therefore, both the courts and the Legislature were right in their respective ways and true to their procedures and precedents.

The powers and jurisdictional limits of our Legislature, Executive and Judiciary were clearly defined and delimited by the Constitution. Every organ was bound by the Constitution and accountable to the people who alone were supreme and sovereign.

The process of expulsion followed would have appeared to have been more convincing if it was not so hurried and more reasonable time and assistance of an advocate was allowed to the accused as was done in the Mudgal case. But, these were matters of procedure, were no more relevant and in any case outside the purview of the Court. Very appropriately and wisely, the Supreme Court (i) declined to interfere with the electoral process for filling up the vacancies created by the expulsion of MPs and (ii) refused to go into the correctness of procedure followed for the expulsions. As reported, the court agreed only to examine whether the powers and privileges of the Houses of Parliament under article 105 extended to expelling MPs. This was entirely in keeping with the existing law as earlier declared by the Supreme Court. Whether a particular power/privilege existed could always be enquired into by the courts but once existence was established, the exercise of power/privilege could not be questioned by the courts, that is, the courts would not look into the 'correctness, propriety or legality' of the commitment for breach of privilege, the punishment awarded, the procedure followed, that is, the manner of the exercise of power. (1959 *Searchlight* case and 1965 *Keshav Singh*'s case)

Article 105 lays down the powers and privileges of the Houses, Committees and Members of Parliament. Important powers and privileges like freedom of speech in Parliament and immunity to members from any proceedings in courts in respect of anything said or vote given in Parliament are stated in the Constitution. In other respects, unless codified, parliamentary powers, privileges and immunities are to be the same as those of the British House of Commons at the commencement of the Constitution.

The power of the House to punish for its own breach of privilege and contempt is 'akin in nature to the power of the Supreme Court to commit for its own contempt from which there is no appeal'. In the case of its own members, punishment may include 'suspension... and expulsion from the House'.

It is important to remember that there is a clear distinction between disqualification for being a Member under articles 102 and 103 and expulsion from the House under the powers given by article 105. The most relevant constitutional provision apart from article 105 is article 122, which categorically bars the courts from enquiring into the validity of any proceedings in Parliament on the ground of any alleged irregularity of procedure. Those with constitutional powers for regulating the conduct of business and procedure or maintaining order in Parliament are not 'subject to the jurisdiction of any court in respect of exercise' of those powers.

In *Tej Kiran vs Sanjeeva Reddy* (1969), when notices were issued to the Speaker and four members to appear before the Delhi High Court, the House decided to ignore the notices. Subsequently, the case was dismissed by the court. In 1975 also, a court notice was ignored and the relevant papers were passed on to the Minister of Law for taking such action as he deemed fit to apprise the court of correct constitutional position. Again, the case was dismissed. In July 1988 when two court notices were received, the Speaker observed that as per well-established practice and convention of Lok Sabha, he had decided not to respond to the notices and that he had passed on the relevant papers to the Minister of Law and Justice for taking necessary steps to apprise the court of the constitutional position and the well-established conventions of the Lok Sabha in that regard. There were similar instances in the years 1990 and 1991 and the same stand was taken by the Speaker. It could, therefore, be seen that the decision to ignore the court notices and not to make an appearance on behalf of Lok Sabha could not be faulted with so long as established practice and convention were adhered to.

It has been held that the control of the House over its proceedings is 'absolute' and cannot be interfered with by the courts. In the UK, the House has unquestioned disciplinary powers over the conduct of its members both inside and outside the House and include the power of expulsion. Our Parliament has always claimed that it has *inter alia* the power to expel its members for breach of its privileges, contempt or lowering the dignity of the House or conduct unbecoming of a member. This power was actually resorted to in the Mudgal case in 1951 (even though he escaped expulsion by resigning) and in Mrs Gandhi's expulsion from Lok Sabha in 1978 (although later the expulsion was retrospectively rescinded by the House itself in 1981). The Judgements of the High Courts were conflicting and the Supreme Court till then had had no occasion to pronounce on the power of the House to expel a member. It was, therefore, very wise and appropriate for the Court to refer the matter to a Constitution Bench to clarify the constitutional points.

It is not a sign of good health, to be hyper-sensitive about one's position or prestige—either at the individual or at the institutional level. As if the all party meeting was not enough while the matter was before the Supreme Court, the Presiding Officers Conference was convened. There did not seem to be much justification for queering the pitch. The Conference incidentally entailed huge expenditure from the public exchequer at the level of the Union and the States.

The court notice was issued also to the Attorney General and the Union Government. In parliamentary polity, Government was actually part of Parliament and when the Government was represented and the Attorney General was there, the constitutional position regarding the powers, privileges and precedents of Parliament could doubtlessly be presented before the apex court.

In the JMM Bribery case, the Supreme Court had held that the MPs taking bribe for voting could not be proceeded against in any court because of article 105. Where the Parliament itself had taken action under article 105 against the bribe-taking MPs, how could the Court question the power of Parliament to punish the bribe-takers by expulsion? As it turned out, the Supreme Court upheld the right of the House to expel its members.